DARK EYE

The Films of DAVID FINCHER

DARK EYE

The Films of
DAVID
FINCHER

James
Swallow

REYNOLDS & HEARN LTD
LONDON

For Mum, Dad and Mandy

First published in 2003 by
Reynolds & Hearn Ltd
61a Priory Road
Kew Gardens
Richmond
Surrey TW9 3DH

© James Swallow 2003

A CIP catalogue record for this book is available from the British Library.

ISBN 1 903111 52 8

Designed by Peri Godbold.

Printed and bound in Great Britain by Biddles Ltd, Guildford, Surrey.

Contents

Acknowledgments

The author wishes to thank the following people for their support and assistance, without which this book could not have been written:

David Fincher, with appreciation for his time and for lunch.

John Brancato, Clare Cernick, Jonathan Clements, Christina Esposito, Peter J Evans, Michael Ferris, Marcus Hearn, Stephen Howard, Stewart Jamieson, Jim McLennan, Richard Reynolds, Jonathan Rigby, Adam R Rosser, Louis Savy, Keith Topping, Linda Tresham, Jamie Walton and the staff of the British Film Institute library.

Introduction

'I have demons you can't even imagine.'

AN ALIEN CREATURE stalks a lone woman through an industrial waste-
land; two detectives hunt a malignant, zealous serial killer; an emotionally
detached millionaire is given the ride of his life; a disconnected young man
discovers a path to redemption through self-destruction; a mother and daughter
are trapped alone with three dangerous criminals. David Fincher's visions of
cinema are tapestries of darkness and light, reaching into all the night-filled
places where we often fear to tread. The matter of his films runs the range from
thriller to horror, from suspense to science fiction, from drama to black comedy
and all points in between. In each of Fincher's movies, he takes us on a journey
into realms that lie half-glimpsed off the tangent of the real world, grim domains
where the gloom hides things that draw out uncomfortable emotions, scare us,
dare us and force us to answer questions we'd prefer to ignore.

A maverick amid the Hollywood mainstream, David Fincher has earned critical respect and cult stardom for his challenging, hard-edged and often uncompromising movies, but he has also come under fire for his handling of subject
matter that many find objectionable and uneasy viewing. In this book, I hope to
provide an insight into this talented director's canon and examine the circumstances that went into the making of his films, as well as the influences that have
shaped his creative vision and the personal philosophy that drives David Fincher
to tell stories that live, both literally and metaphorically, in the shadows.

Dark Eye: The Films of David Fincher covers the life and career of the director
from his childhood to the present day and beyond. The opening chapter highlights Fincher's early life, from his boyhood fascination with Super 8mm cine
cameras to his work with George Lucas's special effects studio, Industrial Light &
Magic, and his earliest directorial experiences in the flashy world of music video
and commercials. Each of his five studio feature films to date – *Alien 3* (1992),
Seven (1995), *The Game* (1997), *Fight Club* (1999) and *Panic Room* (2002) – is
then granted a chapter to itself, with remarks from Fincher, his actors and his
crew, as well as critical commentary.

The overview and analysis of Fincher's films begins with 'Third in Line',
discussing *Alien 3*, the most controversial film of the *Alien* series, with its grim
setting, downbeat finale and tortuous backstory. 'Deadly Sins' looks at *Seven*,
Fincher's first film with actor Brad Pitt, and the first time that Fincher was let off

the directorial leash to craft a moody, visceral drama that broke the mould of the serial killer genre. 'A Player' examines the complex rules of *The Game*, a feature film often overshadowed by the movies that Fincher made before and after, a taut and precise psychological thriller showing his growing maturity as a feature director. 'Hit Me' covers the dark humour of *Fight Club*'s destructive and revolutionary narrative, considered by many to be the director's true breakout movie, a maverick drama that put David Fincher firmly on the map. 'House Arrest' considers the locked-box drama of *Panic Room*, the most recent film in Fincher's arsenal and a new take on his particular brand of Urban Gothic cinema.

Following the coverage of his movies, 'Fincher's Future' looks at exactly that, with a view ahead to the films currently being considered by the director for his next project, such as the coming-of-age drama *The Lords of Dogtown*, the World War II true story *Fertig* and the Arthur C Clarke science fiction epic *Rendezvous with Rama*. This chapter also examines Fincher's role as an executive producer on films from his former production company Indelible Pictures, and considers a few of the films he never made. Finally, *Dark Eye* concludes with an exhaustive resources section featuring a complete filmography for the director and an in-depth bibliography with website listing.

The core chapters of the book covering Fincher's five films to date follow a common format, including the vital statistics of each movie (cast and crew credits, information on box-office takings, release dates and so on); a detailed view from behind the scenes; critical evaluations of each film from contemporary sources, including a look at audience responses; coverage of lost material, alternate scripts and cut scenes, along with extensive quotes from cast and crew members. Although some film guides will coyly shy away from providing complete story synopses, *Dark Eye* is written for an informed readership already familiar with the films in question; thus, the plots are presented in toto and 'spoilers' abound. If you don't know which character plunges into the vat of boiling lead on Fury 161 or what Tyler and Jack have in common, go watch the films before you read this; I'll still be here when you get back.

The rationale behind this book is to create a resource for viewers who want to learn more about both the creator of and the creative process behind David Fincher's films. I've ended each film chapter with some of my own thoughts, but for the most part *Dark Eye* tells the story of these movies from the viewpoint of the people who worked on them. I firmly believe that creators should speak for themselves when their art is placed under the spotlight, and to that end I've done my best to allow David Fincher to tell us, in his own words, what *he* thinks of his works. The material contained in *Dark Eye* has been culled from over ten years' worth of interviews with Fincher, his casts and his crews, plus articles on his films and his career. The book also features an extensive amount of exclusive interview material taken from conversations with the director during 2002 and

2003, between completion of *Panic Room* and pre-production work on his sixth feature film.

In writing a work that focuses on the character and output of one man, I feel that it is important to give the reader some sense of who David Fincher is. With that in mind, I conclude this introduction with an anecdote that recalls my personal impressions of my subject.

I met David Fincher for the first time in 2002 in Los Angeles, several months into the writing of this book. I'd been attempting to secure an interview with him for a while with little success; upon my arrival in California, Fincher had been unavailable, jetting out of the country on a location-scouting mission to Panama, searching for potential sites to shoot the World War II feature *Fertig*. I had expected not to get the audience I wanted; directors are a mercurial lot, and finding a few hours in a schedule top-heavy with development meetings and script sessions just to speak to some passing British author was probably quite a way down his list.

In an earlier telephone conversation, Fincher had expressed surprise – and even a little embarrassment – at the idea that I wanted to write a book about him and his work. 'I'm not John Huston,' he said. 'I haven't made hundreds of films. Would people want to read a book about me?' Yes, I argued, the films he has made are contentious, dynamic, seditious – and largely undocumented. *Dark Eye* was a book that I wanted to read; it was a book that I knew I wanted to write.

And now, on the day before I was due to leave Los Angeles and return home, I fully expected to go back to my keyboard empty-handed. But I was wrong. I got a call from Fincher's assistant, Stephen Howard, that I thought would be a polite brush-off. Instead, Howard provided directions to an exclusive café off Hollywood Boulevard, just a few blocks from my hotel. We'd meet just after 1.00 pm – and inwardly I groaned. An interview over lunch in a crowded restaurant in the midst of the midday rush would not make for ideal recording conditions ... but I was willing to take what I could get.

I arrived at Las Palmas Avenue early and, after a moment of confusion, I found the concealed doorway that leads to the café. I followed it through to a Mediterranean-style bistro that sat like an oasis of greenery between the Walk-of-Fame car park and the tacky souvenir T-shirt stores; it's a stealth restaurant, the discreet kind of place that, if you don't know is there, then maybe you're not supposed to. Perhaps Friday was their slow day, or maybe they closed the café just for him, but that afternoon Fincher and I had the place to ourselves. In case you're interested, he had the chicken.

I'd listened to him speaking about his work on the audio commentaries for *The Game*, *Seven* and *Fight Club*, and meeting David Fincher in person made it clear to me that the personality you hear talking about lighting problems, or making Monty Python jokes with Brad Pitt, is who he really is. Fincher is without artifice when he speaks; what he says is raw and unfiltered, honest and direct, and the nature of his artistic process brands itself even on his speech patterns.

Sometimes you'll ask Fincher a question and he'll reply three times; he approaches the answer from one angle, discards it, then another, discards *that*, and then finds precisely the right way to express his thoughts before reeling it off like a high-speed data download. Fincher talks like he directs, careful to find the exact approach that will transfer what he's thinking to you. He doesn't want to waste time having you interpret what you *think* he means – he wants you to be sure. Fincher's a storyteller too, underlining points by playing out conversations for you, dropping snatches of dialogue into his descriptions like scenes from a script. Speak to the director for more than a few moments and it becomes clear that he communicates with you in the same way he communicates with an audience through his films.

For the rest of the afternoon, we spoke about his childhood and his early ventures shooting commercials and pop videos, plus mundane things like our mutual bafflement with cellular telephone technology and the weather. But mostly we spoke about film. Fincher's passion for cinema is infectious; he's informed and informative, energised by discussing the movies that shaped his viewpoints and open about his own works.

I hope in the following chapters that I'm able to help David Fincher transfer a little of his creative vision to the reader; I can personally say that, in the months I've spent writing this book, I've learnt more about the craft of directing from Fincher than I have from 15 years of working in media journalism. Thanks to him, I know my Skypans from my Kino-Flos and my CCEs from my ENRs. I look forward to the time when he *has* made hundreds of films, and to all the dark places he has yet to take us.

ONE

Dark and Light

'Directing ... it's kind of a masochistic endeavour.'

ON 28 AUGUST 1962, David Fincher was born to parents Howard and Claire in Denver, Colorado, and two years later the family's relocation to San Anselmo in Marin County, California would start him on the path to becoming one of modern film's most challenging directors.

Fincher's parents were an early influence on the young David, encouraging his interest in cinema and the creative arts. His father, who wrote under the name Jack Fincher as a bureau chief for *Life* magazine, would take him on regular trips into San Francisco to visit movie theatres, while his mother, a mental health nurse who worked in drug addiction and methadone maintenance programmes, did her best to expose him to contemporary and classical culture. While still a boy, he took classes in painting, drawing and sculpture, searching for the right creative outlet for his talents. 'It was a beautiful place to grow up,' Fincher says of California, '[a] very sunny and happy and very safe environment.'

Given the director's dark visions on the silver screen, one might imagine Fincher's childhood was similarly gloomy, but the opposite is true. 'Although, for about six to eight months, the Zodiac Killer was around,' he adds. 'We were all being followed by the California Highway Patrol in our little yellow school buses, but that was kind of the only thing to break the idyllic patina.' Fincher still equates the 'play' of being a director with the childhood endeavours of his youth: 'When I was a kid I loved to draw, and I loved my electric football sets, and I painted little things and made sculptures and did matte painting and comic books and illustrated stuff, and took pictures, had a darkroom, loved to tape-record stuff. [Directing is] all of that. It's not having to grow up.'

But before he had even reached his teens, Fincher was already being driven by his artistic urges. 'I would spend hours in my bedroom drawing. I could never get my hands to do it the way I had it in my head. I used to always go, "Someday you'll have the skill to draw exactly what you see in your head, and then you'd be able to show it to somebody, and if they like it, then you will have been able to transfer this thing through this apparatus to this, and then you'll truly know your worth." And I gave up drawing and then painting and then sculpture and then acting and then photography for things that were that much more difficult – to get that idea in your head *out there*.'

The possibility that filmmaking might be the avenue through which Fincher could express himself took hold early on. 'Dad used to take me to the movies on the weekends, and he would take me into San Francisco and we'd go to revival houses and see things like *Singin' in the Rain*, Danny Kaye movies, *The Exterminating Angel*, *Robin Hood* and *Gunga Din* – he took me to see those when I was about six years old. He took me to see *2001: A Space Odyssey* when I was seven, so to me movies were always part of what you could do. My dad's always loved movies; he had enough working knowledge to spark my interest, he was the one trying to rudimentarily explain how animation is done, what persistence of vision is and those kind of concepts, and he took me to a *lot* of movies – and that's kind of what was the genesis of my interest there, being exposed to a lot of stuff.'

It was the 1969 feature film *Butch Cassidy and the Sundance Kid* that inspired the young Fincher's dream of a career in cinema: 'I saw a documentary on the making of *Butch Cassidy* and I saw it when I was about eight and a half. It had never occurred to me before then that movies weren't made in real time, that there was a real job to make a movie. It just seemed to me that if it took place over three days, it took three days to shoot. The documentary that I saw was narrated by the director, George Roy Hill – I think it's actually on the DVD of the 25th anniversary edition of *Butch Cassidy and the Sundance Kid* – and it was kind of amusing to hear him talking about the different processes. He was talking about this behind the scenes footage and talking about why he chose the people and that they had to shoot stuff in slow motion to make the explosion look bigger, and all these things that I had just never thought about. The documentary talked you through the whole process, and I was kind of like, "Wow! These are adults building full-scale balsa-wood trains, just to blow them up. How do you get involved in that?" From that point on I was thinking, "That would be a good job."'

Hill's movie still has a strong personal resonance for Fincher over 30 years later. 'The first movie that I loved, that I thought was for me – not my dad showing me the movies that *he* loved – the first movie for *me* was *Butch Cassidy*, it was the first movie that I could look at and say "This is my experience" – and it's probably still my favourite all-time movie. I mean, it's a Western, it's the first buddy movie, but that was *the* movie; in retrospect you look back on it and go "This has a great cast, a great director, a great screenplay, a great costume designer, a brilliant cinematographer, great sets, great locations" – every single thing, and I remember being so swept away by how everything was working. It's probably some of Hill's best moments in that movie, it's so amazingly well done, and it has action and romance and humour. That was the seminal movie for me, where I went "There can be nothing better than this." And then there was *The Sting, Jaws*, I remember seeing *Lawrence of Arabia* on television in pan-and-scan, and *West Side Story*, I loved that movie too.'

While Fincher's father steeped him in film, his mother introduced him to other interests. 'She would pile me in the car and take me to the museums in San Francisco, like the Palace of Fine Arts, to see stuff,' he recalls. 'We'd go to the symphony, even if you didn't like it, so you could have that experience. I used to take painting classes and drawing classes from a very young age. It's not like my parents used to sculpt together ... we didn't have a painting room or a studio or anything, but they were always like "Whatever you want to do," as long as it wasn't violent – my parents were great because they were very anti-violence.'

With a smile, Fincher notes that it was this trait in his family that allowed him to start his filmmaking career in earnest. 'What it was, I swindled them into getting me a movie camera when I was nine. I very specifically asked my mother for a BB airgun for my birthday and she said, "I won't get you a BB gun. What else would you like?" And I said, "Well, I either want a BB gun or a movie camera." The BB gun was about $13 and movie cameras were about $170 or something, but they went and bought me the movie camera.' He joked in *Interview* magazine that his earliest Super 8mm films had such plots as 'Boy ties younger sister to railway tracks, causing death and dismemberment,' so even at this tender age his trademark style was emerging... 'I kind of always wanted to make movies but I didn't really make a *lot* of Super 8 movies, I made a handful or something with my friends. We did our versions of *The Six Million Dollar Man*, *I-Spy* and stuff like that, we did *It Takes a Thief*. I think we mostly did our versions of television shows, with kids from the neighbourhood. We didn't do a lot of cutting, it was just like goofing around – but I always wanted to make movies from the time I was about eight years old. I was like "That's pretty much the gig I want."'

The Fincher home was also in close proximity to that of a filmmaker whose career was just about to enter a new phase: George Lucas. 'And then when I was ten years old, George Lucas moves in two houses up the street,' Fincher recalls. 'They filmed *American Graffiti* on 4th Street in San Rafael, which was literally five blocks from my house, and we would walk down there and watch the cars drive back and forth, the giant mikes on towers and the camera platforms, so we were sort of exposed [to filmmaking]. There was an initial interest in me and the interest was fed, the fire was fanned, but there was also this access because things were happening in Marin County at that time and people were making films.' He continues: 'It meant the idea of making movies was very immediate, because Lucas, the guy who made one of my favourite movies, was this guy who I'd see getting his paper in the morning in his bathrobe. It demystified it. There were no big gates and a driveway with a Bentley with smoked glass driving in, he was just the guy next door with a beard. That was very encouraging – it was like, "You can do it."'

Fincher was also impressed by the work of British director Ridley Scott on *Alien* (1979). '*Star Wars* was an important film for me as a kid, but nowhere near as important to me as *Alien*. When I saw *Alien* I said, "That's what movies should look like." That was the first time I was aware of a visceral response to art direction, the first time I was aware that I was being told things about the people and the story through their surroundings and not through exposition.'

Fincher remained in San Anselmo until he was 14 and then moved once again, this time to Ashland in Oregon. There, Fincher attended Ashland High School and, along with his academic studies, took jobs that would push him further along the road to becoming a filmmaker – including one that would later be referenced on screen in *Fight Club*. 'I was a non-union projectionist at a movie theatre called the Varsity, which at the time was two theatres – I think it's like five or ten now in the same space, they've cut it up into viewing closets. The Varsity 2, which was the upstairs theatre, was very small, it was basically a theatre built onto the balcony; they had walled off the balcony and put another projector in there, and they showed a lot of foreign films.'

Among the European movies Fincher saw at the Varsity for the first time were the Paul Verhoeven films *Soldier of Orange* (1979) and *Spetters* (1980), and Edouard Molinaro's *La Cage aux folles* (1978). 'I took the gig because they had these films that I just wanted to make myself aware of,' he admits. Unlike *Fight Club*'s fictional Tyler Durden, Fincher is at pains to maintain that he never spliced frames of pornography into the movies he projected. 'I wanted to work in the movie theatre because I wanted to see 35mm film and see how it worked, and get comfortable with the machines; and also I wanted to watch a lot of movies. I got to see *All That Jazz* 175 times, which was a big thing for me. I got to see a lot of movies that I wouldn't normally have seen and I got to scrutinise them, so that was entertaining.'

He also mentions Bob Fosse's *Star 80* (1983). 'When I see a movie like *Star 80* and I go, "That's interesting, we're gonna start with the murder, so what is this movie going to be about?" The movie is about how much like this guy, the murderer that Eric Roberts plays, we all are, that his jealousy is not that different from our jealousy and how relatable this situation is; I love that.' He continues: 'I saw so many movies; I went and I took the college course in film appreciation and I saw *The Pawnbroker, Open City* and the whole Luis Buñuel series. I was kind of just a big sponge.'

In addition to absorbing knowledge from films, Fincher had several other roles that added to his skills. 'I had a bunch of jobs in high school. I worked a lot, slept a lot through school, but I worked a lot outside school and I did lighting for plays and theatre for the drama department. On weekends, I worked at a TV station shooting ENG (electronic news gathering) camera of burning barns and 'snowfall in valley for the first time in three years' or whatever, just going out and setting up cameras and shooting videotape. And then for about four or five nights a week I worked as a projectionist from six o'clock after school to about one in the morning, so I was always doing stuff. I saw a lot of movies, shot videotape and worked in the theatre. It was a good theatre community because of the local Shakespeare festival, so we were exposed to a lot of interesting stuff, but it was mostly out of boredom that I got involved.'

That boredom translated into a need to develop insights that would later serve Fincher as a feature film director. 'Early on, I kind of came to realise that a director needed to know a little bit about everything, so I was never going to be in a position where I was wasting any time, because there was always something to be gleaned that a director could use. Like, if you have a lay-over at an airport, you go and you sit and you listen to people's conversations and you hear how people talk; if you're in the lobby of a hotel and you see someone being angry, you can study the way that people get worked up about stuff – there's always something of value to gather. You could always watch a movie on TV, and this was the beginning of the VHS era, at the beginning of HBO and so on. I'd sort of decided that if I wanted to be a director, I needed to be able to do a lot of different things, so I studied a lot of photography in school and I studied it out of school, painting and drawing too ... I didn't want to be a canvas chair dilettante. I wanted to be able to do it.'

After graduation from Ashland High, Fincher returned to Marin County but, unlike many of his contemporaries, he rejected the notion of going to film school. He would tell *Premiere's* Maximillian Potter years later: 'Directing isn't about drawing a neat little picture and showing it to the cameraman. I didn't want to go to film school, I didn't know what the point was. The fact is, you don't know what directing is until the sun is setting and you've got to get five shots and you're only going to get two. The Teamsters are going, "We're out of here, we're in triple time," the production manager is going, "You have to stop, there's no more money."'

The closest Fincher came to the film school experience was during a brief period in the early 1980s. 'I went to a place called the Berkeley Film Institute for a summer programme with a grade school friend of mine, and we just thought it was a joke. It was very impressionist, very Berkeley. There were all these people who were there to communicate and change the world, to do all these lofty things – and then they made these really shitty, stupid little movies. And we were kind of like, "I'm not here for this, I'm just here to pull cable." We were the youngest people there and we ended up being the grips and electrics on everybody else's movies, and it was pretty good those six or seven weeks, we got to shoot Panaflex cameras and make a married print – it was in black and white and you made these little cheese-ball movies, but at least you were making *something*. It was kind of like film school in that way, but those who can't do, teach, and those who couldn't teach, taught there. They tried, they just didn't want to get dirty with it, they didn't want to get in up to their necks. It was all very patrician.'

But his experiences at the Berkeley Film Institute did lead Fincher into his first industry job at the animation studio Korty Films, in Mill Valley. 'One of the guys I met there got a job for John Korty, who I had known before – my sister had done voice-overs for the *Sesame Street* shorts that his studio had made back in the early

1970s – and so in 1981 a friend who was building their dark room got me a job there as a production assistant. I was just moving Xerox machines around and helping out. I helped out there as much as I could for about a year and a half, and helped rewire animation cameras and worked in the dark room, shot some second unit stuff, and did assistant camera work.'

Fincher received his first screen credit here, on the 1983 animated feature *Twice Upon a Time* – under 'Special Photographic Effects' – but he was already looking beyond it to the mould-breaking visual effects house that George Lucas had built, Industrial Light & Magic. Contrary to some reports, Fincher didn't get a job at ILM just because he had lived on the same block as Lucas. 'I had met him as a ten-year old. I was walking down the street and George was out getting the newspaper in his bathrobe, and I went "Hi" and he went "Hi."' But Fincher *had* been inspired by the second *Star Wars* movie, *The Empire Strikes Back* (1980). 'I think to this day [that film] is one of the finest amalgams of cinematic disciplines,' he notes. 'My roommate in Fairfax was working at ILM and they were hiring for one of their stage units, and he told me about it and got me an introduction to [visual effects supervisor] Dennis Muren – they hired me to load Vistavision cameras and take meter readings and shoot Go-Motion.'

Muren, whose work includes movies such as *Close Encounters of the Third Kind* (1977), *ET the Extra-Terrestrial* (1982), *Empire of the Sun* (1987) and the *Star Wars* saga, was one of Fincher's self-confessed idols. 'It was a great place to learn,' he recalled. 'I learnt a lot about the editorial process, we shot a lot of inserts and we did second unit stuff. There was a lot to be exposed to and to learn from.'

During his time at Industrial Light & Magic from late 1981 to 1984, Fincher was credited on the third *Star Wars* feature *Return of the Jedi* (1983), as an assistant cameraman in the Miniature and Optical Effects Unit, and on *The NeverEnding Story* and *Indiana Jones and the Temple of Doom* (both 1984) in the matte photography department. 'I didn't have much responsibility on those shows, really. I was the second assistant and everything else was simply glorified PA work.'

For Fincher, it was a sobering experience as well as an educational one. 'I got to see the beginnings of the whole unionised, mechanised and disgruntled world of Lucasfilm. I did that for about two and a half years. I came into ILM at the end of a golden age; there's periods to everything. There was a period of time in music videos when things were really fun and exciting, when money was being spent and there was attention on it, it flourished and kind of sparkled – but then it got boring and stupid and then you moved on to commercials. I came to ILM at a time when things were sort of dying off, and all the people that were the reason that I wanted to be there were leaving. Richard Edlund had gone and Phil Tippett was taking a leave of absence, Joe Johnston was coming south to try and make movies, the place was sort of fragmenting. Dennis Muren was taking time off and there were a lot of *Star Trek* movies being made, things were kind of getting off track. They couldn't keep the band together.' Fincher would later work with Edlund on *Alien 3*'s visual effects, while Tippett and Johnston would go on to their own directorial careers.

'To me the highlight of anything ever achieved at that place was *The Empire Strikes Back*,' Fincher reiterates. 'In every single category, it's beautifully lit, it's beautifully designed, it's really well cast – who would have thought, Billy Dee Williams for this? – and there's incredible risks taken with it. I mean, they made a main character a Muppet! You sit there and think, "Who risks a hundred million dollar franchise by having a pivotal character that's a Muppet?" And then they went, "We don't know how to do this thing with the tanks." "Well, we'll do it stop-motion." "Nobody does stop-motion any more." "Well, we'll do it. We'll do it motion-control and it won't look like it and we'll take these rooms and fill them with baking soda and people will come up through trap doors with masks on and move things..." Who has the sort of confidence to create this potpourri of techniques? I thought that the guys who did the effects for this movie, the guys who had the discipline to set up those tables and take one frame every 25 minutes, I could learn something from them.

'The kind of myriad disciplines that had gone in to achieving this whole thing were awesome, and that had kind of ended, they were doing *Starman* and *Explorers* and there was a lot of this "Just get it done" attitude. "Here, make a rubber worm and pull it with a wire, and that's fine..." I was going, "I didn't sign on for this," so I split and came to Los Angeles.'

Fincher's incentive to jump ship was a commercial created for the American Cancer Society that he and a few other discontented Industrial Light & Magic technicians had created on their own time. 'We did it on the weekends, me, this guy Tony McVey and Kirk Thatcher.' McVey was a sculptor who had worked on *Sinbad and the Eye of the Tiger* (1977), *Superman* (1978) and *The Dark Crystal* (1982), a veteran of *Return of the Jedi* with Fincher and Thatcher (who would go on to be a writer-director for the Muppet movies series).

'We were just bored. Most of us worked at ILM and we were kind of bored [with it], so we went to this low-rent optical house just outside of Berkeley where they had motion-control equipment and stuff. This friend of mine, who was a truck driver who wanted to become a producer, went to the American Cancer Society and said "What if we do a commercial for you for really cheap? We've got all these people, we've got all this expertise, we can do it really inexpensively."' The striking concept behind the ad spot was a powerful image for the anti-smoking lobby. 'We sold them this idea that we thought was really funny,' Fincher recalls. 'We were all sitting around a table at a restaurant in Larkspur and came up with this idea of seeing a foetus smoking a cigarette *in utero* – we pitched it to them and they said "Great," and I think they gave us about $7000 – and we just *did* it, my friend Ren Klyce wrote the music and we just *winged* it.' Klyce would also work with Fincher years later when the director moved to the big screen.

The dark imagery of the 1984 'Smoking Foetus' commercial quickly brought Fincher to the attention of producers. 'Some people saw it and then I got a call to come to LA to talk about doing music videos.' Fincher came to the city during the summer of the same year. 'I moved to Los Angeles during the Olympic Games, and I thought "God, there's hardly any traffic. LA is great!" Of course, everyone had left for the games.'

Fincher moved into an apartment in Westwood, decorated in a bland 1980s pop-architecture style he nicknamed the '*Miami Vice* hospital' look; the flat would later serve as the model for Jack's 'Ikea catalogue' home in *Fight Club*. The young director wanted the American Cancer Society promo to be his calling card into the world of advertising; but his new employers took a different view. 'I came to LA and signed with a video company hoping to do commercials. I thought that because Ridley Scott had come from doing commercials, that would be a really good way to break into the movie business – but at the time, nobody would let us do any commercials because they didn't think we were good enough.'

With the growth in music video culture and the rise in popularity of MTV, Fincher instead joined a brigade of new talent being funnelled into the nascent pop promo industry, a breeding ground for many directors who would later go on to careers as feature film directors. People like Fincher, Peter Care and Dominic Sena would graduate from music video in the same way the British commercial directors like Alan Parker, Adrian Lyne and Scott brothers Ridley and Tony had crossed over from ads to movies.

David Fincher is dismissive of his earliest effort, the rock concert movie *The Beat of the Live Drum* (1985) featuring Rick Springfield of 'Jessie's Girl' fame. 'My first videos were for Rick Springfield and we shot that up in San Francisco. [It's] not a feature film, it was just a compilation of videos. That was just something to do; they came to me and said "Will you shoot these videos?" and I started shooting them, and then they said "Do you want to come and shoot this concert too?" and I was like "I've never done that before," and I fucked the whole thing up, it's truly awful. I got into it to do the videos, they hired me to do the videos and then tried to stream it together. We tried to do something different, but it was stupid.'

In the same year, he directed two more videos for another act, The Motels, with 'Shame' and 'Shock'. 'Shame' earned him a nomination for American Video's Best Video Award, and he later directed 'Don't Tell Me the Time' for the band's lead singer, Martha Davis, when she launched her solo career in 1987.

In 1986, Fincher changed his representation: 'I did The Motels and then I got signed at this company called N Lee Lacey.' Nesbitt Lee Lacey's most famous advertisement was one of the classic 1970s Coca-Cola television spots, featuring gridiron star 'Mean' Joe Green. 'He had these beautiful offices on Melrose Avenue and he represented three guys, David Hogan, Greg Gold and Dominic Sena, and I really liked their work, these guys who I thought were doing some beautiful stuff, real simple, really well staged and photographed.' Hogan would go on to work with Fincher as *Alien 3*'s action sequence unit director before directing *Barb Wire* (1996); Gold would direct 1987's *House of the Rising Sun;* and Sena would helm *Kalifornia* (1993), starring *Seven* and *Fight Club* lead Brad Pitt, *Swordfish* (2001) and *A Normal Life* (2003).

At the time, Fincher had been turned down by one set of producers: 'I was looking around for a company to go to and I sent my reel to Steve Barron and Simon Fields – and they politely declined to represent me.' But N Lee Lacey saw Fincher's potential, even if their vision of how to use it didn't chime with his. 'They wanted me, so I signed there, worked there for a couple of years and it didn't really work out. There was a 'bottom-feeder' mentality there – just keep the record companies happy, don't spend too much money, do what you're told. [They felt] we were providing a service, that it was an ancillary thing, videos aren't the be-all and end-all, we're just part of selling the record. I was like, "Don't *you* represent *me*? To me, they're the be-all and end-all." I continually couldn't get jobs because my ideas were too big and too expensive, and this was a company whose attitude was that to stay competitive, you have to stay cheap.

'They had this mentality of "We'll tell you what you have to spend, and then you'll have to figure out how to do it," and, really, like most of the entertainment industry, it was a lot of little people sucking all the lifeforce and juices out of a good endeavour. They said to me, "You have a commitment to doing lower-budget videos because that's where the industry's going." I just sort of lost it with them. I thought, "You guys are morons if you can't see that the music business is ego-driven, and that if there's lucre out there, there's going to be some to spend on how to package and market these artists."' During his time at the company, Fincher directed two promos for The Outfield, 'All the Love in the World', and 'Every Time You Cry' from their 1985 album *Play Deep*.

Fincher had been signed to the company by Beth Broday, a music video representative, and it was her departure from the production company that provided the catalyst for the next evolutionary step in his career; the creation of Propaganda Films. 'Beth got us all together and said, "I'm leaving and I'm going to be a development executive at this company that hopes to get into making motion pictures,"' remembers Fincher, 'and she said, "You'll be well taken care of because the person who's coming to replace me is really good and blah, blah, blah..." I was sitting there with David and Greg and Dom and a couple of other people, and they were saying, "I guess Beth is gone, we should stick around and see how it goes..." And I said, "These people don't want to get us into commercials, they don't think we're good enough, this is like a totally shit-ball bottom-feeder business. Let's start our *own* company." And they all thought "Maybe," and then *en masse* we were approached by Joni Sighvatsson, who thought he could get the money together to start a video company with his then-partner Steve Golin, and that they would run it and take care of all the headaches and we could just go and be creative.'

After recruiting record executive-turned-video director Nigel Dick to the team, Sighvatsson and Golin were ready to create their own enterprise; Golin would later serve as a producer on Fincher's film *The Game*, while Sighvatsson would go on to produce *Wild at Heart* (1990), 1992's *Red Rock West* (the screen debut of *Panic Room*'s Dwight Yoakam), *Arlington Road* (1999) and *K-19: The Widowmaker* (2002). 'They stole Nigel from another company, he came over and we started Propaganda.' Sena came up with the name, which Fincher thought 'would subvert the commercial identity.' He continues: 'We got everybody to kind of agree on this notion that we were going to reclaim this bad, dark word 'propaganda', which is kind of what music videos are, how the artist wants to be seen, how the artist *should* be seen to be attractive to the multitudes.' The director explained the 'mission statement' for the company during an interview: 'There's this place; it's a factory and you don't know what goes on there, but you put your money in one end and your cassette comes out the other.' From its formation in late 1986, the company would become a living, breathing entity that would be home to Fincher for the next decade.

'Propaganda became a huge commercial music video factory,' says Fincher. He jokes about pressuring Sighvatsson to make Propaganda Films into a fully fledged production facility. 'Joni, because he's so cheap, wanted to run the whole thing out of his kitchen, so we had to go beat Joni up and get him to understand that we weren't going to sign with a company that was run out of his kitchen. If we were going to do this, we were going to do this on a big scale. That became Propaganda and that did well.'

In the company's inaugural year alone, Fincher directed videos for acts such as Patti Smith, Eddie Money, Ry Cooder, The Hooters, Loverboy, Mark Knopfler and Wire Train; the latter group's lead singer would make a brief cameo in Fincher's second feature, *Seven*. 'Basically, you'd set the tone for what people wanted to see with music videos, then sell the ideas back to commercial companies for ten times the money – "We did this video and we can tell you exactly how much it's going to cost to do it for your client and their stupid soft drink."'

Perhaps Fincher's best-remembered music video from Propaganda's first 12 months was for 'Englishman in New York' by Sting; matching the tone of the song about the flamboyant British expatriate Quentin Crisp, Fincher's work was an evocative piece in black and white. Opening with a series of snapshots establishing the location and winter season, the video follows Sting and Crisp through New York's snowy streets while a saxophonist plays; the song's lyrics about non-conformity merge smoothly with the sense of exile and melancholy conjured by the imagery.

'It was a really interesting time,' recalls the director. 'Videos were important then and people really cared. MTV was a cultural force, it wasn't just fashion, and people tuned in to see what was happening. I don't think agents watch MTV nearly as much now as they used to 14 years ago. It was a fun time and I really liked it; I looked at it as these people were going to finance my film school. It was a sandbox, it was somewhere to play. If I had this idea about a lightning machine – let's try that. I have the idea of making everything look like [old] Horst photographs – what would those kind of images mean to 14-year-old kids, how would people respond? It was kind of an interesting petri dish and to a certain extent we were in charge. It wasn't like MTV would say, "Hey, thanks very much, not interested," and they wouldn't play it. If you made a video, they'd play it, and if you made a good video, they'd play the *shit* out of it. So it was kind of like instant gratification, and it was a fun exercise – there it was on TV, and Johnny Carson talked about it.'

He continues: 'I only did fairly mainstream rock videos, I never got to do any true subversives like, say, Nine Inch Nails – [although] I guess Madonna was seen as a sort of a provocateur. It was the training ground to make features in the 1980s. In the 1960s it was film school, in the 1970s it was commercials. Eventually every window closes, every niche gets filled, and the next thing comes along. The movie business says, "Okay, we've had enough of those guys, now what's happening?", which is good. Music videos are probably the most creative filmmaking being done right now. They're also close to *true* directing, creating context for the under-standing of an idea. I still feel that films are nowhere near as abstract as they could or should be, and I know there's an audience out there who would understand those abstractions. It's too bad so many movies end up being so literal.'

In 1988, Fincher directed two promos for British band Johnny Hates Jazz and returned to experimenting with coloration on 'Roll with It' for singer Steve Winwood. Set in a blues club, the sepia-toned video makes thorough use of a long 'snorkel' lens to take the point-of-view into tight niches. Fincher also directed LA Lakers cheerleader-turned-singer Paula Abdul, with 'It's Just the Way That You Love Me'. Two versions of the video were made, one with additional material, casting Abdul as a woman in love with a rich millionaire who showers her with fast cars, champagne, pearls and other gifts, even though she loves him for his personality and not for his money. In the following year, Fincher worked with the singer again on three more videos: 'Cold Hearted', a piece perhaps inspired by *All That Jazz* (1979), blending risqué dance moves as the singer and her dancers perform for a group of stoic 'suits'; 'Straight Up', another high-contrast black and white film, with a cameo by actor Arsenio Hall; and 'Forever Your Girl', which was left incomplete by the director. 'It was never finished,' he notes, 'and they just cut a video together from what was there.'

As well as working with Jody Watley and Don Henley, 1989 also brought Fincher two of his most striking videos to date, the grim 'Janie's Got a Gun' for Aerosmith and Madonna's Gothic romance 'Express Yourself'. The Aerosmith song tells the story of a young girl, pushed to the edge by her father's abuse, who finds a handgun and kills him before going on the run. A night-time chase ends in a gloomy rail yard, with the girl pursued by the probing beams of the cops' flashlights – a clear visual cue that returns on a number of occasions in *Seven*. Fincher admits his attraction towards 'the idea of peering into darkness,' but adds that he felt 'that video didn't really turn out as it was supposed to.' Still, his direction of 'Janie's Got a Gun' lay some of the groundwork that would mature in Fincher's feature film endeavours.

'Music videos are fun,' says the director. 'There's nothing more gratifying than shooting, cutting, scoring and mixing a scene that works. It has a beginning, a middle and an end. When you watch that scene with an audience and they react to it, it's amazing. You've got to them, you've touched them. It's also an amazing thing to be able to take a piece of music and put pictures to it that may or may not be related to the lyrics and to create this whole other thing. You kind of force abstraction [from it]. The best ones don't tell the story of the song, but offer an alternative way of thinking about what's being sung. They're jumping-off points for other ideas, things which, while being singular, don't become the definitive interpretation.'

'Express Yourself' brought Fincher together with pop diva Madonna for the very first time, starting a collaboration that would lead to four outstanding videos and several industry awards. Shot in Los Angeles in November 1989, the song from her *Like a Prayer* album was married to a cool, moody vignette inspired by the 1926 science fiction film *Metropolis*, directed by Fritz Lang. In the video, Madonna is the confined wife of a suited 'overseer' who rules a mechanised undercity populated by well-muscled men; while she pines to escape her gilded gage, one of the slave workers breaks his shackles and the two are brought together. *Slant* magazine named 'Express Yourself' as their 'Greatest Video of All Time' and called it 'the embodiment of queer chic' and 'a bombastic masterpiece'; the promo won several other accolades, including a Best Direction Award for Fincher.

Like *Metropolis*, the 'Express Yourself' video is about a repressed woman destroying the contrivance that controls her, touching on the rebellious attitudes that characterise much of the director's work. The video also plays with dark industrial imagery that prefigures the penal colony seen in *Alien 3*, and the conflicts between the shirtless workers prefigures the basement bare-knuckle boxing of *Fight Club*.

Madonna and Fincher collaborated again in 1990 on a video for another track from *Like a Prayer*, the heartbreaking 'Oh Father'. Widely regarded as one of Fincher's best pieces, the director drew on visual techniques and motifs from the Orson Welles classic *Citizen Kane* (1941). Both the song and the video move through the memories of a woman as she thinks back to her childhood, the death of her mother, and her life growing up with a father who cannot handle her. The stylised expressionist tone of this black and white short plays to Fincher's skill of creating singular, memorable images; singing cherubs, a rain of pearls from a broken necklace, the child stretching up to a distorted door handle.

But perhaps the best known Fincher video for the singer was her dance hit 'Vogue'. Shot in March 1990, 'Vogue' showcases Madonna in Marilyn Monroe/Marlene Deitrich mode as she performs complex routines in 1940s-style clothing, once more shot in monochrome with the deep blacks that characterise Fincher's night scenes. The 'Vogue' video was a key element in the singer's re-invention of herself for the 1990s, winning multiple industry nominations and awards for Fincher and editor Jim Haygood, who would go on to work with the director on *The Game, Fight Club* and *Panic Room*.

The director's last video for the performer was shot three years later, after he had completed his work on *Alien 3*. From the *Erotica* album, 'Bad Girl' guest-starred Christopher Walken and *The Game*'s James Rebhorn in a narrative following Madonna as a power-dressing executive driven to dangerous relationships. In a homage to the 1987 Wim Wenders film *Wings of Desire*, Walken is cast as an ethereal 'angel of death', following Madonna around New York City as she seeks solace in self-destructive casual sex. Again, Fincher's effective use of imagery explores the plotline through economical storytelling – an excellent match-cut between a roadway and a bar top, the surreptitious removal of a wedding ring, an unbuttoned blouse, a refrigerator full of vodka, all setting up her eventual murder at the hands of one of her lovers. Like Fincher himself, Walken watches events unfold from a camera crane, playing with the idea of the director as the 'god' of a movie, and by the end of the video, Madonna has joined her angelic observer as they both watch the murder scene from a distance. Fincher had used a similar motif in 'The Director', an earlier commerical for Chanel.

Fincher's work with the singer did much to cement her image at that time in the minds of her audience. 'Madonna is Madonna,' the director notes, 'but she's also this foul-mouthed, funny, sincere girl from Detroit. There's the thing that you're selling and the thing that the people were – I've had some very bad experiences with artists, I've done really good work for those who really didn't deserve it, and I've done really bad work for people who deserved so much more. But I've always liked musicians, I thought the people were incredibly stimulating. I really enjoyed [working with them] because they were so different from my experience. Some of the most interesting and most talented people I have ever worked with are musical artists.'

Along with 'Oh Father' and 'Vogue' for Madonna, in 1990 Fincher also directed videos for Iggy Pop, George Michael and Billy Idol. George Michael's 'Freedom '90' is memorable for its plethora of supermodels at play on a country estate, including Tatjana Patitz, Cindy Crawford, Christy Turlington and Linda Evangelista; the concept for the video came from the singer, with the addition, at Fincher's suggestion, of a scene where a jukebox explodes, to symbolise the destruction of Michael's old pop persona and the birth of a new one.

For Billy Idol, Fincher directed more conventional fare, with 'Cradle of Love', a tie-in to that year's box-office flop *The Adventures of Ford Fairlane,* and a cover of 'LA

Woman' to coincide with the release of pop biopic *The Doors*. In the tradition of several hard rock videos, 'Cradle of Love' answers the prayers of a lonely guy when a gorgeous girl invades his room and dances on his bed, while 'LA Woman' follows Idol and his girlfriend in a game of hide-and-seek through the seedy club-land underbelly of Los Angeles; however, Fincher did not complete his work on the latter. 'It was never finished. I went off to do *Alien 3* and somebody else from the record company came in.'

Fincher was one of the first directors of the video generation to move to features. 'It was obviously going to be the video guys [next],' he notes. 'The studios eventually said, "Okay, this guy's never made a movie before but he's shot a bunch of interesting videos, let's give him a shot." I guess with any movement, the things that are good are going to be aped by people who are stupid, who pollute the language and make it crap. But I think there are more talented technicians working today because of music videos than ever before. I think there are more skilful cameramen working today because a lot of people had the opportunity, through music video and commercials, to shoot film.'

However, some commentators would forever brand Fincher and his fellows as being all style and no substance. Kenneth Turan of the *Los Angeles Times*, a frequent disputant against Fincher's films, described the post-MTV directors as 'Cold ... They're technically proficient, they're not hacks, but characters and emotional content do not seem to concern them.'

At last, Fincher's plans to make music videos a stepping stone to movies seemed to have come to fruition, but the director would spend the next two years fighting an uphill battle to make the third film in the *Alien* saga as *he* saw it, only to come away soured by the entire experience (see Chapter Three). 'I thought I'd rather die of colon cancer than do another movie,' he said in a *Sight & Sound* interview, and so Fincher returned to Propaganda Films, back to directing videos and, for the first time in years, directing commercials.

In 1991, Fincher had been involved with developing an advertisement for Pepsi called 'Pop Rock' (the piece subsequently became known as 'Bullet the Blue Sky'). 'It was just a rough-cut that we did of something that they never bought [based on] the U2 music we used.' But the director continued to make commercials and the following year created the Nike spot 'Barclay on Broadway', featuring basketball star Charles Barclay. Fincher teamed with Haygood and production designer Jeffrey Beecroft (*The Game*) for this and other Nike ads such as 'Temple of Flight' and 'Instant Karma', along with commercials for Budweiser, Chanel and the award-winning 'BladeRoller' promo for Coca-Cola Japan, inspired by *Blade Runner* (1982) and *Rollerball* (1975).

Throughout the mid-1990s, Fincher continued to direct television spots for major concerns like Nike, Levis and AT&T. These included the dynamic 'Magazine Wars', in which tennis star Andre Agassi comes to life on the cover of a magazine (winner of a Silver Lion award at the Cannes International Advertising Festival), 'Young Miss', featuring an early part for actress Angelina Jolie, and 'Escape', an advert for the 1995 Honda del Sol that was never broadcast. Fincher's sole venture into car commercials was a 30-second espionage-thriller parody; the commercial cut so close to the James Bond films that the ad was pulled following legal action from MGM. The director recalls: 'It was terrible. Too Bond-ish. We were trying to do *The Avengers*, but they were just too young to understand it.' The advert featured actress Claire Forlani, star of *Highbinders* (2003) and *Meet Joe Black* (1998) with Brad Pitt, who also played a role in another Fincher commercial, the Levis spot 'Restaurant'. Fincher would later become involved with another car company when BMW produced their short film series *The Hire* (see below).

Between *Alien 3* and Fincher's next feature, *Seven*, Fincher's music video output slowed, with just 'Who is It?' for Michael Jackson in 1993 and 'Love is Strong' for The Rolling Stones a year later. The video for Jackson (subtitled as 'Version 2: Break-up Dangerous Story') recalls Fincher's narrative promos for Madonna, casting the singer as a reclusive millionaire pursued by a high-class call girl who longs to leave her 'stable' and become his lover. Reaching the rich man's mansion, she discovers dozens of silver cards with the names of other call girls and realises that he has many lovers, before returning – heartbroken – to her old life. More striking is the monochromatic 'Love is Strong', where the Stones wander the city of New York as giants; like the opening titles of *Panic Room*, the scenes of the band striding across the Big Apple's streets are both impressive and unsettling, and the video spawned several imitators, both in commercials and other pop videos.

Amidst pre-production preparation for *The Game*, Fincher directed '6th Avenue Heartache' for The Wallflowers in 1996, returning to motifs similar to those he used for Sting's 'Englishman...' video. Like the 1987 short, '6th Avenue Heartache' is shot in black and white on the streets of a chilly New York City, but Fincher constructs the piece as a series of old, careworn photographs from a scrapbook, brought to life as the viewpoint moves across them. But the video for The Wallflowers would be Fincher's last for Propaganda Films.

Back in 1987, Steve Golin and Joni Sighvatsson had initiated a relationship between Propaganda and PolyGram, producing Nigel Dick's *PI Private Investigations* for the home video market; PolyGram bought the company whole in 1992 to begin what Golin called 'a slow push into the movie business', which came to fruition in 1997 when Fincher's third feature *The Game* became the debut for the company's new film division. But by 1998 Sighvatsson and Dick had left the company and Propaganda had become a wholly owned part of the PolyGram Filmed Entertainment Corporation.

Fincher remembers the progression of events: 'Propaganda went out of business. It was sold off to PolyGram and a few people made some good money, but then PolyGram got out of the movie business and sold all of its assets to

Universal. Universal didn't want Propaganda, and they sold it to a cartel of investors from Texas who brought in their own management people.'

The disappointed Fincher found himself in the same situation he had encountered years earlier at N Lee Lacey. 'I left because I didn't want to be tied to a place that was kind of a shadow of its former self. I think I originally had a deal that had television, internet and all these different projects that I had access to, and I didn't want that, because I didn't like these new people – so I went and started a commercials and videos thing just to do those.' This new production company was Anonymous Content, co-founded by Steve Golin. 'I added my name to that, then partnered with Art Linson to produce *Fight Club*, and we went to New Line to get the money to make movies.' Fincher and Linson created Indelible Pictures in 1999, signing an exclusive three-year production deal with New Line Cinema to produce and direct; *Panic Room* (2002) would be the first Indelible feature.

Under the Anonymous label, Fincher's next music video came in 2000, after completing work on *Fight Club*. Filmed for the band A Perfect Circle, 'Judith' was put together on a relatively short production schedule to fit around the group's current tour. With Allen Daviau as director of photography, the video exhibits a mix of stylistic elements, including high-contrast depth of shadow and artificial distortion effects layered into the film itself, as the band play their song on an abandoned movie set. The band's lead singer would later be offered a role in Fincher's next film, *Panic Room* (see Chapter Six). Fincher's concept for the video keeps the band's faces blurry and mysterious, gradually 'distressing' the look of the film to the beat of the song.

In the same year, Fincher also directed spots in Nike's 'Invincible' series of commercials for the Summer Olympic Games in Sydney. Working once again with musician Ren Klyce, editor Angus Wall and visual effects house Digital Domain after *Fight Club*, Fincher's adverts mix live-action film of sprinters with computer-generated imagery; the finished commercials appear to show moving strips of celluloid back-lit against a lightbox, shot through a macro lens. Following the conclusion of the *Panic Room* shoot in 2002, the director also produced 'Mechanical Legs', an award-winning commercial for Adidas starring a set of robotic limbs giving a pair of trainer shoes a work-out, and an entry in Coca-Cola's 'Real' campaign, shooting real-life celebrity couple Courtney Cox Arquette and David Arquette in a sitcom-style scenario.

But perhaps the most dynamic commercials to have come from Fincher in recent years are the short films that comprise *The Hire* series for BMW. With the formation of Anonymous Content, Fincher was able to step back from the directorial position and assume a producer's standpoint. 'All I did was say "Here's an idea, here's how it could be executed, here's what you could sell, here's why it's good for you, here's how you should position the vehicle, here's what this character is, here are some names of some people I think are talented that I know might be interested." I was just getting the ball rolling.' But although confined to an executive role, Fincher's stylistic fingerprints are still visible on these mini-movies.

The shorts all feature British actor Clive Owen of *Croupier* (1997) and *Gosford Park* (2002) as the nameless Driver, the extraordinary wheelman who puts the Beemers through their paces. For the first movie in the series, *Ambush*, the late John Frankenheimer, director of *The Manchurian Candidate* (1962) and *Ronin* (1998), was called upon to direct a script by *Seven*'s Andrew Kevin Walker about a gang of goons intent on gutting the driver's charge, a smuggler who has swallowed a fortune in diamonds. *Crouching Tiger, Hidden Dragon* (2000) director Ang Lee took on the second story, *Chosen*, centring around a balletic, swooping car chase as the driver protects a Tibetan child from villains driving – no bias here – a Mercedes.

Hong Kong's Wong Kar Wai, director of *Happy Together* (1997) and *Chung King Express* (1994), eschews the high-octane approach in *The Follow*, where a suspicious husband played by Mickey Rourke hires the driver to track the wife he believes is being unfaithful to him; the script came from the pen of Andrew Kevin Walker once again, while *Panic Room*'s Forest Whitaker featured in a supporting role. *Star* is the work of British director Guy Ritchie, of *Lock, Stock and Two Smoking Barrels* (1998) and *Snatch* (2000), and starred Brad Pitt. Ritchie cast his wife Madonna in the lead as a bitchy celebrity given the ride of her life. The final film of the quartet is *Powder Keg* by Mexico's Alejandro González Iñárritu, the director of *Amores Perros* (2000). Co-starring Stellan Skarsgard as a bullet-wounded war reporter, Iñárritu's film is a monologue for the actor on the role of the observer and the observed in wartime as the driver speeds him across a battle-zone wilderness. In addition to these main features, the director of *Boiler Room* (2000), Ben Younger, has helmed a series of 'hidden' films featuring a chain of incidental characters, which fit in between the other five stories.

However, Fincher notes that the original concept for *The Hire* was very different. 'The advertising agency had been given a directive by BMW to get into the internet in a high-profile way, and they came to me with this stupid idea of making *Mission Impossible* by way of *Timecode*. It was like an action-adventure thing where everybody's trying to find this car that's been stolen, and these five different characters would stream in real time and you'd be able to hop from one channel to the other and all these stories would intertwine.

'I said, "It is technologically unfeasible, you would never be able to download this much data to be able to pick and choose streaming video channels, you would never figure out a way to intertwine these stories in a way that will be satisfying." A movie is the by-product of choosing specific moments that are seen and help you understand a narrative. You can't take where everybody crosses over and extrapolate [what happens] when this person left. As William Goldman says, most of the time you come into the scene at the last possible moment, just so you get the high point. You don't want to see what happens before it and you don't want to see what happens after it. When characters leave and go off, it's probably not the most interesting part of the movie, because if it is, then the movie is in the wrong place.'

For all BMW's high-flown words about *The Hire* as a project intended to push the boundaries of digital cinema, the five shorts are still glorified adverts for the company's top motors, but, that said, they are accomplished with enough elan to elude the radar of even the more resistant viewer. The cookie-cutter car ad is commonplace, where some free spirit go-getter takes his shiny ride through a clean, perfect highway landscape, but *The Hire*'s films are sharp bites of motor vehicle porn for fans of German engineering technology.

Fincher's reaction against the typical car advertising model was strong. 'I said, "So you want me to do this story where everybody is in this amped-up, super-charged situation, and their primary concern is Where Is This Car?" That doesn't even work in a *Mission Impossible* thing. We have to make the people believable, otherwise it's just a corporate positioning statement. I said, "You guys have an image problem, because your cars are synonymous with yuppie me-decade [thinking]." Every time you see a BMW, it's on a turntable, it doesn't exist in the real world, it's in some beautiful shot of a horse-breeding ranch, it's this aspirational, unattainable thing. It says, "You can't afford it, but if you could, this is the one you'd want." I think that the notion here is to take the BMW and, like the same way it's used in the James Bond movies, make it *disposable*. Make it a Bic lighter, so it gets shot up, it gets run off the road, it gets crashed and the guy gets another one.'

Fincher refers to Walter Hill's 1978 movie *The Driver* as *The Hire*'s touchstone. 'It's a really simple, existential set-up for a hero, and it's a guy who transports people from one place to the next, and that's it. Whomever he meets is what that story's about. [I said:] "You should do them in five or six minutes and get great directors, different ones to do each one," and that's what they did.' Underwritten by BMW at an alleged $1 million budget, produced by Anonymous Content and presented exclusively through a website portal, the shorts were also made available on a DVD for potential car buyers; as a marketing campaign, *The Hire* was a hit for BMW, earning advertising industry accolades like the Grand Prix for online advertising at Cannes, plus the Clio, One Show and AICP awards, as well as snaring an all-important potential car owner demographic of affluent males. 13 million viewers watched the streaming video of the five films, and BMW's sales jumped by over 17 per cent compared to the same period the previous year.

Despite the success of Fincher's production, BMW announced in 2002 that the second run of three more movies, *The Hire Phase 2*, would go ahead without his stewardship. Initially, Fincher, Spike Jonze and Lars Von Trier had been tipped to direct the first three *Phase 2* shorts, but apparent 'creative differences' meant the project was turned over to Tony Scott's production house; however, BMW retains a relationship with Fincher in order, potentially, to produce other commercials in the future.

But, considering Fincher's anti-commercial rabble-rousing in *Fight Club*, some observers wondered how the filmmaker could reconcile his art with the hucksterism of an ad campaign for one of the world's largest, most conspicuously status-symbolic auto companies. 'I'm totally anti-commercialism,' the director states firmly. 'I would never do commercials where people hold the product by their head and tell you how great it is, I just wouldn't do that stuff. It's all inference ... The Levis commercials I did weren't really about jeans, the Nike commercials weren't about shoes. The 'Instant Karma' spot was some of the better stuff I got offered, and it was never about people going, "Buy this shoe, this shoe will change everything," because I think that's nonsense. Anybody looking outside themselves to make themselves whole is delusional and probably sick.'

Fincher maintains that adverts can be more than just blatant product promotion. 'When I started making television commercials in the mid-1980s I was certainly privy to a lot of that kind of "lifestyle packaging", but I give the audience far more credit than most people do ... There's this assumption that commercials are just close-ups of celebrities holding up products, but some of them are great art. It's not the art of the surrealistic painting or the poem, but it *is* art.'

And Fincher isn't afraid to attack some of the very trademarks he's worked for. 'The thing that I hate most about advertising and corporate imaging is "brand-centred thinking." Coca-Cola does this, and I think they're some of the worst offenders. They do these commercials where you see a bunch of teenagers, youthful, good-looking, sweaty people at a bonfire in the middle of a forest and they're all wearing red and white, and they're all drinking Cokes, so it's almost this kind of pagan idolatry of the curved bottle – and it has nothing to do with the rest of the world. Nowhere in the world do people set bonfires in groves of trees, because it's just stupid. Nowhere do people all wear red and white, unless it's at a football game, and even then there are some stragglers, and nowhere are people so concerned with their soft drink choice that it becomes the focus of their lives.'

For Fincher, *Fight Club*'s acid take on the commercial mindset speaks volumes regarding his opinion of advertising: 'There are certain easy truisms that we all adopt. Beautiful people are stupid. Smart people have the potential for evil and should be watched. Commercials are supposed to sell you something, and therefore must be bad. But the best commercials are the ones that are anti-corporate. I never thought, "Oh, *Fight Club* is my chance to get back at all those people," because I never did anything I didn't want to do – to me, *Fight Club* is a natural extension of the stuff I was doing.'

'Filmmaking encompasses everything, from tricking people into investing in it, to putting on the show, to trying to distil down to moments in time and ape reality, but send this other message. It's got everything. It's four-dimensional chess, it's strategy, it's being painfully honest, and unbelievably deceitful, and everything in between.' David Fincher's comments on the craft of directing are, like the man himself, direct and heartfelt. 'A director's job is to feel like everything that they're doing is worth the amount of money, worth the cost of human life and blood, sweat and tears. That's the job, that's what it is. Designing shots is a [small part] of your life. The [rest] is holding everything together while there's total chaos, maximising the amount of hours that you have in order to get stuff, pulling something out of your ass to fix things, being able to work on your toes. It's not all about going, "We'll do this, and then we'll do that." Well, now do it with a Teamsters strike, with 150 people who are exhausted, who think that everything you're doing is, you know, gilding a lily – "You don't need that shot." I love it when people say that.'

Although he shies away from the *auteur* label, Fincher is very quick to underline the value of a strong directorial hand on the tiller, especially when taking a stand against the concept that any form of 'interactive' entertainment might make them obsolete. 'This is the cynicism of the new media people. I remember initially, when people were building these companies with this dot-com money, there was this idea that you were going to be able to someday make a movie and choose what the ending was – and I remember having heated arguments with these people, going "Look, people don't *want* to choose what the ending of the movie is, they just want to see a satisfying end to the movie." You may show them an end to the movie that they don't like and they may wish in hindsight that another choice had been made, but that's not what storytelling is.

'Storytelling is when the most competent person around the campfire says "Once upon a time..." and that's how that person gets their reward, that's their skill. It doesn't just happen by accident. This is why not everyone is a comedian; the art of comedy is when you stop, when you pause and what you say and how it strings together to get to the joke – that's storytelling. This notion that we're suddenly going to have this reverse-auteurism, that you're going to be able to posthumously impose narrative structure on something based on momentary whim, is stupid.'

For Fincher, the story is the core of his work. 'I don't want to be constrained by having to do something new. I look at it as – what are the movies that I want to see? I make movies that other people aren't making. I'm not interested in *The Hero with a Thousand Faces* – there are a lot of people that do that. A friend of mine used to say there's a pervert on every block, there's always one person in every neighbourhood who's kind of questionable. I'm looking for that one pervert story.'

According to Fincher, directing 'is thinking the thing up, designing all the sets, and it's rehearsals, and then the creative process is over. Then it's just war, it's just literally "How do we get through this day?" It's 99 per cent politics and one per cent inspiration. I've had days of shooting where I went, "Wow, that's what it is, that's what it's like to be making a movie." Everything's clicking, people are asking questions, and the clock's ticking, but you feel like you're making progress. But most of the time it isn't that. Most of the time it's, "How do you support the initial intent of what it is you set out to do, and not undercut that by getting pissed off and letting your attention get away?" It's priority management. It's problem solving.

'Oftentimes, you walk away from a scene going, "That wasn't what I thought it was gonna be." But it's also knowing that you don't have to get it exactly the way you see it. You want to be able to provide something, and you're pissing down a well. It will suck you dry and take everything you have and, like being a parent, you can pour in as much love as you want and your kid still says, "Just let me right out here, you don't have to take me all the way." You're working to make yourself obsolete. My movies are fairly obvious in what the people want and what it is that's happening. It is not that internalised. What's internalised is how you process the information from the singular, subjective point of view. And that becomes the subtext of it. I'm not Elia Kazan, I'm probably not going to reinvent an actor for the audience or for themselves, but I pay meticulous attention to getting the environment right so that the people have to do less work to pretend to be that person.'

Fincher dismisses the 'stylist' label he's often saddled with. 'I don't know what that means. My background has never been about *flash*, but about *economy*. Being called a stylist has always seemed like a backhanded compliment to me.' He continues: 'I think there are people who just know that I'm a malcontent and a miscreant who, for better or worse, goes out on a limb. I don't like the idea of having a style, it seems scary. It's so weird – what is it that makes your style? It's the things that you fuck up as much as the things that you do well, so half your style is stupid mistakes that you consistently make.'

The director feels that his viewpoint 'comes from a more voyeuristic place' than more conventional filmmakers. 'I have a philosophy about the two extremes of filmmaking. The first is the "Kubrick way", where you're at the end of an alley in which four guys are kicking the shit out of a wino. Hopefully, the audience will know that such a situation is morally wrong, even though it's not presented as if the viewer is the one being beaten up; it's more as if you're witnessing an event. Inversely, there's the "Spielberg way", where you're dropped into the middle of the action and you're going to live the experience vicariously – not only through what's happening, but through the emotional flow of how it's presented. It's a much more involved style.

'I find myself attracted to both styles at different times, but mostly I'm interested in just presenting something and letting people decide for themselves what they want to look at. I look for patterns in coverage, and for ways to place the camera to see what you need to see, from as far away as possible. I'll say to myself, "Am I getting too involved in the action? Am I presenting this to someone who's uninitiated to these people and doesn't want to be in the middle of this argument? Maybe we should be doing over-the-shoulders, as if the spectator is experiencing the scene after returning from the water cooler." I try to remain detached. I want to present the material without becoming too involved.'

Fincher is unquestionably a technically expert director, and he answers charges that he's a 'control freak' by simply replying 'I'm a film director.' He adds, 'If you're in a medium that requires so many disparate disciplines to get to the final product, it didn't seem to me to be a wise idea to not know how it goes together if you wanted to be specific about what you were saying – it seemed like you would make things more difficult for yourself if you had to go, "Can we do this?" So I always sort of like the jigsaw puzzle [of film] and I love the process of it, it's a fascinating, elaborate, labyrinthine process.

'But I don't think of myself as a technical person, I just have a lot of interests. I like painting, I like drawing, I like sculpture, I like taking pictures. I like choosing costumes, I like the psychology of that stuff, about what people's hairstyles say about them, what choice of shoes ... I like all of those things, either building a case for someone to be taken at face value or building a face value for someone to be incorrectly taken at. I like the sleight of hand of that, so I tend to get involved in all of that, because I think that if you just go, "Okay," then this girl walks into [a scene] wearing a red dress and you're not supposed to be looking at her but you do ... You've got to kind of know at what point in the story you want information to come out. It's about having, if not control – which you *can't* have because there's too many decisions to be made – you owe it to yourself to make sure that you didn't do something that was the exact opposite of what you intended to do. My interests in photography and lenses and filtration is because I don't want something to get in the way of me and what I'm trying to say, or what I'm trying to fool people into thinking.'

Pre-production also forms a major part of Fincher's directing credo. 'I think it's best always to have a plan even if you throw it out, even if you say, "Oh, this is rubbish, your idea is much better." I think it's always best if you're spending tens of millions of dollars of other people's money, to show up on the day and go, "We gotta get these two pages done today, she says this and he says that and then he's supposed to be over here, they go down the stairs." But how do you get the camera down the stairs? You better not [have to] find that shit out on the day; you have to go "Isn't there a Steadicam here?" "No, there's no Steadicam." "Okay, we'll do it in pieces." But why wing it? It's a medium where you can literally do anything, now what do you want to do? So at least coming in with what you want to do, even if it pisses down with rain and the electricity goes out and you have to figure out how to do it in two hours instead of eight, at least you started from a design.

'There's so many elements in film, like the quality of light on somebody's face, the amount of light that's in their eyes, the top-light and how skeletal their face looks, the nature of how soft and out-of-focus or sharp the background is, how three-dimensional somebody looks on a 35mm lens as opposed to how much flatter they look on a 40mm lens ... Those are all your tools, that's your power. So, you're trying to take away anything that's going to get in the way of your intent. It seems to me that if you are sculpting in three dimensions with people and what they are wearing and what they are saying, you have to kind of know what it's all gonna do; because otherwise somebody is going to come up and make a compromise for you, because you don't know the answer to your own question. "Could I make the camera go from here up to there?" "No go." "Oh. How about if we used a Louma crane?" "Oh yeah, you could do that."'

Fincher is one of the key directors of the DVD age, where film has been placed under a scrutiny far beyond anything it has previously experienced; the special edition releases of *Seven* and *Fight Club* are practically a lecture series for cineastes and the director feels it is important to use the medium to the fullest. 'It's the record of what you did, and if you can help people understand the context that went into the decisions that were made, I think they'll understand better what the movie is. The thing is, you finish a movie and you turn it over to these people who market movies. Most of them don't like movies, you get the distinct impression that they don't go to movies, it's their day job and you get all of their neuroses on who it's going to appeal to, what demographic and all this stuff.

'Ultimately, two years later there's going to be a record of that movie and DVD is that record; if you can get everybody to understand it then the product has a longer shelf life, because I think you can use them to teach. For me, it goes back to that behind-the-scenes documentary on *Butch Cassidy and the Sundance Kid*, you can show people all the thought that goes into it and maybe they won't so easily dismiss things that make them uncomfortable, because that seems to be [some] people's criteria for movies. I enjoy movies that make me uncomfortable, because it's very difficult to make me uncomfortable. I love movies like that.

Two

Third in Line

'It was a bloodbath – a constructive bloodbath.'

TO SAY THAT David Fincher's debut feature was a troubled production is an understatement. This was a film that brought the 27-year-old director to the attention of Hollywood not because it was the explosive debut of a fresh new talent but because it was the end result of a stormy voyage through production hell. Fincher's film was savaged by the critics, disliked by many fans and mired in controversy before he even stepped in to direct it, taking on a task two other directors had already walked away from.

James Cameron's *Aliens* (1986) had shifted the concepts of Ridley Scott's *Alien* (1979) from the haunted-house-in-space of the original into a high-octane roller-coaster ride. But, with conflict raging behind the scenes that would have broken a less dogged spirit, Fincher elected not to try to top Cameron's work, but instead to take the series back to its roots, into a confined industrial hell stalked by a flesh-ripping nightmare.

Along the way, he earned the respect of actors and crew, as well as a harsh lesson about the nature of the industry. In the aftermath, the director was famously quoted as saying that he would rather have cancer than take on another studio picture. Still, he was back three years later with *Seven*, and at last Hollywood woke up to the fact that he was a force to be reckoned with – something the cast and crew on *Alien 3* had already learned firsthand. Perhaps appropriately, the birth of Fincher's film career was like that of the alien itself, an event accompanied by bloodshed and plenty of pain.

——— ALIEN 3 ———

20th Century Fox, Brandywine Productions Ltd.
Director: *David Fincher.*
Writers: *Vincent Ward (story), David Giler (screenplay), Walter Hill (screenplay), Larry Ferguson (screenplay), Dan O'Bannon and Ronald Shusett (characters created by).*
Cast: *Sigourney Weaver (Ellen Ripley), Charles S Dutton (Dillon), Charles Dance (Clemens), Paul McGann (Golic), Brian Glover (Andrews), Ralph Brown*

(Aaron), Daniel Webb (Morse), Christopher John Fields (Rains), Holt
McCallany (Junior), Lance Henriksen (Bishop II), Christopher Fairbank
(Murphy), Carl Chase (Frank), Leon Herbert (Boggs), Vincenzo Nicoli (Jude),
Pete Postlethwaite (David), Paul Brennen (Troy), Clive Mantle (William), Peter
Guinness (Gregor), Dhobi Oparei (Arthur), Philip Davis (Kevin), Niall Buggy
(Eric), Hi Ching (company man), Danielle Edmond (Newt).
Crew: Gordon Carroll (producer), David Giler (producer), Walter Hill
(producer), Ezra Swerdlow (executive producer), Sigourney Weaver (co-producer),
Elliot Goldenthal (music), Alex Thomson (cinematography), Terry Rawlings
(editing), Norman Reynolds and Michael White (production design), James
Morahan (art direction), David Perry & Bob Ringwood (costume design), Susan
A Cabral & Greg Cannom (special makeup effects), Martin Brierley (second unit
director), Jonathan Angell, Clive Beard, John Brown, James Camomile, Chris
Corbould, Terence J Cox (special effects), H R Giger (creature designer).

Tagline: 'The Bitch is Back'

SYNOPSIS

The Colonial Marines Corps starship *Sulaco* cruises through space carrying the only
survivors of a failed mission to planet LV-426 – Ellen Ripley, former navigation officer
of the cargo ship *Nostromo*, who has twice faced the alien xenomorphs and lived;
Corporal Dwayne Hicks, the last man standing from his marine squad; Newt, a
colonist child rescued from the planet; and the remains of the android Bishop. All
four of them are locked in suspended animation chambers, sleeping away the
journey home until an alarm is triggered aboard the ship. An egg, left by the alien
queen just before Ripley killed it, has hatched into a facehugger, which penetrates one
of the hypersleep tubes and starts an electrical fire. The *Sulaco*'s automatic systems
kick in, and the survivors are ejected into space aboard a lifeboat – an EEV unit.

Crashing through the atmosphere of the nearby planet Fiorina 161, the EEV
lands in the sea close to a penal facility run by Ripley's former employers, the
Weyland-Yutani Corporation. The prison is a lead works, a desolate, Gothic place
with only 25 inmates and three staff members; all the prisoners are lifers, double-Y
chromosome category hard-cases. As the EEV is dragged out of the water, a prisoner
named Murphy climbs in and discovers Ripley alive inside her hypersleep pod.

A message is sent to the company reporting the crash; meanwhile, as a crane
winches the EEV from the water, Murphy's dog confronts a facehugger inside the
pod. The prison warden, Andrews, addresses the inmates and describes the situation.
Dillon, the spiritual leader of the convicts, is concerned that the presence of a woman
in their all-male community will be disruptive, but Clemens, the chief medical officer,
promises to keep Ripley out of the way until a rescue team arrives. Ripley awakens in
the infirmary, where Clemens tells her that Hicks, Newt and Bishop did not survive

the landing. Investigating the EEV, Ripley discovers an acid burn mark on Newt's cryo-tube; she insists on seeing the girl's corpse, fearing an alien infestation. When she finds no exterior signs, Ripley tells Clemens that Newt may be carrying a virus in order to make him conduct an autopsy – but her corpse is perfectly normal.

Nevertheless, Ripley demands that the bodies be cremated. Dillon leads the prisoners in a funeral service as Hicks and Newt's remains are burnt but, unseen in Murphy's quarters, the dog is killed as a newborn alien bursts out of it. Clemens explains that Dillon's 'religion' is what keeps the remaining prisoners at the colony as custodians. When Ripley asks Clemens his reasons for being on the planet, he ducks the question, and when he asks why she wanted Newt autopsied, she counters by making a pass at him. They sleep together, and she sees the barcode tattoo that marks Clemens as a prisoner.

Down in the tunnels, Murphy discovers a sloughed skin from the growing alien, and he is killed when he falls into the blades of a massive fan after the thing spits acid in his face. Aaron, the assistant warden, has Clemens examine Murphy's remains, and he discovers the same kind of burn mark found in the EEV. Ripley recovers the *Sulaco*'s flight recorder, and Clemens confronts her about his building suspicions. Seeking out Bishop's remains in order to access the data records, Ripley recovers him from the rubbish tip; a few of the prisoners assault her, intent on rape, but Dillon arrives and stops them with a little violent 're-education'. Meanwhile, Andrews grills Clemens on Ripley, threatening to reveal his sordid past to her. In the tunnels, prisoners Golic, Rains and Boggs are on a foraging mission when the alien attacks them; only Golic, insane with fear, escapes alive.

Ripley manages to reactivate the wrecked Bishop. The android explains that an alien started the fire aboard the *Sulaco*, and confirms that it was on the EEV; moreover, the flight recorder data has been sent to the company, who are no doubt on their way to the colony intent on recovering the alien intact. Golic, blood-soaked and raving about a 'dragon', is brought into the infirmary, confirming for Ripley that the alien is loose; Andrews dismisses her description of the creature, telling her there are no weapons on the planet. Ripley is still feeling the after-effects of hypersleep, and Clemens confides in her, explaining his reasons for being on the colony – he is an ex-prisoner, disbarred from medicine after an error of judgment killed a group of patients. But no sooner has he opened up to her than the alien attacks and kills Clemens. The creature approaches Ripley but strangely leaves without harming her. She races into the mess hall to warn the prisoners, just in time to see Warden Andrews suffer the same fate as the doctor.

The remaining prisoners assemble, looking to Ripley for some way to fight the beast, and a plan begins to form. Using flammable chemicals left over from the lead works to set fires, they can try to flush the alien into a toxic storage tank, with walls thick enough to trap it inside. Under Dillon's leadership, the prisoners begin, but the plan backfires when the alien attacks and the fire is triggered too soon. In the flames, ten inmates are killed and the creature is still loose. Ripley's sickness is worsening, however, and she returns to the EEV to run a medical scan on herself; to her horror, the neuroscanner reveals the presence of an alien embryo – a nascent egg-laying queen. She realises that if the company get hold of the embryo, the alien threat would be unstoppable.

Heading into the tunnels once again, Ripley finds the creature and tries to goad it into killing her, but the alien will not attack while she is carrying the baby queen. Ripley implores Dillon to do the deed instead, but he refuses while there's still a chance they can kill the alien. Rallying the survivors, Dillon plans to force the alien into the foundry's main mould, where they can drown it in hot lead. With the company rescue unit in-bound, the prisoners use themselves as bait to draw the creature out; one by one the alien kills them until only Ripley, Dillon and Morse remain. In the mould chamber, Ripley and Dillon confront the beast; meanwhile, Aaron leads the company soldiers into the prison. Ripley climbs out, but Dillon sacrifices himself to hold the alien in the mould and Morse dumps the liquid lead onto the creature – but the alien survives the deluge and bursts out of the molten metal, burning hot. Ripley douses it with a flood of cold water and the shock explodes the beast, finally killing it.

Waiting for Ripley is Bishop – the human template for the android – sent by the company as someone she can trust. He implores her to surrender herself to them, to let them remove the embryo; but Ripley knows they won't destroy it, that the company will use it to make bio-weapons, and she refuses. As Bishop cries out for her to stop, Ripley lets herself fall into the vat of molten lead, holding in the chest-burster as it tries to escape from her. With Aaron killed at the hands of the company marines, Morse is the sole survivor of Fiorina 161 and, at last, Ripley's battle with the alien is finally at an end.

ORIGINAL TREATMENTS

With the myriad changes that *Alien 3* went through even before a single frame of film was shot, the movie left in its wake a paper trail of discarded scripts, cuts and disposed-of drafts littering the offices of 20th Century Fox. In total, ten scriptwriters worked on various versions of the third *Alien* movie, some of their drafts bearing little or no resemblance to the final theatrical release.

The first writer attached was William Gibson, who penned a draft based on an outline by Walter Hill and David Giler in 1987; Gibson is known for his work as a science fiction novelist and one of the founders of the 'cyberpunk' sub-genre, with novels like *Neuromancer*, *Idoru* and *Pattern Recognition*. While well-respected in the SF literature community, Gibson would not enter the Hollywood scene until the feature adaptation of his short story *Johnny Mnemonic* (1995), which earned a critical mauling similar to *Alien 3*'s and for many of the same reasons.

Gibson's *Alien III* keeps up the same action pace of *Aliens*, widening the world of the films to introduce human antagonists as well as the aliens themselves. With Ripley, Hicks, Newt and Bishop in hypersleep, the *Sulaco* accidentally crosses into space claimed by the Union of Progressive Peoples, a Soviet-style combine locked in a cold war with the corporate Weyland-Yutani; a UPP commando squad boards the ship and steals Bishop, who was unknowingly implanted with an alien egg by the queen in the previous film. The ship continues on its way to Anchorpoint station, where colonial marines evacuate the survivors and encounter a pair of alien warriors hiding in the ship. With Ripley in a coma, Weyland-Yutani agents intent on securing the alien biotechnology confront Hicks and Newt. Breaking arms limitation treaty bans, both the UPP and the company begin experiments to clone the aliens for use as weapons; but the experiments backfire and the samples mutate into a virus that infects and transforms living tissue into an alien analogue.

Pushing the boundaries of *Alien*'s body invasion one step further, Gibson's story has humans shedding their skin as they warp into grotesque 'New Beasts'. With Newt already safely on her way back to Earth, Hicks ejects the sleeping Ripley into space in an escape pod and takes Bishop, released from UPP captivity, on a mission to eradicate the alien infection. Setting Anchorpoint's reactor to explode, Hicks leads the supporting characters through the gauntlet of the alien-human mutants as the countdown to annihilation runs down.

Gibson's story is clearly written with the intent to keep Ripley as a background character – perhaps with the proviso that Sigourney Weaver could appear in the film for a few days of shooting as a cameo; in addition, the closing scene is wide open for a sequel, as Bishop and Hicks discuss seeking out the homeworld of the aliens and destroying it. This script also features an extended escape-and-chase sequence that mirrors the similar events in the later *Alien Resurrection* (1997). The writer dryly noted, 'In my draft, this woman has a barcode on the back of her hand – in the shooting script one of the guys has a barcode on the back of his shaved head. I'll always privately think that was my piece of *Alien 3*.'

Eric Red's 1988 draft took on some of the themes from the Gibson script about the alien as a viral organism and a subject for illicit genetic engineering, but little else. Again opening aboard the *Sulaco* as rescuers investigate the ship, the recovery team is attacked by aliens after finding no survivors aboard. Sam Smith, one of the team members, recovers from the incident at his home on a space station-cum-farming colony. Smith investigates the local marine base where alien cloning experiments are underway and, to his horror, discovers the military attempting to train aliens as troops. The experiment goes badly awry and soon the marines and then the 'redneck' farmers begin to fall victim to the creatures. In a last-ditch battle, the soldiers and the farmers team up to escape the multiplying monsters on the streets of their small colony township.

Red's story has some bizarre elements – the aliens seem to be able to transform anything they touch, leading to all kinds of hybrids; alien cats, alien pigs, alien chickens, alien mosquitos, as well as alien cows and alien dogs, the latter making appearances in other drafts of the *Alien 3* script. The rapacious alien DNA also subverts metal, leading to a finale where the entire space station becomes a massive hybrid monster. The script featured none of the *Aliens* cast, intimating that they had been killed by the discovery of alien eggs in their sleeping capsules and a torn, bloodstained fragment of Ripley's uniform. A more conventional, almost B-movie take on the series, Red ramped up the gore, gunplay and sexual content, but dissatisfied the producers and the current director in the process.

David Twohy's take on the storyline included the first incarnation of the prison colony seen in the final film, here an Earth-orbiting space station called Moloch equipped with an iron foundry and a drugs lab. A group of new prisoners, led by a chancer named Styles, are considering a breakout when an unpleasantly familiar creature begins killing off convicts on the station's lower levels; unknown to Packard, the station's doctor, the company is using Moloch's labs to breed aliens, and the prison populace are being used as test subjects. Styles befriends Packard before making an escape attempt and in the process encounters an escaped alien 'rogue'. When company executive Lone arrives to take over the prison, Packard investigates and the truth is revealed. After an accident in the landing bay, the station begins to decompress as Styles, Packard and a prison guard race to escape, with the alien on their tail.

Twohy's first draft, like Red's script, had no *Aliens* characters, referring just once to Ripley when a computer screen lists her as 'deceased'; but following Fox's decision to include Sigourney Weaver in *Alien 3*, the writer produced a revised version that included her. Twohy's story was the last to feature the genetic engineering thread, with the company technicians on Moloch experimenting to create new subspecies of alien including the heavily muscled 'Brute' and the deadly 'Newbreed', which stalks Styles and Packard during the climactic scenes. A sequence where several alien clones are discovered prefigures the Ripley clones from *Alien Resurrection*; in addition, the roots of the supportive doctor character Clemens in *Alien 3* can be seen in Packard.

Vincent Ward's approach to the storyline, co-written with John Fasano, represented the most radical departure yet for the series; while Ripley was now included as a key character, the setting was Arceon, a Gothic artificial world made of wood. On this man-made planetoid exists a colony of Minorite monks who have rejected technology, seeing themselves as the contemporary equivalent of their Dark Age counterparts, who protected libraries of knowledge during the Black Plague. Earth has apparently been destroyed by a technological computer virus, and the monks are slowly dying as Arceon succumbs to entropy. Into this environment comes an escape pod from the *Sulaco*, carrying Ripley and a dead Newt – Bishop and Hicks having already been killed off-screen – and the order's Abbot places her in the care of their doctor, Brother John.

Ripley fears that she has brought the alien with her, and John's encounter with a chestburster emerging from an infected ewe confirms this; but the Abbot convinces the monks that Ripley is to blame, that she's the servant of the Devil. Ignoring her warnings and John's concerns, Ripley is locked in Arceon's hellish lower levels where she meets Anthony, a maddened android who has visions of death and destruction. As the alien matures and begins to kill off the monks, the creature exhibits a new trait, changing like a chameleon to blend in with cornfields and the wood of the buildings. John descends into the planetoid, finding Ripley, Anthony and the Abbot, who has fled the carnage above.

After confrontations with the alien, Ripley realises that the monks cannot defeat the creature and that their only chance is to get back to her ship and escape. The Abbot and Anthony are killed by the alien, but Ripley and John face it in the monastery's glassworks – the creature is doused in molten glass, escaping only to be bombarded by cold water, which causes it to explode. Ripley, realising that she carries an alien embryo, attempts to send John into space alone, but the monk uses an alchemical potion to make her reject the creature, which he absorbs instead. As Ripley escapes the burning planetoid, John willingly dies to kill the alien and be with his Brothers.

By this draft, many of the key elements of *Alien 3* are in place: Ripley is the only living survivor from the *Sulaco* aboard an escape pod; Brother John is clearly the prototype for Clemens and the Abbot for Warden Andrews; the alien-impregnated ewe prefigures the ox/dog of the final versions; the alien is drowned in a vat of white-hot glass and then drenched in water to explode it; and most importantly, Ripley is carrying an alien embryo inside her. In addition, John's death-in-flames sacrifice also mimics Ripley's eventual suicide.

Rex Pickett was hired just four weeks prior to the start of principal photography on *Alien 3* to rewrite a previous Walter Hill/David Giler script, mixing their scenes and his with a completely new second half as ordered by Hill; Pickett noted that several scenes were included in the script despite his objections to them. Much of the material in the Pickett version was shot but later excised from the final cut (many of these scenes, such as Clemens' discovery of the escape pod and the alien-bearing ox, are listed later on in Cuts and Changes). The most notable elements are the smaller details, such as the origins of Dillon's religion in the prison's large library of devotional books and his more formal, sermon-like speeches, or the survival of Aaron to the end of the story, along with the prisoner Morse. Hill and Giler's last draft also featured additional moments during the opening credits montage that would have shown the embryonic queen alien opening Ripley's mouth and sliding inside, after having burst out of Newt.

DEVELOPMENT

The genesis of the third *Alien* movie began almost five years before David Fincher's name was put forward as a potential director. James Cameron's action-packed sequel *Aliens* had proven that additional adventures in the gritty industrial universe created by Ridley Scott were ready to draw in new audiences, and 20th Century Fox were keen to exploit this new science fiction franchise.

Brandywine Productions executive Gordon Carroll, producer on all four *Alien* movies as well as films like *Cool Hand Luke* (1967) and *Blue Thunder* (1982), brought in writer-producers Walter Hill, of *48 Hours* (1982) and *Last Man Standing* (1996), and David Giler, known for *The Parallax View* (1974). Together, the trio came to the table to create a basic premise for a third *Alien* story. Both Hill and Giler had worked on the scripts for *Alien* and *Aliens* and chose to bring in noted science fiction novelist William Gibson to expand on their concept of the alien as a weapon fought over by Earth's superpowers. Gibson's *Alien III* script was completed in 1987, but events at Fox and the then-current strike by the Writer's Guild of America derailed progress on the project, eventually leading the novelist to drop out of the undertaking.

With Gibson gone, his script and the original Hill/Giler plotline were jettisoned; to encourage the studio to up the development budget for the movie, the producers engaged the services of *The Hitcher* (1986) and *Near Dark* (1987) writer Eric Red towards the end of 1988. At the same time, Fox had picked Renny Harlin, later to direct *Cliffhanger* (1993), *Deep Blue Sea* (1999) and *Driven* (2001), to helm the project, straight from completing *Die Hard 2: Die Harder* in 1990. Ironically, Harlin's *Die Hard* sequel would end up indirectly causing a lot of *Alien 3*'s later financial woes, because the blockbuster follow-up to the Bruce Willis action movie had spiralled above and beyond the budget Fox set for it. After swallowing cost overruns on *Die Hard 2* and James Cameron's underwater epic *The Abyss* (1989), *Alien 3* was not to be allowed to follow suit, and by the time Fincher took the reins, he would find himself hounded for every dollar he spent on the shoot.

Harlin's involvement with the nascent *Alien* feature was short-lived, however; after Red presented the producers with his first draft of the script, set on a remote farming colony, the director disliked it so much that he walked. Red blamed Hill and Giler for having a poor handle on what the film should be about, but the producers pointed the finger at Red's script and the writer left. Harlin called the script 'nothing more than a rehash of the two previous movies. At that point I lost all passion for the project.'

David Twohy, who would later cover similar ground with his 1999 feature *Pitch Black*, was taken on and told by the producer to craft a story that would not feature Sigourney Weaver's character Ripley or any of the other survivors of *Aliens*. Twohy's script was set on an orbital prison – the first hint of the Fiorina 161 facility seen in the final version – and the producers were very pleased with his work. But the absence of Ripley from the storyline was absolutely unacceptable to Fox, who disagreed with Hill and Giler's intent that she should only return in the mooted *Alien 4*. Fox's studio head Joe Roth refused point-blank to give the film the green light unless Ripley returned, so the producers approached Weaver with the outline and the actress agreed to reprise the role if the script was acceptable to her. Twohy went back to work, revising his penal colony story to include Ripley, while Fox considered approaching Ridley Scott and horror author Clive Barker to direct the film.

But in the meantime, Hill and Giler had started to move in another direction. After seeing Vincent Ward's film *The Navigator: A Medieval Odyssey* (1988), Hill was convinced that Ward was the right man to replace Harlin on *Alien 3*, and Fox agreed – but the new director wasn't interested in Twohy's script and wanted to write a story of his own (hence his 'story by' credit on the final version of the film). Ward's concept for the movie had Ripley arriving on a wooden planetoid of quasi-medieval technology, populated by monks in a monastery with no weapons or means of defence against the rapacious alien. 'It sort of flies in the face of all the other *Alien* [films],' said the director. John Fasano, who later wrote *Universal Soldier: The Return* (1999) and the *Forever War* TV miniseries, was tagged to co-write this new take with Ward.

Among the elements introduced in this draft, later to be discarded, was the concept of a shape-shifting, chameleon-like alien that could appear to be made of glass or of wood. Design work and preparation for this bizarre effect was started by the visual effects staff but subsequently abandoned – a fate that would befall a number of alien concepts along the way. Fasano believed that the script he and Ward were writing was to be the basis for *Alien 4* – unless they finished it before Twohy's rewrite, in which case it would become *Alien 3*. When Twohy discovered he was writing one of two competing drafts, he called it 'one of the most transparent pieces of studio treachery I've ever heard of' and, after completing his work, left the project in disgust – followed soon after by Fasano, who was off to co-write *Another 48 Hours* (1990).

At this point in mid-1991, pre-production on *Alien 3* was well under way at Pinewood Studios in England, where Fox had chosen to shoot the movie; sets were being constructed, and Ward had moved to London in preparation, bringing a new writer, G J Pruss, along with him. No relation to the Gregory Pruss who served as *Alien 3*'s production designer, this Greg Pruss had been hired by the producers to polish Fasano's version of Ward's script, which he did through several 'arduous' drafts. Alec Gillis, one of the effects experts brought in early on to prepare for the shoot, spoke of the various scripts that passed through his hands: 'One used a king alien, while another had radio-controlled powerloaders fighting an army of queens. But there were practical considerations against making a $150 million movie, because the story's hook is dangling the threat of the aliens getting to Earth. The sequel ideas were like the difference between *Psycho* and *Zulu*.'

By now *Alien 3* had developed a momentum of its own, with Fox paying out huge fees for scripts, sets and actors (some figures quoted as high as $13 million) in addition to giving star Sigourney Weaver a generous $4 million deal, then the highest figure ever earned by a Hollywood actress; she had been paid only $30,000 for appearing in *Alien*. But almost at the point of no return, the relationship between Ward, Pruss and the studio began to fall apart. The New Zealand director was in conflict with Fox over the weight of the movie's narrative, leaning ever more closely to Ward's monk characters and away from the central relationship of Ripley against the alien. 'The movie is called *Alien* because it's about the alien. I couldn't get that across to Vincent,' said Pruss.

Fincher recalls: 'Greg was a friend of mine, and he was called in to do a rewrite for Ward, but it wasn't working out. He thought they were going to fire him – and then they fired Vincent.' Ward was apparently unable to bring Fox and the producers around to his radical take on the *Alien* saga – despite the fact that Giler had stated that Ward's 'far-out' premise was exactly what they had wanted at the outset. Fasano was wooed back for another quick look at the script, but the rudderless *Alien 3* was in grave danger of falling apart even before shooting had begun; Fox needed to find a talented replacement director, and fast. Into the breach stepped David Fincher.

'It would be stupid of me to say that I didn't know what I was getting into. It took me five years to decide what I wanted to do and I always held out for something on this scale because I like this kind of canvas. I like the scope of this kind of thing. *Star Wars* was an important film for me as a kid, but nowhere near as important as *Alien*,' Fincher recalled in an interview with *Starburst*. 'I was 16 [when I saw it], it just changed my life. Finally outer space *looked* like outer space and people on a spaceship *looked* like they were on a spaceship ... [they] put their hair up in rubber bands and drank coffee and talked about union squabbles. It just seemed like it was so real.'

The two previous *Alien* movies had been important steps in the careers of Ridley Scott and James Cameron respectively, and the producers were keen to bring Fincher, another breaking new talent, into the fold. For the director, the chance to take on the *Alien* franchise and follow up what he called 'one of the ten perfect movies of all time' was irresistible. 'So I got a call and I thought, "That could be cool, that could be a really interesting notion to make an *Alien* sequel" ... At least it has a kind of cinematic pedigree and as long as it isn't too stupid it might be great ... So I went in to see them and I was led to believe that my ideas were cherished and I signed on to do this thing under the auspices that are usually given when they want you worse than you want it, which is no expense will be spared, you'll get whatever screenwriter you want, Robert Towne if you want him, blah, blah, blah, it's only in our interests to make a great movie. So you do that and you sign on and the only caveat was that there were some sets and personnel they wanted to keep on, could I work it in? [But] it was downhill from there.'

Fincher barnstormed his way through a meeting at Fox's head office with the daring idea that Weaver, who had signed on to co-produce with Hill and Giler, should lose her hair throughout the film. 'He didn't even have the job at that time,' the actress recalled, 'and I said, "Well, if I have to make the picture bald, I'll want more money" ...' But Fincher notes that Pruss tried his best to dissuade him. 'They went to him and said, "Do you know this guy named Fincher?" And he said, "Yeah, I know him really well." "Do you think he would come in and talk to us?" And he said, "No, he's way too smart to get involved in this."'

Pruss told the producers that Fincher 'wouldn't direct this movie in a million years' but he was soon proved wrong. The director set to work creating his own storyline for the movie, even as Fox brought on board a new face, *Highlander* (1986) and *The Hunt for Red October* (1990) writer Larry Ferguson, for yet more rewrites. From the start, Fincher disagreed with his predecessor's choices for the story, notably the wooden planetoid. 'I didn't feel that Ward's ideas made sense in terms of the previous movies. Some of them were really interesting, but to send that much teak into outer space ... I liked the religious aspect, although much of it was subsequently thrown out.'

While Ferguson worked on a by-the-numbers sequel (in a *Premiere* interview, he equated sequels with Big Macs, citing the need for similarity over innovation), Fincher presented Fox with a huge, expensive concept that sent them running for cover. 'I was just so taken with the legacy that it had to be ... *Apocalypse Now*.' he joked. Of course, Fincher's vision for *Alien 3* was an impossible choice for a studio already into an eight-figure budget, and Ferguson's script similarly failed to find favour. Ferguson retained a screenplay credit on the movie, but his infamous 'Snow White' scene was excised completely. Fincher described it to journalist John Richardson: '[Ripley] was going to be the woman who had fallen from the stars ... she dies and there are seven of the monks left – seven dwarves ... and there was this tube they put her in, and they were waiting for Prince Charming to come and wake her up.'

One Ferguson element that did remain was the theme of the alien as the bane of Ripley's life. 'Larry and I decided that ... it's what she's cursed to do. She's cursed to fight this thing until it's over with. The idea was not to make a whizz bang shoot 'em up, but to deal with this character. Let's put a 40-year-old woman in outer space, not an underwear-clad victim like in the first *Alien*. In a way, we had to rationalise it; here was this woman waking up again and facing the same damn monster.'

Weaver would not make the film unless the script was rewritten yet again, so Walter Hill and David Giler took the story and began to rework it themselves even as the start date for shooting loomed ever closer. The Hill/Giler script merged Twohy's prison colony setting with Ward's supporting cast of religious, semi-monastic characters (a theme both Weaver and Fincher agreed upon) and a straight-shooting ending. 'The idea of no technology, of rubbing sticks together to make fire in the bowels of an oil refinery, appealed to me. We all agreed that we wanted to do something that was dark, mean and adult, trying to return to the simplicity of the first movie.' The revision was completed and everyone liked the new draft. Everyone except the director.

'You learn very quickly with movie studios that the reason there are so many people working there is to deflect blame and to spread culpability,' said Fincher. 'It just became this morass of one person says this, two days later that idea gets shot down because of its content, somebody else says go ahead and try this, the writers that you want for some reason aren't returning calls to the studio – I wanted to get Greg Pruss on, but he wasn't enough of a name for them at the time, but he was fine when it was with Vincent Ward, it was all this kind of double-talk and it just continued for two and a half years. It was a really stupid experience, because we had a lot of really talented people, we had Sigourney Weaver, [editor] Terry Rawlings, Charles Dance, who I think is way underrated, Paul McGann who I love, Ralph Brown, all these people who could do much better work than they were allowed to do. It was just kind of a process of attrition. [Composer] Elliot Goldenthal had like nine days to write a score, it was just like "Get it out". It was just a disaster on every front, we never had the material, we never had the support.'

Alien 3 had originally been scheduled for a summer release in 1991, but now it was the end of the year and principal photography had yet to start. In the run-up to a revised January 1992 kick-off, Fincher went into round after round of arguments and battles with the producers and Fox production executives, as the studio attempted to wring every last penny out of the script, pushing the already-strained budget to the limit. 'When you get into this business from the outside, it is difficult to understand the politics and mechanics. You assume movies cost so much because you always hear how filmmakers go over budget. You believe the budget is coming out of a process where the people financing a movie know exactly what the pitfalls are. You believe they do their best to make the film happen, and that it is their wish to make it right. In reality, it is not.

'When the studio hires you, executives are trembling and sweating for months and months. A lot of finger-pointing is going on and people are trying to cover up. I learned that the people who have made the largest investments in a project, the ones who have the most at stake, are the ones you can trust the least to salvage a film. The whole process is designed around a system where they set up hurdles for you that you can't possibly achieve. Inevitably you fail and the executives say, "Okay, let's go with what we had initially set out to," but instead of really sticking to the original plan, they now force you to do the same thing with half the original budget, and it just keeps going on like that.'

Fincher continues: 'Because it's just a money-making device, because there was nothing that anyone needed or wanted or had any investment in seeing, it was just about "How do we make this as cheaply as possible?" And whenever that happens, you're doomed. You don't have final cut on a movie like that. I didn't have any say in how it was going to be presented and so there were all these cooks in the kitchen.'

Caught between the two camps was Tim Zinneman, an experienced line producer with films like *Bullitt* (1968) and *Pet Sematary* (1989) on his resumé. Zinneman told Fox that they 'were building ... a high rise without plans' but then he was gone, leaving Fincher without an ally on the set. 'How do we solve these problems?' Fincher said. 'How do we get this movie made? I'd love to take the 50 million bucks and just start over again.'

PRODUCTION

On his arrival in the UK, the director went to Pinewood to discover that parts of the set had already been discarded. 'I found that the Gothic columns built for Ward had just been ripped down and thrown away. I was trying to get sets started in construction that would be somewhat multi-purpose, since we still didn't know where the story was going.' Then, just a month away from the start of shooting, Fincher met with Rex Pickett, writer of *From Hollywood to Deadwood* (1989), newly brought in to work on the Hill/Giler script, and explained his concerns over the latest draft. 'I said, "Am I crazy, am I insane?" and he said, "No, this makes sense."' In turn, Pickett reportedly tore Hill and Giler's script apart in a memo to Fox, which Zinneman saw and showed to the producers; they were so enraged that they left London and never returned, while all of Pickett's work on the script was discarded. Only an additional fee from the studio kept Hill and Giler on the project as story consultants.

But worse was still to come; as the studio introduced Zinneman's replacement Ezra Swerdlow – who later worked on *CopLand* and *Wag the Dog* (both 1997) – Fox cut the shooting schedule by three weeks and dropped the visual effects allocation to less than half that of the previous film, *Aliens*. The tight timetable pushed the Pinewood crew to the limit, pressing them to make the movie in three months – despite the fact that both *Alien* and *Aliens* had each taken over four months to shoot. Communications between the studio and Fincher were strained: 'Fox didn't really have the language to be able to speak to me and they weren't even there. The key to this whole thing is how much they want to believe in you, and who was I? Some guy who shoots commercials and did the Paula Abdul video. I just didn't have much credibility.'

He continues: 'The lesson is that you can't take on an enterprise of this size and scope if you don't really have a movie like *The Terminator* or *Jaws* behind you, because in the end the guy in charge of the studio has to look you in the eye and say "Is this extra $2 million worth it?" and it's very difficult to engender that sort of confidence ... It's very nice to say, "This is the guy who directed the biggest grossing movie of all time, sit down and shut up, and feel lucky you've got him" ... it's another thing when everybody's wringing their handkerchiefs and sweating and puking blood because of the money that's being spent.'

Swerdlow found Fincher to be a knowledgeable and impressive director, praising his affinity for lighting scenes and managing visual effects shots. But while he won the new line producer's support, Fincher was constantly being pressed by Fox executive Jon Landau, who stringently measured each scene for cost and pushed to prevent the director from shooting for too long – like many directors who had come from filming commercials, Fincher had a reputation of lensing the same shot over and over in search of the perfect image. 'There's no point in trying to force it before it's done,' Fincher said. 'It's a guy in a rubber suit. If it looks like a guy in a rubber suit, we're fucked. This movie isn't made for people who see a movie one time, it's a movie for people who are going to see it five times.'

The director later described his conflicts with Landau as 'a random and bloody blur', like a prize-fight that left him reeling – and it was Landau who would ultimately make the fateful decision to shut down the production at Pinewood when Fincher refused to comply with Fox's demands. 'The story that I sold them on, how I got the gig, was a really interesting idea,' Fincher notes. 'But the one thing movie studios can't tolerate is difficulties. They don't like difficult actors, they don't like difficult directors and they especially don't like difficult films. And the fact is, nothing good ever came out of a happy set. You can't stay sharp without friction, that's just physics. Plus, this was a franchise being controlled by a studio regime and not by a moviemaker. Every decision was based on, "Well, we spent X on the second one, so we'll spend Y on the third one." I'd go, "But wait a minute, we've got to build a fucking abattoir." They'd go, "No, you don't have to build an abattoir because there was no abattoir in the first two movies." I was like, "I can't fight this logic because it doesn't exist."'

During the British part of the shoot at Pinewood, and on location at a power station in Northumberland and Dawdon Beach in County Durham, filming went ahead despite the absence of a finalised figure for the budget and a finished draft of the script. 'We started shooting with 40 pages and the script changed so much and so fast that we were receiving stuff off the fax machine and shooting it the next day. You'd get stuff where prisoner number 19 is in a shot where his face is ripped off and two days later he's supposed to be in the background. That kind of stuff makes a crew crazy. It was insane ... I did a lot of 'Bay of Pigs' stuff – hit the beach, get as many confirmed kills as possible and move on.'

Weaver and Fincher joined actors Charles S Dutton and Lance Henriksen with a largely English supporting cast that featured Charles Dance, Pete Postlethwaite, Paul McGann, Brian Glover and Ralph Brown, and at last the *Alien 3* machine cranked up to speed. However, the problems didn't go away. Because of the punishing schedule, Fincher found himself and the crew pushing 17-hour days as they entered the second month of the shoot, during the filming of the larger action sequences in the tunnels and the lead works sets. The director managed four film units as well as struggling over script issues when he wasn't behind the camera, all the while fielding Fox's demands to cut costs and rein in his vision for the film. At the same time, the director reluctantly discharged his treasured cinematographer Jordan Cronenweth, a personal hero of Fincher's since his work on *Blade Runner*, and replace him with Alex Thomson of *Legend* (1985) after Fox became unhappy with Cronenweth's pace of work. 'They thought the two of us were in cahoots,' Fincher noted.

To make matters worse, the studio's decision to shoot at Pinewood, which had been made to take advantage of favourable exchange rates, was now backfiring as the dollar began to weaken against the pound. With Swerdlow and Fincher continuing to press

Fox for more shooting time, the studio refused to be moved from their May stop date, and still the script problems with the film's climax were unresolved. While shooting was under way, a small team from Fox briefly visited the location to film *The Making of Alien 3* documentary, which tellingly contained interviews with cast and crew from the film, as well as with the directors of *Alien* and *Aliens* – but not with David Fincher.

'I always thought Ridley Scott was brilliant, and I never really appreciated how brilliant he was until I tried to make this movie,' said Fincher, who met Scott when he briefly visited the shoot on the 007 soundstage at Pinewood. 'He came down to the set when we were setting fire to something. In he walked with his silk suit and one of his big Cuban cigars, looking fabulous. Ridley said, "How's it going?" and I said, "Really bad," and he said, "It never goes well ... this is not the way to make movies, make sure you make a little film where you have some control while they are beating you up" ... When Ridley made the first one, Alan Ladd Jr [Fox's then-president] said, "Okay, you guys can do it if you can make it for $10 million," and so they went off and did this thing, and the best stuff always kind of sneaks in under the wire. If it's too scrutinised, if there's too much expectation, then there's too many middle managers involved. I mean, they were managing the franchise and whenever you're dealing with brand managers, you're doomed. We probably would have been left alone to make a much better movie [if] everyone had thought it was going to be a failure, because we wouldn't have had so many people coming in to proffer a stupid opinion like "Oh, I know – it'll come out of a dog!"'

These were clearly dark days for Fincher. 'You have a multi-million dollar investment before a frame of film has rolled. To walk away from something like that because I didn't have any script approval is, in this town, more detrimental to your career than to plough on with something you think needs a lot of work. It was not the optimum way to make a movie.'

With ill-feeling still in the air between Hill and Giler and the director after Rex Pickett's comments, the wrangling over *Alien 3*'s ending kept up a slow burn for weeks until an explosive telephone conference in early February. Fincher presented his ideas to conclude the script, and reportedly remembers David Giler saying to Fox executive Roger Birnbaum, 'What are you listening to him for, he's a shoe salesman.' – a reflection on the director's previous work for Nike sports trainers. Both Hill and Giler believed that Fox would back them up with the categorical, unambiguous ending they had written, but Birnbaum chose to follow Fincher's ideas even though the concept presented by the writers also had merit. 'If both arguments hold water, I'm going to go with the guy who's shooting,' he said. Feeling betrayed by the studio, Walter Hill and David Giler quit the production.

Fincher's victory in getting the ending he wanted soon became academic when he reached, then passed, the May stop date for shooting while filming the climax on the Fury 161 set. The studio were understandably concerned and, after more than a week of overruns, Jon Landau arrived on set at Pinewood, replacing

Swerdlow and earning the ire of the cast and crew as he made radical demands for production cuts. Sigourney Weaver accused Landau of being 'contemptuous of the effort we were putting in', citing his inference that Fincher was an '*enfant terrible* going mad'. But after two weeks of additional shooting and still no end in sight, Landau exercised his executive control and ordered production to stop, after a total of 93 days of filming. 'If I learned anything,' Fincher said, 'it's that on a 90-day shoot there's so much distance between your idea and the final expression of it that the only thing that can make up for that is preparation.'

Despite Weaver's personal appeals to Joe Roth, Landau's order stood and *Alien 3* shut down; cast and crew were discharged and the American contingent flew home. 'I was glad to get back on the plane,' Fincher recalled. 'We were told they were going to hold the sets until [Roth] could take a look at the picture.'

Fincher subsequently discovered that the massive sets at Pinewood Studios were destroyed while the fate of *Alien 3* was being decided at Fox's highest levels.

A rough cut was constructed, along with a seven-page 'wish list' of additional scenes to be filmed, and Fincher slaved over edits and re-edits as Roth requested cuts to make the movie shorter, to alter pacing and to make it 'more like a traditional horror film', despite Fincher's desire to do just the opposite. With Hill and Giler back on board during the post-production phase of the shoot, Fincher found himself in conflict with them once again as they urged him to up the level of gore. 'We all decided to make a china cup, a beautiful, delicate china cup,' he retorted. 'You can't tell me we should have made a beer mug.'

New sets were constructed and the director's proposed six weeks of follow-on filming was cut down to just eight days. Fincher believes the extra Hollywood photography cost Fox around $12 million of the rumoured $63 million budget, a total that was more than than twice the cost of the first two *Alien* films combined. Despite industry rumours of multiple re-shoots, Fincher was adamant that the additional days were for 'stuff we didn't get before', including dramatic moments like the eruptive birth of the alien chestburster from its canine host. The director had lobbied for the birth scene from the start, but was only allowed to shoot it when audiences at test screenings were confused about where the alien had come from.

But what test audiences giveth, they also taketh away, and the subplot involving Paul McGann's character Golic was excised. '16-year-old kids in Long Beach, California decided that they weren't interested in what happened to Golic,' Fincher said in 1993. 'They weren't interested in what he gave the movie ... it was lost, a whole subplot that I, to this day, feel is very important and certainly answers a lot of the critics' questions about my inability to tell a story.'

The lessons learned were hard ones for the young director, as Fincher noted several years later. 'The one thing you learn from an experience like that is that you're ultimately responsible, so don't do anything you don't want to do. That's why I fight so voraciously up front so that everybody understands what is going to happen – this is what I'm going do, this is going to change, this is not going be like this, this is going to be scary because of this, this and this... I don't wing stuff, so I can talk fairly explicitly about what it is I want to do, but then I want people to know this is what it's going to cost and this is what I'm going to deliver, so I don't ever have to go through that experience again, because there's so much rhetoric and circuitous conversations and you end up spinning your wheels and wasting so much time.

'The thing that I realised on *Alien 3* is that I'm interfacing with these people, Michael London, Tom Jacobsen and Jon Landau, every day for like two years and when it got right down to it, none of them really had the authority to make any decisions without higher directive. It's like you were just pissing into a well, and I didn't have a producer, I didn't have somebody to protect me so I became white noise. All my words, all my complaints, all my warnings – "This is what's going to happen." – just became white noise and they were just like, "Oh, *that's* the guy with all the problems." The thing that you learn from an experience like that is to take all the responsibility, because you're going to get all the blame anyway. So you take all the responsibility and you say exactly what it is – my movies are not inexpensive movies, but everybody knows what they're gonna cost up front, it's never like, "Oh no, I can make *Fight Club* for $18 million" and it turns out at $60. It's like, "This is what it's going to cost, let's have that fight now."'

By the end of December 1992, nearly a year after the cameras had started to roll in England, *Alien 3* was in the can and Fincher had done his best to drag the studio kicking and screaming around to his vision for the film. He told *Cinefex*'s Bill Norton, 'Everybody did a phenomenal job, considering the restraints that we had. In the end, *Alien 3* is $60 million worth of the best ideas we could come up with on any given day ... it was a logistical nightmare, it was a production nightmare and it was a micro-management nightmare. If the movie is only half as scary as the experience of making it, then we'll do very well.'

By virtue of the closed narrative and location, *Alien 3*'s cast was a small group, mostly British and almost all-male except for series star Sigourney Weaver and young Danielle Edmond (who played the mute role of Newt's corpse). Weaver admitted that she had been doubtful about Fincher as the correct choice for *Alien 3*'s director, given his neophyte status and track record for flashy style-over-substance rock videos, but his uncompromising approach at their initial meeting won her over: 'I thought he was tremendously talented and very ambitious, with very high standards.'

Co-producer Weaver exercised her influence over the movie's set-up and found she shared similar ideas to the director. 'I did want to go back to the mystery of having one alien,' she said, 'which Fincher had decided to do, but he wanted a creature we hadn't seen before.' Fincher's handling of one of her key scenes dismissed any remaining reservations the actress had, the distressing autopsy on Newt's corpse. 'It's the most emotionally charged scene ... and I was terrified because [it] was so important to me. If David had been insensitive, it would have been a nightmare, but he was incredibly sweet and supportive.'

On set during the rigorous Pinewood shooting, she later admitted: 'It's tough to make a film like this, and Fincher is the only one who's laughed all the way through it. No matter how tense things get, you can always crack jokes with David.' The actress described the finished movie as standing 'on its own as a brilliant *Alien* picture, very unusual and very provocative.'

Other members of the cast also found themselves warming to Fincher. Charles Dance, a Royal Shakespeare Company member for five years before his breakout role in the 1984 mini-series *The Jewel in the Crown*, called the director 'Extraordinary'. The actor noted, 'David Fincher is a genius, basically, for whom I would jump off London Bridge. I trust him implicitly, I stand awe-struck watching Fincher work.' The role of Clemens had briefly been linked with actors Richard E Grant and Gary Oldman before Dance made it his own, bringing to his role an understated, mournful quality that matched the more introspective Ripley of *Alien 3*; in his scenes with Weaver, Dance provides a flawed-but-human foil for Ripley that remains absent in all the other *Alien* films. Fincher was impressed with Dance's performance and, although the project never materialised, while the director was considering helming the remake of *The Avengers* ('a big, widescreen black and white version, kind of cool, a real mod sixties kind of thing'), it was Dance he had picked to play the role of John Steed.

Other than Weaver, the only returning cast member was Lance Henriksen, playing the dual role of the android 'synthetic' Bishop from *Aliens* and his human template at the film's conclusion. The actor, who became a genre staple after his appearance in *The Terminator* (1984), returned to the series in a lengthy scene at *Alien 3*'s finale, entreating Ripley to let the company save the alien queen embryo inside her (see Cuts and Changes below). Henriksen commented that *Alien 3* was 'so Gothic, in terms of the setting, the sets. I've never seen anything like it.' Of David Fincher, the actor said, 'I don't know where a young guy with such an instinct for scenes came from.' He would later star as Frank Black in the television series *Millennium*, a show directly influenced by Fincher's 1995 feature *Seven*.

Playing the leader of the penal colony's prisoner population with a quiet, powerful menace was Charles S Dutton, a former ex-convict himself who took to acting after serving time for involvement in a fatal street-fight. Dutton spoke of the movie's characters as 'the wretched of the universe' and put forward his opinion of the second *Alien* sequel: 'It is totally unlike the other two in terms of its thrust, its focus.' As the quasi-religious prisoner Dillon, the actor presents a man in search of his own redemption, eventually finding it in giving up his life to destroy the alien.

A number of *Alien 3* actors are founder members of the so-called 'Finch Mob' of talent that David Fincher would return to in his later movies. Holt McCallany (Junior, the prisoner with the tear-drop tattoo), reappears as the Mechanic in *Fight*

Club, and Christopher John Fields (the ill-fated Rains), is seen in *The Game* as Detective Boyle and again in *Fight Club* as the counter clerk at the dry-cleaners.

The visual texture of *Alien 3* is as much a player in the movie as the cast itself, from the washed-out sepia tones of the tunnel sequences with their coffin-shaped corridors through to the Gothic, cathedral-like interiors of the prison and the hellish steam and fire of the lead works. The scenes from *Alien 3* shot early in the production bear the stylistic fingerprints of Jordan Cronenweth, the cinematographer on *Altered States* (1980), *Blade Runner* and *Final Analysis* (1992), a filmmaker Fincher had great admiration for. Although studio demands and Cronenweth's deliberate pace meant that Fincher was forced to let him go him mid-shoot, his work helps paint many of the scenes with the medieval shading that runs through the entire movie. Fincher noted, 'When [he] works, it's like he's playing 3-D chess and the rest of us are playing Chinese checkers. The tonal range is amazing, it's like Ansel Adams.' Cronenweth and his son Jeff first met Fincher on the set of the Madonna video 'Oh Father'; the director went on to work with Jeff Cronenweth on *Seven*, *The Game* and *Fight Club*.

Replacing Jordan Cronenweth for the majority of the film's action sequences shot at the end of production was Alex Thomson, a British cinematographer who later handled more action fare in films like *Cliffhanger* and *Executive Decision* (1995); brought into the midst of this troubled production, Thomson nonetheless managed to retain the moody, semi-decayed tones that permeate the movie.

A genre feature film like *Alien 3* stands or falls on the strength of its visual effects, and, with his background in the field from his time at Korty Films and Industrial Light & Magic, Fincher was determined to apply his exacting standards to every inch of the effects during and after production. Much of the work on the film was given to Alec Gillis and Tom Woodruff Jr of Amalgamated Dynamics (who had both worked on *Aliens*) and Boss Film Studios, Richard Edlund's company, known for their work on the *Star Wars* trilogy, *Ghost* (1990) and *Air Force One* (1997). Gillis recalls: 'When we asked who he was, some people said, "It's David Fincher, king of the pop videos." So we thought, "Another flash-and-trash kid." But the more we worked with him, it became apparent that David's extravagance only showed that he wanted the highest quality work. Since we like to push our effects to the max when everyone else is telling us to make things simpler, it was great to have someone who would push us.'

Edlund recalled the numerous delays, changes in release date and script changes. 'The production started off with one director, one producer and one director of photography, and all three of those changed at various times. [Fincher] was an exciting addition, because he knows a lot about effects and understands how to get the most out of them.' Gillis felt that the director was 'very demanding, because he knew the audience would be cheated if our effects were cut too much. He needed to see the alien's actions occur in real time, without using stuff like reverse photography or undercranking. David wanted *Alien 3*'s reality to exist beyond the film, and that would be our toughest challenge.'

For the titular monster, Fincher demanded a creature he described as 'a freight train crossed with a jaguar', but like the script, the alien itself went through dozens of changes, and several different alien designs – including a new version of the face-hugger – were built but never used. The director wanted to avoid obviously 'stagy' effects shots. 'We went into the effects a different way – to me the alien wasn't just a monster, it was a character, so we decided we were going to see the whole thing this time. We wanted the creature to walk on the ceilings and really sell the idea that this thing is a bug from outer space.'

Using the conceit that the alien would adopt genetic traits from whatever host the embryo was implanted in, initial thoughts were of a powerful, muscled creature that would be born from an ox. The explosive birth scene during the funeral would have had the alien (nicknamed the 'bambi-burster') clawing its way out of an ox's corpse on a meat hook, but when the production crew couldn't train an ox for the previous scenes where it would drag the crashed EEV to shore (see Cuts and Changes below), the animal was changed to a dog instead. 'To really do [the ox] right would have cost a couple hundred thousand and we only had $60 thousand,' said Fincher. 'It looked stupid ... the ox stuff just never played.'

Although the smaller incarnation of the dog-like alien was a mechanical puppet, the effects team first attempted to use an actual dog – a whippet – in an alien costume for the monster's earliest evolution. 'The whippet looked great, but it wouldn't perform on the set,' said Woodruff. 'We couldn't even get it to trot down the hall, which was all it had to do. So I ended up sliding the dog into the shot.' Fincher was aware that a similar dog-alien effect had appeared in John Carpenter's *The Thing* (1982), but he wanted 'something faster and more predatory.'

The director noted that the later chase scenes were improved by having a swift and spindly creature design. 'It gave us exciting points-of-view and explained the ravenous attack mode that the thing was in.' However, permission to film the scene of the creature emerging from the impregnated dog was initially denied by Fox. 'We previewed [the film] and people would ask "Where did the alien come from?"' says Fincher. 'So I said to Fox, "Can I shoot the fucking dog now?"' The scene was added just months before *Alien 3*'s release date.

For the beast's larger form, a combination of a human actor in a rubber suit (Woodruff, in an outfit of spandex and foam rubber) and rod puppets allowed the director to capture the mixture of realistic yet insectoid movement he wanted. Mutations from the original H R Giger designs eventually did away with the 'stove-pipe' protrusions on the beast's back and gave the *Alien 3* beast lips with which to snarl – 'We gave it Michelle Pfeiffer's lips ... these big, luscious, collagen lips!' Fincher said jokingly.

The suit, he added, 'was beautifully sculpted, but it was still very difficult to hide the human form inside.' Fincher would direct Woodruff through a radio built into the alien head, and Sigourney Weaver recalls his technique: 'I thought Tom was being particularly specific and very good, considering the fact that he can't really see me; but when I get around the corner, I hear Fincher literally screaming into the microphone "You hate that bitch. Get her, *get her*!" He was whipping up Tom into this frenzy of hatred ... it was wonderful, and so funny.'

The director's challenges to the effects team to make the alien look *truly* alien led to Edlund's Boss Films team developing a computer-operated motion-control camera system that could be assembled on a set and later used to duplicate movement, pans and zooms on a visual effects stage; combined with a new technique they christened 'Mo-Motion', the alien rod puppet could be integrated directly into live-action scenes with actors and practical effects like fire and smoke. 'There was something really interesting, a more animal feeling, about bringing five (puppeteers) to bear on a single puppet,' noted Fincher, comparing the creature's movement to that of a tarantula. 'The tail was what made it look organic and the head was what made it look alien. When those two things were in sync, that was usually when we had a take that we liked.'

Another major effect was the animatronic version of Bishop, the mangled remains of the android left over after being bifurcated by the alien queen in *Aliens*. The original radio-controlled puppet was poorly thought of by Fincher, who underlit the scene and favoured Ripley to mask the unsatisfactory effect; on the set, the British effects crew nicknamed the wrecked Bishop puppet 'Bosh-Up'. A second version also failed to perform the required lip-syncs with Lance Henriksen's dialogue and in the end the scene was re-shot when the production returned to Los Angeles.

One alien element that was cut entirely from the film, like Gillis's 'super face-hugger', was a series of cocoons. In the original *Alien*, Ridley Scott had shot a sequence where Ripley discovered the half-dead remains of the *Nostromo*'s crew, webbed into cocoons and incubating new alien embryos; Fincher planned to use the same concept in *Alien 3*, but the script change that altered the alien growth inside Ripley to a baby queen made the scene redundant. Woodruff had assembled just one of 20 planned cocoons when the sequence was cut. 'He [Fincher] liked it ... he had it on the set with him and would occasionally climb into it for inspiration. He called it his 'thinking shell'...'

For the climax of the film in the hellish lead works, the effects team prepared a pair of tanks that held 2000 gallons of fake molten metal, made from aluminium paste and methocel; Woodruff, fully suited as the alien, was deluged over numerous takes. In post-production there was some concern about the similarity of the lead works scenes to the climax of James Cameron's *Terminator 2: Judgment Day*, despite the fact that Cameron's film had begun shooting after work started on *Alien 3*. The secene was eventually left as it was.

Ripley's final fall into the lead bath and the emergence of the chestburster was the subject of more serious contention. Originally, the beast was to break out of Ripley's body, only for her to hold onto it and dive into the molten metal, but Fincher found the shot 'inelegant all round' and instead filmed a 'stigmata effect' version, with blood blooming on her chest as she fell. 'Everybody felt it was too religious, and to be honest, I thought it was vulgar. If she gets ripped apart before she falls into the fire, that's not sacrifice, that's janitorial service. To knowingly step into the void carrying this thing inside her seemed to me to be more regal.'

But when test audiences responded badly to Ripley's death-dive, Fincher was forced to shoot a third take on the scene at Boss Films' effects stage in Hollywood; in the final version, the alien emerges during Ripley's fall, and she drags it with her into oblivion. 'I didn't want to have the alien come out, I never felt it was necessary to show the creature ... I just didn't want to do the *Carrie* ending. I felt that if we left the movie with [that], no matter what cathartic experience we could expect from seeing the strongest images from the first movie, the chestburster and the character of Ripley, if we left the movie with her choking on her tongue, [the audience] would feel worse going out of the film than they do now. I said, "Whatever happens, she has to be in peace at the end".'

After *Alien 3*'s production at Pinewood Studios had been shut down and moved back to Los Angeles, Fincher spent 72 hours on a rough cut that he estimates was approximately '60 per cent complete' by the time he stopped work. 'This assembly used 100 per cent of the film available to us, but of course I hadn't filmed everything in the script.' This work-in-progress clocked in at two hours and 17 minutes, and was of course missing the additional scenes Fincher still required. From the rough cut, Joe Roth ordered edits to change the pacing and trim the length, as well as allowing Fincher to film several minutes of new footage. Still, after almost a year in the editing suite, a large number of scenes were pared away to give the studio the film they thought they wanted. When *Alien 3* was released, it was down to just under the two-hour mark, with a good 20 minutes lost from Fincher's rough version. The majority of the cuts were minor, but others, most notably the fate of Golic and the brief capture of the alien, punched obvious holes in the narrative.

'When I finished *Alien 3*, I showed it to Joel Schumacher, who is one of the most wonderfully gregarious and most politically astute people you could ever meet, one of the smartest men on how to work and survive in the business,' Fincher said in a 2002 interview. 'At the time, I was deeply disturbed, horrified. It was so out of my control, so unbelievably fucked up. I showed him the movie and he goes, "Well, first of all, it's not bad, it's okay. The good news is you're aiming high. The bad news is you're not able to achieve what it is you want to do. You're an over-achiever, so you're miserable. That's number one. Number two is you put yourself in a position where they have more power than you because you care more about the movie than they do. You can never let that happen again."

'And he was right. If you're not prepared to say "Forget it, let's not do it," you have no power over the situation. Unless you're prepared *not* to make it, you're never going to get to make the movie your way. That was the learning experience of *Alien 3*. I really wanted to make a great *Alien* movie – I loved those movies. And to this day, I believe I was the right guy for the job. I just had the wrong franchise, the wrong script and the wrong studio.'

CUTS AND CHANGES

In the opening moments of the film, Clemens is walking on the beach outside the facility and watches the *Sulaco*'s EEV escape pod crash into the bay. Discovering Ripley alive inside, he carries her indoors wrapped in a cloth (this moment appears in one of the film's trailers), sending some of the prisoners back to get the pod. In the final cut, Clemens doesn't appear until Andrews addresses the inmates.

As Ripley, Clemens and Kevin walk down the spiral staircase to the morgue prior to Newt's autopsy, Clemens asks her if the girl was her daughter, and why she has to know about how she died.

Spike, prisoner Murphy's unlucky dog, is the first victim of the alien and its unwilling host, but originally the host was to have been an ox (named Babe, after the mythical blue ox of Paul Bunyan). The scenes would have the EEV pulled from the sea by a team of oxen, but one dies and is taken to the colony's abattoir to be butchered for stew – a reference to the abattoir remains in later dialogue from the warden. Murphy and Frank discuss why the ox died and their less-than-noble intentions towards Ripley before Murphy finds the remains of the facehugger, discarding the creature thinking it is a dead jellyfish.

Boggs and Rains complain to Dillon in the mess hall about Golic's insanity and poor personal hygiene prior to being sent out on the foraging mission; Golic smiles at the comments and Dillon tells them they have to go, complaints or not.

Ripley's line 'I've been out here a long time' to Clemens just before they sleep together was not in the original cut.

Murphy sings the Rick Evans song 'In the Year 2525 (Exordium and Terminus)' just before he is killed, but the tune was originally 'Paint It, Black' by The Rolling Stones in the earlier cut.

After Murphy's death, Dillon tells Golic to light a candle for the dead man as Golic sets off into the dark tunnels with Boggs and Rains.

When Andrews presses Clemens for information about Ripley, the dialogue continues for a few more lines; the warder intimates he knows about their liaison, and Clemens tells him that she was a member of a marine unit that was destroyed, before Andrews, unsatisfied, throws him out.

While Ripley speaks with the reanimated remains of the Bishop android, Golic appears in the mess hall, covered in blood and babbling madly; he panics Eric the cook, who drops a tray of dishes before Clemens, Aaron, Andrews and Dillon subdue him and take him to the infirmary.

Golic also had more dialogue in the scenes where Clemens and Ripley are speaking, telling them, 'In an insane world, an insane man must appear to be sane.' Moments later, after the alien kills Clemens and Ripley rushes to the mess hall,

Golic studies the face of the creature and calls it 'Magnificent'. Golic's fascination with the alien sets up his later actions at the toxic waste tank, which are also cut.

In the mess hall, Andrews explains that 'at 14.00 hours, prisoners Boggs, Rains and Golic left on a routine foraging mission in the underground network' just before he's dragged into the roof space and killed.

When Morse threatens to put Ripley's head 'through the fucking wall' she coolly replies with, 'Sounds good to me.'

In the final cut of the movie, the attempt to trap the alien in the toxic waste tank appears to fail, but in fact scenes were shot where Ripley's plan succeeds; after the explosion, Ripley and Dillon tend to the wounded, but Junior (one of the prisoners who tried to rape Ripley earlier) is chased by the alien and, despite the attempts of the others to lure it away, the creature follows him into the tank. Locking Junior in with it, Ripley and Dillon hear the prisoner die at the hands of the alien even as they trap it. Finally, they trigger the sprinklers and douse the fires.

When Ripley steals away to the EEV after she starts to feel unwell, Dillon asks, 'Where did she go?'

In the aftermath of the explosion, Dillon leads a prayer service, watched by Ripley and Aaron, who explains that Andrews used to call the prisoners 'Dillon's God Squad.' Ripley questions Aaron's religious beliefs; 'I've got a job,' he retorts. Ripley then asks what he's heard from the incoming rescue team and suggests that they may want to take the alien alive, not kill it.

Guarding Golic in the infirmary, Morse talks to the crazed prisoner while shaving his head; Golic gets him to loosen his restraints as payback for all the times he gave Morse cigarettes, but then he knocks him out with a fire extinguisher and races off to see the alien.

Ripley has Aaron send a message to the network telling them they've trapped the alien and requesting permission to kill it, in order to test the company's intentions; Aaron has to ask her how to spell the word 'xenomorph'. The company reply is a negative, justifying Ripley's distrust.

Golic slits the throat of the prisoner guarding the door to the toxic waste tank when he refuses to let him in to talk to the alien; releasing the creature, he promises it he'll do whatever it wants and calls it 'brother'. In early versions of the subplot, Golic would believe that he and Ripley were to be spared by the alien to become an 'Adam and Eve' on the desolate planet. 'That idea basically got cast aside because it was considered to be strange,' Fincher recalls.

Ripley tells Dillon that the company want to take the alien alive, but he doesn't care, and when she says that innocent people will die, Dillon tells her that 'the world outside does not exist' for them any more. Then Morse arrives to tell them what Golic has done and, at the rubbish tip, Aaron blames Morse for letting it happen.

When Dillon refuses to kill Ripley with the fire axe, he prefigures the end of the film when he tells her, 'Go kill yourself.'

As Dillon rallies the prisoners to kill the alien, he invokes their religion by claiming that the task is 'one of the steps to heaven.' Aaron wants to wait for the rescue team, but Ripley questions who – or what – they are actually coming to rescue.

During the chase sequence, Ripley asks Dillon about 'the plan' and he replies that although she's immune to the alien's attacks, the others are not, so they're 'improvising'. When Dillon finds Troy's corpse, he says his name in farewell, while the prisoner with the scissors impales himself on them by mistake, dying with the words, 'For fuck's sake!'

Aaron confronts the company rescue team as they arrive, telling them that Ripley has been impregnated. 'We know that,' says Bishop, as his men bring in a cage for the creature. In what might be a *Jaws* homage, Aaron tells them, 'You're gonna need a bigger cage.'

As Ripley entices the alien into the piston chamber, she dares it to kill her.

Just before Ripley activates the sprinklers to kill the overheated alien, she says to herself, 'For the last time.' In the original cut, Ripley uses the water spray on the creature without being told to by Morse – apparently his voice-over was added later to explain her actions to the audience.

When Bishop confronts Ripley, her hesitation over what choice to make is much more intense and he has more dialogue before she shuts the gate on him, talking about her courage and describing the queen embryo as a 'malignancy'; the Weyland-Yutani technician explains that it will only take two hours to remove the alien chestburster from her, with no ill-effects.

When Morse asks Ripley, 'What do you want me to do?', she replies, 'You'll know.'

After Aaron is killed for striking Bishop with the metal rod, Bishop is revealed as a human when he clutches his blood-soaked ear and yells, 'I'm not a droid!'

In the original cut, Ripley falls into the bath of molten lead without the chestburster breaking out of her torso, and the injured Morse crawls over to the edge of the rim to look into the pit.

And finally, the last scenes of the Fury 161 plant being shut down were originally in a different order, with the shot of the EEV's empty hypersleep pods and the replay of Ripley's *Nostromo* log coming after the read-out screen.

AFTERMATH

Alien 3 weathered a deluge of critical negativity on its initial release, a response that took the director to task over what was seen as his violation of expectations for the *Alien* saga. Some critics were confused by early promotional material for the film that intimated it was going to be set on Earth, a logical step up from the earlier movies, only to be presented with a movie taking place in the bowels of a dingy outer space toxic waste dump. Others pilloried Fincher for a perceived lack of substance beneath the glossy visuals generated by this 'MTV whiz'.

Sight & Sound's Mark Kermode called it a 'dreary and incoherent conclusion to the otherwise extraordinary *Alien* movies', while *Cinefantastique*'s Thomas Doherty labelled it as 'a downer to the third power'. Adam Goldberg of the *All Movie Guide* said it had a 'stifling and redundant narrative', while Marc Savlov of the *Austin Chronicle* chastised Fincher's 'MTV sensibilities' in a 'beautifully shot and utterly uninteresting sequel'. Both fans and critics were united in their uproar over Fincher's bold choices to first kill off *Aliens* survivors Newt and Hicks barely five minutes into the movie, and then eliminate the heroine of the series by plunging Ripley into a vat of boiling lead; here was a second sequel that all but erased the whole meaning of the preceding film and turned the courageous lead into a terminal victim, ticking away the running time towards her bloody death.

Says Fincher: '*Alien 3* takes place in a prison, it was supposed to be about the wretched of the world. The other ones had heroic marines or those unsuspecting truck drivers in outer space. We thought, "Here are the fucking wretched, nobody cares if these people live or die." The task was to make people care and think, "Hold on, we have a duty to everyone," but it didn't really work. We failed to give people the broad, safe entertainment that, in the United States at least, they seem to want. They want to go to the cinema and get away from it all. We tried to bring it down to right here and now, and I just think in terms of the world box-office we may have chosen wrong. If we failed to do one thing in this film, and we failed to do many things, it was to take people out of their everyday lives. It's not a scare movie but a queasy scare movie and I think people resent that.'

At the time, the director told the *Independent*, 'I want people to realise that I'm not embarrassed by the film, there are certain things in it I really like. At least we were taking some chances. If I make ten shitty movies, I'll deserve the flak, and if I go on to make ten great movies, this'll probably be looked upon as my first bungled masterpiece.'

Alien 3 is undeniably a striking film, and a handful of commentators were willing to buck the trend and praise it. Peter Travers of *Rolling Stone* defended the feature's 'austere, low-tech, darkly funny' narrative and said of Ripley's swan-dive, 'Her final scene, a war between her maternal and killer instincts, is bold and haunting. So is the movie.' Travers also tapped into the consensus of many viewers that the film was 'the first $50 million thriller that also functions as an AIDS allegory', an element that *Sight & Sound*'s Amy Taubin also saw 'in the metaphor of a mysterious deadly organism attacking an all-male community.' Desson Howe at the *Washington Post* called it 'too interesting to make an exciting summer flick' and, commenting on the later DVD release, Bill Hunt of *The Digital Bits* said of Fincher's visual style: 'much more so than either of the first two films in the series ... Fincher successfully creates an air of depression and despair throughout the film very reminiscent of *Seven*.'

After *Alien 3*'s utterly final ending and its poor reception, some observers considered the *Alien* franchise over. At the 1993 box-office, the film grossed

$55.47 million and later added another £31.76 million in rental fees across the United States, but, bracketed by major hits like *Lethal Weapon 3* and *Sister Act*, *Alien 3* lost out in a year that was ultimately dominated by family films *Aladdin* and *Home Alone 2: Lost in New York*. The film was nevertheless nominated for a handful of awards, winning none of them; *Alien 3* earned Oscar recognition for Richard Edlund, George Gibbs, Alec Gillis and Tom Woodruff Jr. when it was nominated in the Best Visual Effects category in 1993, and the team were also nominated for the BAFTA for Best Special Effects in the same year. The MTV movie awards chose the tunnel chase sequence as a nominee for the Best Action Sequence, and the World Science Fiction Convention's Hugo nominated the film for the Best Dramatic Presentation award.

In the years that followed, especially as a fourth *Alien* feature was added to the canon in 1997, *Alien 3* gained a little more of the respect it deserves through hindsight, but still the film remains the most contentious and fought-over entry in the series. In Doherty's words, the film is 'a sad, nihilistic finale to what is, all taken, a brilliant trilogy.'

For several years after *Alien 3*, the film was something of a dead issue to Fincher, a work he had moved on from and declined to revisit. In 2002, he candidly told *Cinescape* magazine that 'I hate it.' He later categorically said, 'I have no plans to revisit *Alien 3*. There was a kind of famous encounter about that, when footage was cut, and I remember saying, "Can we possibly save this stuff for the laserdisc?" I was told by someone with great relish, "There are no plans ever to do that." You know, it was flawed from its inception and it was certainly flawed – actually pretty fucked-up – well before we started shooting.' Half joking, he added, 'I have no interest in seeing that movie preserved. I remember, I was finishing the movie during the LA riots, and I was just hoping that the DeLuxe film laboratory would be burned to the ground. "Is all the negative at DeLuxe? Oh thank God, thank God."'

But despite Fincher's comments, *Alien 3* will be rescued from this ignominious fate by the release of the oddly named *Alien Quadrilogy* box set, a massive nine-disc set of DVDs scheduled for late 2003. The new version of *Alien 3* included in the set restores all the missing footage – especially the Golic scenes – as extras or as part of a new cut created by Terry Rawlings. This remains the closest approximation to Fincher's original, unadulterated vision of the film.

My own first exposure to *Alien 3* was in the home of a cineaste associate, clustered around a bootleg copy of the movie that had been hastily sent to London by an American friend, a whole gang of us ready to be hit between the eyes by the latest instalment in the saga. None of us was sure what to expect, what we would get from a director whose only reference was pop videos and Nike ads. But in moments we were reeling from the sucker-punch Fincher's daring opening gave us. His cold-blooded killing of Hicks and Newt, the two characters we'd sweated and prayed to see safely escape from planet LV-426, shredded the rules that Scott and Cameron had so painstakingly established. Suddenly, all bets were off, and the rumours I'd heard that Ripley wouldn't survive to the end credits were now not so easily dismissed.

As a fan of the *Alien* films I was dragged unwillingly into Fury 161's dark world, hoping that somehow this horrific tale could all be a mistake, a bad dream; flinching each time the creature appeared, afraid that the alien – and Fincher – would do something else that broke the rules. Watching the first *Alien*, we never knew what would happen next, and to recapture that sense of dread in *Alien 3*'s viewers Fincher warped the narrative environment to confound our expectations. It was a nightmare in the already-nightmarish *Alien* world, a nasty wake-up call which told the audience that, yes, there were worse things that could happen. I had come to *Alien 3* comfortable and complacent, but, in return for my presumption and that of my fellow audience members, we were made to recall the fear that *Alien* had first shown us. By the time the credits rolled, Ripley was dead and so were our preconceptions – and then we began an argument about the movie that lasted for hours.

The cold entropy of *Alien 3* was what made many people hate it, the creepy and sullen sense of gloom that permeated the entire film from the EEV's crash on the black beach to the dark closing moments. And yet it is the same fatalistic thread that Fincher was praised for when he used it again in *Seven*. And, like *Seven*, *Alien 3* shows us the edges of human life trying to make a little warmth in a cold, unforgiving universe, as Ripley gets the first opportunity in three movies to be something more than a warrior-mother figure, and experience a moment of love. Fincher's film goes back to the roots of the *Alien* series by resetting the mythos to zero and still manages to advance the key character of Ripley. (Granted that, beyond Clemens and Dillon, the rest of Fury 161's population don't rise above the role of hapless victims, but this isn't their story.) *Alien 3* is the final movement in Ripley's life – and this is discounting her reborn self in 1997's *Alien Resurrection* – where she learns that her awful fate is to face the monster again and again, losing all that matters to her until the very end.

This is a film that rediscovers the Haunted House fear of the *Alien* universe, a fear that we lost when *Aliens* turned the franchise into a war story. It's right there, even in the dialogue as Ripley tells Aaron she's off to 'the basement' to look for the beast. 'This whole place is one big basement,' he replies, and he's exactly right. Thanks to the cuts and omissions of key subplots, the movie we see will never be the one that was made, and because of the distressed evolution of *Alien 3*, it will never be the film that Fincher *could* have made. This is obviously a director's first feature, obviously the work of someone used to finding the perfect shot waylaid by the vagaries of time and money. There are places where the pitch and movement of *Alien 3* go off-balance, where the underlit scenes and the oppressive doom of it all are almost too much to sustain.

But beneath it all, even if you hate it for gutting the emotional core of the series, *Alien 3* is true to the nature of the beast – uncompromising, harsh and challenging.

THREE

Deadly Sins

'I've always been interested in movies that scar.'

A DARK SERIAL killer story with one of the most powerful endings and bleak narratives in contemporary film, *Seven* was the movie that pulled David Fincher's directing career from the doldrums and brought his talent to light in Hollywood. After his harsh experiences on *Alien 3*, the gun-shy Fincher was careful to select a second feature project that would not only allow him to exercise the creative range he had been previously denied, but also to blow the lid off an established genre. *Seven* confounded critics who had savaged the director for the perceived shortcomings of his earlier work and brought Fincher into the orbit of other creatives – writer Andrew Kevin Walker, cinematographer Darius Khondji, producer Arnold Kopelson and actors Brad Pitt, Kevin Spacey and Morgan Freeman – whose talent would inform his later projects.

Seven is Fincher free to film. In this tale of two detectives on the trail of a murderer, one educated but world-weary, the other brusque but vital, the director crafted a movie that takes on the cops-hunt-killer stereotype and smashes it. Audiences were pushed into a cold, gloomy world by the tale, confronting horrific acts of evil – and it is the movie's dynamic reversal of expectations in the later scenes that left such an indelible mark on the cinema of the 1990s. At last, after a harrowing apprenticeship, David Fincher had arrived.

SEVEN

New Line Cinema
Director: *David Fincher*
Writer: *Andrew Kevin Walker*
Cast: *Morgan Freeman (Detective William Somerset), Brad Pitt (Detective David Mills), Kevin Spacey (John Doe), Gwyneth Paltrow (Tracy Mills), Andy Walker (Dead Man), Daniel Zacapa (Detective Taylor), John Cassini (Officer Davis), Bob Mack (Gluttony victim), Peter Crombie (Doctor O'Neill), Reg E Cathey (coroner), R. Lee Ermey (Police Captain), George Christy (workman), Endre Hules (cab driver), Hawthorne James (George, library night guard), Roscoe Davidson (library guard),*

Bob Collins (library guard), Jimmy Dale Hartsell (library janitor), Richard Roundtree (Martin Talbot), Charline Su (TV news reporter), Dominique Jennings (TV news reporter), Allan Kolman (forensic man), Beverly Burke (TV anchor woman), Gene Borkan (Eli Gould, Sin of Greed victim), Julie Araskog (Mrs. Gould), Mario Di Donato (fingerprint forensic man), Alfonso Freeman (fingerprint technician), John C. McGinley (California), Robert J Stephenson (cop on SWAT team), Harrison White (cop on SWAT team), Michael Reid MacKay (Victor, Sin of Sloth victim), Richard Portnow (Dr Beardsley), Tudor Sherrard (coupon man), Mark Boone Junior (greasy FBI man), Pamala Tyson (homeless woman), Lennie Loftin (policeman), Sarah Hale Reinhardt (police sketch artist), Emily Wagner (Detective Sara), Martin Serene (Wild Bill), Michael Massee (man in massage parlour booth), David Correia (cop at massage parlour), Ron Blair (cop at massage parlour), Cat Mueller (Hooker, Sin of Lust victim), Leland Orser (crazed man in massage parlour), Lexie Bigham (sweating cop at massage parlour), Evan Miranda (paramedic), Harris Savides (911 operator), Rachel Schadt (additional 911 operator), Paul S. Eckstein (paramedic), Heidi Schanz (beautiful woman, Sin of Pride victim), Brian Evers (Duty Sergeant), Shannon Wilcox (cop behind desk), Richard Schiff (Mark Swarr), John Santin (helicopter pilot), James Deeth (helicopter pilot), Charles A. Tamburro (SWAT helicopter pilot), Richmond Arquette (delivery man), Duffy Gaver (marksman in helicopter).

Crew: Stephen Brown (co-producer), Phyllis Carlyle (producer), William C. Gerrity (line producer), Nana Greenwald (co-producer), Lynn Harris (co-executive producer), Dan Kolsrud (executive producer), Anne Kopelson (executive producer), Arnold Kopelson (producer), Gianni Nunnari (executive producer), Sanford Panitch (co-producer), Michele Platt (associate producer), Richard Saperstein (co-executive producer), Howard Shore (music), Darius Khondji (cinematography), Harris Savides (additional photography), Richard Francis-Bruce (editing), Arthur Max (production design), Gary Wissner (art direction), Clay A Griffith (set decoration), Michael Kaplan (costume design), Jean Black (makeup supervisor), Rob Bottin (special makeup effects), Peter Albiez (special effects co-ordinator), Peter Frankfurt (visual effects producer)

Tagline: 'Seven Deadly Sins. Seven Ways to Die.'

SYNOPSIS

In an unnamed city, police detective William Somerset begins his final week on the job, counting down the seven days to his retirement. His replacement at the homicide unit is David Mills, a younger cop from the country who has moved to the city looking to make a difference, and Somerset resigns himself to chaperoning Mills for the next few days.

Monday: the two detectives are summoned to the site of a particularly gruesome murder, where the body of a hugely obese man is found face down in bowl of spaghetti. An autopsy discovers the victim was forced to eat himself to death, and despite Somerset's unhappiness at being given such a case as his last, Mills embraces it with gusto.

Tuesday: Mills investigates another killing, of a high-priced lawyer in his uptown office. This victim died after being forced to cut off a pound of his own flesh, and the word 'Greed' is painted in blood on the office floor. Meanwhile, evidence found in the stomach of the obese man leads Somerset back to the first crime scene and he discovers a previously hidden clue – behind the victim's refrigerator is the word 'Gluttony' written in grease, along with a note featuring a quote from *Paradise Lost* ('Long is the way and hard that out of Hell leads to the light'). Despite his misgivings, Somerset finds his interest piqued by the crimes and realises that the killer is following the pattern of the seven deadly sins; that evening, he visits the library while Mills tries and fails to find a lead among the evidence.

Wednesday: Mills, sceptical and less well-read than Somerset, is dismayed by the elder man's suggestion that they search for clues and motives in the books of Chaucer, Dante and Saint Thomas Aquinas, but the two cops are eventually brought together by Mills' wife Tracey, who invites Somerset over to their noisy, cramped apartment for dinner. Later that night, while Tracey sleeps, the detectives pore over the evidence from the 'Greed' crime scene before locating a possible lead. Tracey awakens to find herself alone as they visit the lawyer's wife; in turn, the wife points out a wrongly hung painting in the lawyer's office. At the scene, Somerset removes the picture and discovers fingerprints on the wall from an unknown party, spelling out the words 'Help Me'.

Thursday: A fingerprint match from the police's records leads to an address for Victor, a known felon who fits the typical serial killer profile, but Somerset is not convinced that he is their suspect. Following a SWAT team raid, the detectives enter Victor's apartment to discover that he has been tied to his bed for a year, degenerating into a near corpse-like state; his hand has been removed to plant the clues at the 'Greed' murder, and Victor is in fact the third victim, 'Sloth'. Mills is angered at losing the killer's trail and berates a photographer who appears at the crime scene. That night, Somerset gets a call from Tracey, who is looking for a sympathetic person to talk to.

Friday: Somerset and Tracey meet at a diner. Tracey admits how much she hates life in the city, that she is only there for her husband, and confides to the elder detective what Mills himself doesn't yet know – that she is pregnant. Somerset regretfully tells her of his own experiences, of how a relationship he had with a woman was destroyed by the harsh reality of city life, before he is called away.

Back at the precinct, the two cops find themselves at a dead end until a chance comment from Mills leads Somerset to a new avenue of investigation. Using a contact at the FBI, Somerset gains access to secret files that track the movements of library books on contentious subjects such as police techniques and serial killing, procuring an inventory of readers cross-referenced with titles that their murderer may have read. The list produces a likely suspect, Jonathan Doe, and the detectives visit his apartment; confronting Doe, the two men are shot at and the killer attempts to escape. Mills almost catches Doe, but the killer turns the tables on him and puts a gun to his head – for a moment. Instead of killing him, Doe inexplicably lets Mills live and vanishes into the city.

Returning to Doe's home, Mills subverts due process and kicks the door in, paying a false witness to cover his unwarranted entry. Inside the dark apartment Somerset finds thousands of Doe's notebooks, full of his crazed ramblings on sin as well as grisly souvenirs from the first three murders and a lead on a fourth, as yet undiscovered, victim. Mills realises that they had the killer in their grip and didn't know it when he finds photographs of himself taken at Victor's apartment – the cameraman he ejected was Doe. Despite the wealth of evidence, the police find no traces of Doe's identity, even down to his fingerprints. The killer telephones Mills to taunt him, hinting at the murders yet to come.

Saturday: the lead on the fourth victim takes the detectives to a leather shop, where the owner has sold Doe a custom-made sex toy – a razor-sharp bladed dildo. Nearby in a seedy brothel, the police find the fourth victim, 'Lust' – a prostitute, stabbed to death when Doe forced her client to wear the dildo and have sex with her. After interrogating the hysterical client and the brothel owner, Somerset and Mills discuss the case at a bar and the older detective speaks about the damning, apathetic nature of the city. Returning home, Somerset is unable to sleep, conflicted by his need to catch Doe and his intention to retire and leave the city's squalor behind him.

Sunday: Doe calls the 911 operator and confesses to another killing, and the detectives arrive at the scene of the 'Pride' murder. Doe tortured a beautiful model by cutting off her nose before gluing a telephone to one of her hands and a vial of sleeping pills in the other – giving her the choice between being rescued but living on disfigured, or taking a suicidal overdose. As they return to the precinct, Somerset tells Mills he has decided to forestall his retirement until the Doe case is closed – and unseen by the two men, Doe exits a cab and enters the station behind them. Covered in blood, the killer gives himself up to the police – but the case is not closed. Doe's lawyer tells the police officers that the murderer is willing to plead guilty to his crimes – but there are two more victims whom he is willing to show to them. However, Doe will only do so if Mills and Somerset are the ones to accompany him.

The three men drive out of the city, trailed by a police helicopter. On the way, Doe resists any attempts to uncover his identity – his fingerprints having been cut off with razor blades and no other records of him having been found – and instead goads Mills with his reasons for murdering his sinning victims at God's behest. Arriving at a dense stand of overhead power pylons, Doe leads the detectives into the bleak desert as the hour reaches seven o'clock; and suddenly, a delivery van approaches them. Leaving Mills with Doe, Somerset intercepts the van. The driver is carrying a package addressed to Detective David Mills, and after sending him away, Somerset warily begins to open the box.

Meanwhile, Doe speaks to Mills, telling him how much he admires the police officer, how much he admires Mills' ordinary life with his wife Tracey. Somerset looks inside the box and reacts with horror, racing back to Mills and calling for him to drop his weapon. Doe tells Mills that he visited his home that morning and tried 'to play husband' with Tracey, but failed – so he took a souvenir; 'her pretty head'. Doe admits that he is a sinner and his is that of envy, of Mills and his life – and suddenly Mills realises what is inside the box, that Tracey is dead. As Somerset tries to talk Mills into giving up his gun, Doe provokes the young cop further, revealing that Tracey was pregnant with David's child. Wracked with anger and horror, Mills shoots Doe, killing him and becoming the final victim, of the sin of wrath. As Mills is taken away under police custody, Somerset realises that Doe has won even with his own death; and regretfully he knows that he can never retire, telling his captain that he'll 'be around'.

DEVELOPMENT

After *Alien 3*, three years would elapse before the release of David Fincher's second picture. *Seven* was the dark serial killer drama that would ultimately put him on the directorial map. In the interim, he was connected to scripts for *The Game* (which he would later shoot in 1997) and the big-screen remake of *The Avengers* television series. 'For about a week,' he notes of the latter. 'Then they told me that Warners would do the budget...'

But by his own admission the director refused to look seriously at any other scripts for a year and a half, instead returning briefly to the world of commercials and music videos, producing promos for stars like Madonna, The Rolling Stones and Michael Jackson. 'I looked at stuff, but I got sent stupid crap, I got sent stuff commensurate with my station in life – "You're the guy who fucked up what should have been an interesting movie" – and that was true. I just didn't feel like I wanted to go into a situation where you say, "I want to do it this way," and have all these people saying, "Yeah, yeah, that sounds good," and then as soon as you leave they say, "Look what he did with *Alien 3*...."'

Fincher's first exposure to *Seven* came when his agent sent him an early version of the script – accidentally forwarding him what was, at that time, the 'wrong' draft. He recalls, 'I read [the script] and I thought there's something so perverse about this.' *Seven* had originally been taken up by Penta, an Italian production company, with *Benny & Joon* (1993) director Jeremiah Chechik in the hot seat and actor Denzel Washington in the frame to play Mills; after an initial look at the property, Chechik had chosen to lighten the storyline, to lose the blacker-than-black ending. It was this draft that Fincher had been meant to see, but an office mix-up meant he saw the version with the 'head in the box' climax, and it blew him away. But for this error in postage, *Seven* might never have been produced.

Fincher remembers that 'I didn't know what was going to happen in the end ... I kind of thought to myself, "Well, maybe this could happen, but they'll never do that, they'll never do that to those guys in this movie, it's just not the Hollywood way to do it..." I liked the fact that the movie was so ruthless ... [that it] just kind of fucked with their ideas of what entertainment should be. That was the point of *Seven*, dragging you through the whole gruesome nightmare. I liked the idea of a mass entertainment that has all those nasty trappings. I like the idea of a movie that takes its toll on the audience.' It was the can't-look-away effect inherent in the story that snared him. 'I liked how it tapped into the push-pull, attraction-repulsion relationship we have with serial killer mythology. I got sent the script for *Seven* by Mike DeLuca. He had seen *Alien 3* and obviously thought there was some promise, I met with the guy and he said "I'd love you to do it." They paid me well, and I went off and made it my second movie.'

Seven was the creation of writer Andrew Kevin Walker and, as with Fincher, the movie would help to mark Walker as a major creative force in the industry. Walker was a former Pennsylvania State University film student. Working as a production assistant on B-movies like *Robot Holocaust* (1987), he had later slaved over scripts for low-budget straight-to-video projects like *Brainscan* (1994) alongside a day job at Tower Records in New York City. *Seven*, with its nameless, brutal and filthy metropolis, was his cynical 'love letter' to the Big Apple. 'New York is an amazing place, but it's a cauldron of unpleasantries. I lived there for about five years and I was miserable for just about every minute of every day,' he remembered. 'I just couldn't adjust to living in a big, angry, loud city, so part of [*Seven*] was a reaction to that.'

In three months, *Seven* was sold and Walker moved to the sunnier climes of Los Angeles to further pursue his writing career, where the script earned him work on *Hideaway* (1995) and an early draft of *X-Men* (2000). When Penta and Chechik left the project, *Seven* was picked up by New Line Cinema and David Fincher entered the frame at the behest of Arnold Kopelson, the producer on films like *Platoon* (1986), *Falling Down* and *The Fugitive* (both 1993). 'I called my agent and said, "This movie, are they going to make this? There's this head in the box at the end, it's just amazing. Are they really going to do this?" And he said, "No, you've got the wrong draft."'

Fincher read the new, 'softer' draft, the draft he'd been meant to see, and rejected it – 'It was awful. I said, "This is just crap, the first one is much better".' New Line's Michael DeLuca, an executive producer whose later projects would include *Dark City* (1998), *American History X* (1999) and *Simone* (2002), concurred with Fincher's decision to lobby for the original ending. 'We thought it was very original in the world it depicted,' DeLuca noted. 'The film is full of moments that are arresting on a visual level.'

More than ten drafts of *Seven* had been written between the remorseless original and the more lightweight version, a script that Fincher called a more 'kick ass, take names cop movie'. The director took the challenge to producer Kopelson. 'Fincher impressed me with his highly stylised manner of shooting,' he said. 'Once we began discussing David's vision of how he would approach each scene, the screenplay literally came alive. His descriptions left me unhinged.' But Kopelson was still convinced that a film with such a hard ending would never be made. Fincher remembered his words. 'He said, "There's no way that there will be a head in the box at the end of this movie, there is absolutely no way that that will ever happen, don't even talk to me about that".'

Nevertheless, Fincher continued to campaign for the original finale, going back to Kopelson with endorsements from lead actors Brad Pitt and Morgan Freeman after they signed on to the film. Pitt in particular put his weight behind the scene, refusing to play the role of Detective Mills unless it was retained. As pre-production began, the director finally won Kopelson over with an appeal to the producer's sense of movie immortality. 'I said, "Arnold, 50 years from now there's going to be a bunch of 20-year-olds at a party and one of them is going to say, "Remember when you were 15 and that movie was on TV, I don't even know who was in it, but at the end there's the head in the box and the guy drives up in the middle of the desert?" And everybody's going to go, "Oh yeah, I love that movie." That's how this movie is going to be remembered, so how can you cut the head in the box?'

Both the director and his actors would be proved right in the years that followed. Still, during casting and recruitment of the film crew, Fincher encountered resistance from some talent who refused to work on *Seven* because of its content. 'A lot of agents said "I'm not sending this to my client – it's evil and misogynist".'

Another part of the appeal of *Seven* for Fincher came from its changing, evolving nature; opening as a fairly typical buddy-cop story before morphing into a tense thriller, and then a final, dizzying drop into horror territory. 'I got 20 pages into it and I thought, 'Oh God, it's just a buddy movie, and it's like I am the last person in the world to do one ... But then all of a sudden it took this turn, and I found myself getting more and more trapped in this kind of evil ... Although I felt uncomfortable about being there, I had to keep going.' Expecting a riff on the *Lethal Weapon* series, Fincher was rewarded by a script that inverted the expected narrative progression. 'Everyone said, you have to have the scene where you see the killer stalking the victim – she's in the shower, he's outside the window – but the thing I found gripping about the script was the connect the dots aspect.' Walker deliberately broke the standard model for the procedural detective story by bringing the antagonist out into the open early in the third act, as the killer simply surrenders to the police.

The icing on the cake was when John Doe gives himself up,' said Fincher. 'I was holding the script and I knew how many pages were left in the movie and I thought, "Holy shit, if I'm sitting in a theatre, this movie could go on for another hour, this could be the middle of the movie." I just felt so much at the end,' he said, comparing the script to *The Exorcist* (1973). 'You don't have any control over this, you're just along for the ride. From the time he opens the box ... it's like you realise that the end of this movie's been written in stone and it's been there for like eight or nine hours and you don't have any choice. The big sequence in the third act of most movies, with the big chase across town, [with] the guy in the car going "C'mon! C'mon!", honking the horn and driving on the sidewalk, and there's the window being opened in the back and the woman drawing the bath ... this script doesn't even *care* about that, because it's already happened ten hours ago and you just kind of go "*Oh!*" That's what I liked about it, it's like a kick in the stomach. All of a sudden it becomes a horror movie ... it becomes a morality play, it becomes about confronting evil.'

The director felt that *Seven*'s ability to fracture the rules of conventional plotting was its biggest strength. 'Movies make a pact with the audience, there's an expectation. You pay your eight bucks and you're going to be taken *this* far but not *that* far ... I don't like those sort of movies. I feel most alive at a scary movie when I truly feel like this could go places even I couldn't predict.' In an interview with *Empire* magazine, the director said 'I don't know how much movies should entertain, to me I'm always been interested in movies that scar. The thing that I love about *Jaws* is the fact that I've never gone swimming in the ocean again. I was 12 when I saw *Jaws* and I thought it was amazing.'

PRODUCTION

After just six weeks of pre-production and planning, the film rolled into action, and Fincher found a degree of freedom that had been lacking on *Alien 3*'s shoot. '*Seven* is the first time I got to carry through certain things about the camera,' he said in a 1996 interview. 'I thought I was making a tiny genre movie, the kind of movie Friedkin might have made after *The Exorcist*, a little handheld hippie movie.'

He later joked that the film would be 'a lurid little footnote in everyone's career'. 'I tried hard not to have a hundred trucks, but every time you take the camera out of the box, it gets complicated.' Helping the director with that complexity was Darius Khondji, the cinematographer on *Delicatessen* (1991) and *The City of Lost Children* (1995). Khondji's association with Fincher had started on a Nike commercial and the two men would later work together on the early parts of *Panic Room*'s shoot. He remembers, 'One of the first things [Fincher] told me was, "It's got to be *scary...*" I had only seen his film *Alien 3*, but immediately knew he was a great director. I wanted to do a film like *Seven* for a long time; I grew up dreaming about it.'

Fincher told him: 'Make it dirty, make it about decay, make it real.' *Sight & Sound*'s Chris Darke would later call Khondji's work 'a virtuoso trawl through the barely illuminated antechambers of Hell'. But the cinematographer's dark, moody footage was not liked by everyone at New Line, especially the producers who saw Khondji as a relative unknown. 'The studio, the unions – they had to accept me and everything had to be arranged ... but the pictures were coming to me.' Intending to draw on the techniques used in an expressionist Nike advert they had shot together in Paris, Fincher went for a 'clash of elements' on screen; he asked, 'How do we make black *black*?'

The shared vision of Khondji and Fincher created the colour palette for *Seven*, in its range from moist, fungal greens through to sepia browns and rich blacks, and throughout the shoot, the cinematographer worked to maintain the perfect look; in interviews, Morgan Freeman jokingly recalled Khondji's constant tinkering with the lighting between each shot as he fine-tuned each scene. At the scene of the 'Gluttony' killing, the crew placed cardboard panels in strategic places throughout the set, to let the actors light themselves by reflecting their flashlight beams. The use of colour unites many scenes in the film; from the red of the 'Lust' murder scene that evoked the image of a ghost train for Khondji, to the pools of green light in the library and the dim apartment interiors of Victor and John Doe.

Seven's visual darkness (as opposed to its thematic darkness) grows out of Khondji's abuse of atypical film stocks and a processing regime that he first employed on *Delicatessen*. After the film's colour negative was developed and fixed it was 're-souped' and run back through the baths as black and white; these 're-silvered' prints created an image where the colour elements were de-saturated and the black elements deepened – typically, most movies have less silver to create a lighter image. 'Silver retention is necessary to make film look like it should look, but doesn't,' said Fincher. 'Kodak makes such thin print stock these days because it is cheaper. They run the bath hot and fast. What happens is, that with this print stock they try to tweak every penny out of the process in the labs and in the end you get these incredibly thin prints. It's nothing like a 35mm slide. These prints are grey, they have no density and no saturation at all.'

Despite the director's intent, only a few hundred of the cinema prints of *Seven* that used this retention (known as a 'CCE process') were distributed among the 2500 first-run reels, making them a rarity among film aficionados. Luckily for collectors, the silver print was used as the basis for the 2000 DVD release of the movie. Ironically, in the concluding scenes of the film amid the power-line pylons, *Seven* is at its brightest visually, while approaching its darkest moments narratively.

'I look at *Seven* and I see something that was trying to be realistic, ' said the director. 'It may be incredibly stylised, but it was always the intention, the thing at the forefront in everybody's mind was how to make it raw, how to make it real.' Fincher and Khondji took the video-verité look of the reality TV series *Cops* as their starting point for the film. 'We wanted to do something immediate and simple ... The camera is in the back seat peering over people's shoulders, like the runt following the pack, in a vulnerable position.' Fincher also traced visual connections to what he called 'these kind of weird movies of the 1970s ... it just sort of reminded me of *Klute* and *Vanishing Point* ... to have this "we don't know exactly what we're doing but it could be a movie" kind of attitude to it.' Indeed, he makes an overt visual reference to *Klute* (1971) in the scene where Somerset and Mills are being fitted for wires prior to their desert drive with Doe.

Fincher and Khondji held religiously to the conceit that the film was shot 'in the real world'. '[We] talked about psychologically where we wanted to be in any given room. We decided we wouldn't build any flyaway walls. If the kitchen is only 12 feet, then hem him in.' The claustrophobic look of scenes such as the 'Gluttony' murder and even the close-in moments inside Somerset's car reflect this intent clearly. 'We wanted to continually remind the audience of how we're constantly rubbing elbows, glancing off other people – and yet in this beehive of bodies, people come in and are snatched out, dispatched. The killer is among us, it's Jeffrey Dahmer, it's the guy in 3c who's running a saw in the middle of the night.'

One of the most striking scenes comes at the 'Sloth' murder site, when the supposedly dead Victor suddenly comes to life; the corpse-man is not a prop effect, but actor Michael Reid MacKay under special make-up by effects expert Rob Bottin. Fincher was inspired by videos from the band Nine Inch Nails (who played the movie's opening music) and let Bottin – 'an awesome fucking genius' in his words – 'go mad'.

Many negative comments about the film stem from the perceived brutality in the movie, but in fact *Seven* has very little on-screen violence – rather, it is the film's harsh vision of the after-effects of violence that is shocking. The director appreciated the sleight of hand he could exercise in this way: 'I loved the underpinning of "I'm going to show you something you absolutely don't want to see" – or, in fact, "I'm *not* going to show you something you absolutely don't want to see and you're going to sit there breathlessly waiting to see it".' The stark images force the impact of the killings on the viewer. 'There's a psychological trauma that the movie is inflicting on you,' said Fincher, 'because it's making you think about things that you don't want to think about – it's psychic violence ... it's not just a white chalk outline on the floor, it's right there.'

The director wanted *Seven*'s serial killer to mirror the real horror of his true-life counterparts. 'I'd say I'm a realist. If you make a film about a serial killer, you do your research. When you pull the pictures out of the files, man, it's bleak. It's fucking *bleak*.' Production designer Arthur Max, who had worked with Fincher on a number of commercials, appreciated what he saw as a sense of 'visual corrosion' in building the movie's reality. 'It could never be dark enough,' Max noted, with intent to make the film's projected image 'leak' into the viewing theatres. 'It would melt into the real world.' Arranging the interiors of both location-based settings and fabricated sets, he felt it was important to have 'something slightly *off* about everything', designing rooms to 'squeeze you both physically and psychologically.'

Outside the grim inner world of *Seven*'s nameless city, the rain-soaked exteriors helped create much of the film's gloomy texture, but the choice to shoot through a downpour was less a stylistic conceit than a logistical one. Brad Pitt was only available to the production for 55 days of shooting, due to the actor's prior commitment to a role in Terry Gilliam's *Twelve Monkeys* (1995), and as filming began in a rainy Los Angeles, the director elected to keep things wet. 'We knew that we would have to match in the exteriors to stuff that was being shot interiors. We did it to stay on schedule, because we knew that if it ever really rained we would have been fucked ... also, it was a way to make it kind of not look like Los Angeles, because Los Angeles is always seen in the sun.'

However, Fincher's decision to use the rain to unify the film's look backfired when it caused Pitt to injure himself on set just a few days into production. Shooting the scene where Mills and Somerset chase Doe after encountering him in the apartment building, the actor lost his footing running over a wet-slick car bonnet and fell hard, putting his hand through the vehicle's windscreen. 'Acting is a rough sport,' Pitt joked, suffering a severed tendon that required microsurgery at a nearby hospital, and he was back on set within the week after a course of painkillers. To cover the sudden appearance of the actor's cast, his accident was written into the film. Kopelson remarked, 'He wasn't supposed to break his arm, but that's what we've done. We worked his injury into the storyline.'

Pitt wasn't the only one to suffer during *Seven*'s shooting, however – an ankle injury Morgan Freeman had sustained the previous year while falling from a horse was aggravated by the running he had to do during the desert scenes, and after the end of filming the actor was forced to wear a brace for a considerable time. Freeman had assumed after reading the script that the film would be set in a 'wet' city like Seattle, but, with the use of rain towers, *Seven* was largely shot in Los Angeles, with some brief scenes in Chino (the unused footage of Somerset's retirement home). 'We wanted to shoot in Oakland,' Fincher recalled. 'Beautiful clapboard houses, but we didn't have enough time, so it's all downtown LA.' The actual name of the city in *Seven* is never mentioned, and the only location name clearly visible at any point is 'Bardach County Jail', written on the back of Doe's orange prison fatigues – but even this is a gag reference to Elinor C Bardach, the film's costume supervisor.

Fincher also ensured that the mood of *Seven* leaked into its titles, as designed by Kyle Cooper; an early 'draft' version of the opening credits over the song 'Closer' used the handwriting and photos from Doe's books, but motionless. Fincher subsequently decided to have the credits show the 'making' of the books and Doe's removal of his fingerprints, to demonstrate the mindset of the dangerous, deranged killer. 'The only way to do that in two minutes was to do something that was really abstract, made up. It had to travel a pretty good distance because you had to establish that somebody was out there and they were pretty fucked up. [The books] had to be obsessive, compulsive.' Fincher would later use a similar look in a music video for 'Judith', a song by the band A Perfect Circle.

Manufacturing nearly 50 of John Doe's Mead Composition books, each full of rambling screeds and disturbing imagery, was the job of Clive Pearcy and John Sabel, and the process cost the production $15,000. Sabel did the writing in what Pearcy called his 'amazing calligraphic hand', scribbling the bizarre stream-of-consciousness rants alongside images inspired by photographers like Robert

Frank. Sabel recalled visiting his local printing shop to get film transfers of some of the alarming pictures and freaking out the staff there. 'These kids in their blue aprons would look at this stuff and go "What is this guy?!"'

Like much of *Seven*'s set dressing, the Devil is in the details; the designers used a chance-found cache of stationery left untouched since the 1950s, with colour-coded library tape on the books' spines, each colour relating to a separate sin. The books were hand-stitched with thread and surgical needles before being baked to age them – but perhaps the most shocking inclusion was an actual tear-stained suicide note left behind by a convict. The traits of Doe's mindset were also underlined in other items of set dressing, like the warped, distressed photos shot by Melodie McDaniel and seen in the killer's darkroom.

An integral part of *Seven*'s mood comes from its sound, and in particular the film's uses of music to underline narrative themes. The opening song 'Closer' carries not only the ominous feel of the title images but also has resonance within serial killer 'culture' – artists Nine Inch Nails recorded the song (from their album *The Downward Spiral*) at the home of killer Charles Manson. Similarly, the David Bowie/Brian Eno end theme 'The Hearts Filthy Lesson' has hidden meaning; the song is taken from the concept album *1.Outside*, which centres on a detective who investigates 'art-murders' akin to Doe's staged acts of homicide. These grimmer tunes are lightened by the music favoured by Somerset and Tracey, like Thelonius Monk's 'Trouble Man' and Charlie Parker's 'Straight No Chaser', as well as the gently emotive use of Bach's 'Air on a G String' during the library sequence.

But it is Howard Shore's score that ties all the elements together without artifice, with a rising and falling series of rhythms along the low register. *Seven* represents a dark audio landscape that Shore's music had previously visited in films like *The Silence of the Lambs* (1991) and *Single White Female* (1992); he would later rejoin Fincher to score *The Game*. It was Shore's work on *Silence* that brought him to the director's attention after a track from the movie was suggested as a temporary score for *Seven* when the film was exhibited at the industry's ShoWest event. Among the outstanding elements he brought to the film was what Shore called 'the Macbeth theme' for Mills, a musical motif that emphasised the character's doomed quality.

'There's sound everywhere [in the film],' Fincher notes. 'When Somerset goes back to the 'Gluttony' apartment and there are kids playing across the street – that's the real world.' This dense ambient background was as important to the director as the visuals; 'I wanted to exhaust the audience with sound ... It's not just the kid crying and the dog barking, it's the game show going on and the people on the steps above you thump-thump-thumping. That's the world we live in.'

Creating this was the job of *Seven*'s sound designer Ren Klyce (an Korty Films-era associate of Fincher's who would also work on *The Game* and *Fight Club*), providing the remainder of the movie with elements that vary from strident sirens to the peculiar woolly noise of voices in a distant apartment. Klyce spoke of

Fincher's desire 'to paint an audio tapestry', and Klyce's skill is best noted in the scene where Somerset uses his metronome to get to sleep, masking the noises of the harsh city – and by extension, the world outside. Even for so fleeting a detail, the designer asked two homeless people to stage an argument and recorded them at an alleyway location so that the sound picture of the scene retained an air of reality.

Leading *Seven*'s cast is Morgan Freeman as William Somerset. Fincher described him as 'elegant all over', and Freeman's gravitas as the learned older cop is the lynchpin of the story, the matching intelligence that brings Doe's crime into sharp relief. But at the same time, Somerset's worn, cynical exterior is a stark contrast to his junior, David Mills. During shooting, several of Somerset's lines were cut to underline his quiet, introspective manner. 'We trimmed stuff for Morgan,' Fincher noted. '[Freeman said] "I can just look at this guy and do all this, you can cut this stuff".' The actor said of the character, 'He's trapped by his own need to solve the puzzle. The whole weight of the script is telling you he's pretty much burnt out ... his heart is full, he needs to go fishing.' For his part, Darius Khondji saw Somerset as 'an old samuraï'.

Freeman has most recently been linked with David Fincher on the planned screen adaptation of Arthur C Clarke's science fiction novel *Rendezvous with Rama*, although the project has yet to schedule a start date. The actor spoke about the director with enthusiasm: 'When I first met David Fincher, I was struck by his personality, his warmth. His intelligence is almost intimidating, and then you talk to him ... I just really took to him, he's just so bright.'

The antithesis of Freeman's studied intellectual Somerset is Brad Pitt as David Mills, the vigorous younger man who lacks the elder's book smarts but compensates with his drive to do good. Where Somerset's speeches were reduced, Mills got more to say, and Pitt, cast alongside his then-current fiancée Gwyneth Paltrow, played the cop in a restless, wound-too-tight fashion to complement Freeman. Initially, Fincher didn't see Pitt for the role, which had first been conceived as a slicker kind of guy – 'I had always seen somebody who was more sort of a fuck-up,' the director said, '[but] he was incredibly enthusiastic ... he was like "I'm in, I want to do it".' 'Finch keeps us in line, on focus' said the actor, and Fincher remarked that working with Pitt was comfortable for him, down to sharing Monty Python jokes on set – 'We're of the same ilk'.

Looking back on the film, Pitt simply said, 'It's the closest I've been to a perfect movie.' Earning a $4 million fee for *Seven*, Pitt was on $17.5 million on re-teaming with Fincher to play Tyler Durden in *Fight Club*. Post *Fight Club*, Pitt has worked with Steven Soderbergh on *Ocean's 11* (2001) and *Full Frontal* (2002), where actor and director both played themselves.

As *Seven*'s female lead and in many ways the emotional heart of the film, the part of Tracey Mills was loaded with import and an exceptional actress was needed to fill it. Fincher recalls that Gwyneth Paltrow, who had come to his attention as Ginnie in *Flesh and Bone* (1993), was his first choice, but the producers were sure she would not be interested in the role: 'Everybody kept saying Gwyneth's not going to do it ... she's too picky, she doesn't want to play the cop's wife.' Eventually, after seeing dozens of actresses for the part but choosing none of them, Pitt prevailed on Paltrow to meet with Fincher and Kopelson. 'She came in and she sat down for about two seconds before she said, "I have to go to the bathroom," and left ... straight away Arnold said "She's perfect."' Paltrow described Tracey as 'a very unique woman; she's very centred, very direct. She knows that her husband can be a bit immature when he's out in the field, so she takes it upon herself to smooth things over between the two cops. She brings Somerset into their lives to show him the vulnerable side of Mills.'

For the chilling John Doe, Fincher cast Kevin Spacey in circumstances of great secrecy. In order to retain the mystery and the surprise reveal of his character, Spacey insisted that his name be removed from any promotional materials such as posters or press kits and opposed the producers' intent to list him in the opening credits. The actor instead gets first billing in the closing credits. In the same year as *Seven*, Spacey took the Best Supporting Actor Oscar for his part in *The Usual Suspects*; he would later receive the Best Actor award in 1999 for *American Beauty*. To get him Spacey for *Seven*, Fincher and Pitt both fought with New Line to push the budget for the actor; the director remembers Spacey's screen test – 'We put a video camera on him, he did two takes and you just went, "Okay, that part's cast."'

Of his character, Spacey said, 'He's a bad, bad man, truly evil.' Fincher jokes: 'When we made *Seven*, Spacey had just finished *The Usual Suspects*. None of us knew what that was about. We didn't know he was Keyser Soze, and that Keyser Soze was this evil genius mastermind, so of course when the two movies came out, not far apart, I was appalled. I said, "Spacey! Why didn't you say something? How many times do you want to be the evil mastermind?"'

The film's supporting cast included Richard Roundtree, the star of *Shaft* (1971) and its sequels, as district attorney Martin Talbot; John C McGinley of *Platoon* and *The Rock* fame as California; and former US Marine Corps drill sergeant R Lee Ermey of *Full Metal Jacket* (1987) and *Sommersby* (1993) as the precinct captain. (Ermey got the captain's role after reading for the part of John Doe.) *Seven* also features a few faces from the Finch Mob collective: Richmond Arquette, the delivery van driver, appears in *Fight Club* as Jack's doctor; *The Game* cinematographer Harris Savides, who worked second unit on *Seven*, has a brief cameo as the 911 operator who takes Doe's 'I've gone and done it again' call; Cathryne Muller, a music video set director who worked with Fincher at Propaganda Films, plays the prostitute victim of the 'Lust' murder; and Heidi Schanz, a model who appeared in one of the director's commercials for Levis, is the dead woman at the 'Pride' crime scene. Morgan Freeman's son Alfonso appears in the film as the police fingerprint technician.

Andrew Kevin Walker's script grew from seeing aspects of the seven deadly sins in the city around him. 'You could point them out in New York', he recalled, and the simple, high-concept theme of seven murders in seven days was exactly the idea he wanted to take to the screen, inverting the clichés of comfortable cop cinema along the way. 'The beaten path is extremely beaten,' he noted. In preparing to write *Seven*, he spent time researching police procedures and forensic medicine to bring a level of realism to the script, in his words just enough to create the impression of Somerset's 'iceberg of knowledge'. As well as law enforcement technical manuals, the writer also studied the manners and attitudes of cops to get the right texture to his dialogue. Fincher followed this up by using real police officers in some sequences, most notably in the SWAT raid on Victor's apartment.

Walker lays a number of references into *Seven*'s script; as well as the seven murders, the number appears several times, as the time of the dinner date and the delivery of the fateful box, which also occurs on the seventh day; all of the building numbers in the police station begin with 7 (Somerset's office is 714, the same as the badge number of TV detective Joe Friday in *Dragnet*). The writer alludes to many classic works, including the writings of Saint Thomas Aquinas, Milton's *Paradise Lost*, Shakespeare's *The Merchant of Venice*, Dante's *Divine Comedy* and Chaucer's *The Canterbury Tales*, among others. Somerset is named after Somerset Maugham, author of *Of Human Bondage*, a book referred to by the character during the story; Walker later wrote a screen adaptation of Maugham's work for Turner Pictures.

Some of the asides are a little more pop culture, though, touching on the *Star Wars* trilogy ('Just because the fucker's got a library card doesn't make him Yoda'), *Charlie's Angels*, the Al Pacino cop thriller *Serpico* (1973), the Charles Manson book *Helter Skelter* and the 'Glimmer Twins', a nickname for Rolling Stones Mick Jagger and Keith Richards. At the 'Gluttony' murder, there's also a pile of spaghetti sauce cans arranged in an Andy Warhol-esque manner, while Victor's ceiling has a forest of pine tree-shaped car fresheners dangling from it. The script even plays with its own cultural pretensions in the moments where Mills is forced to pick up a set of Cliff's Notes (academic 'digest' books on classic literature) to follow the thread of Doe's reasoning; however, Mills' mispronunciation of the Marquis de Sade as 'Shar-Day', like the female soul singer, was a gag invented on the spot by Brad Pitt during an early reading. A more oblique reference is the SWAT police officer named California; a character with the same name also appears in Walker's script for *8mm* (1999), which was briefly mooted as a Fincher project (see below).

Another member of the Finch Mob, Walker worked again with the director handling rewrites on *The Game* and *Fight Club*. The writer also penned *Ambush* (2001), one of the short films produced by Fincher for BMW's Internet movie series *The Hire*, and he later wrote *Sleepy Hollow* (1999) for Tim Burton. Walker appears on-screen in *Seven* as the sole victim not connected to John Doe, a man shot dead by his angry wife, and again as a down-and-out in a scene cut from the final movie (see below); he would later cameo in *Panic Room* as Jodie Foster's sleepy neighbour.

Walker's harsh, uncompromising ending was part of *Seven* from the start, but, as noted, during the script's tenure at the Penta production office the writer was asked to devise a lighter alternative for what was seen at the time as an unfilmable climax. In a draft from early 1992, the storyline concludes not with the revelation of Tracey's death and Doe's murder by Mills out in the desert, but in a burnt-out church where it is Mills who dies and Tracey who lives to have their unborn child. Retaining the opening but unused scene of Somerset at his newly bought retirement home, the early draft also makes an effort to add more material about Mills and his wife Tracey. Mills has an introductory scene of his own where he single-handedly busts two would-be car thieves before meeting Somerset for the first time. Later, we see more of Tracey as she tries and fails to get a job at a local school (referred to in dialogue with Somerset in the final script), then endures a trip on the subway before meeting Mills at a fruit stall and returning home to make love.

Tracey's pregnancy is also telegraphed by her reading of a book on parenting while home alone, and Tracey and Somerset meet for the first time when the detective stops at their apartment to drop off his notes for Mills. Elements of their dialogue here were later shot as part of the dinner scene, but cut from the film (see Cuts and Changes below). There's also a surprising scene that grows out of their chance meeting at a bookstore, where Tracey and Somerset share a passionate kiss in his car as Doe watches them; a photo of the pair later finds its way to Somerset's desk after the 'Lust' killing.

Several scenes between Mills and Somerset play differently; Mills' annoyance at being sidelined during the examination of the 'Gluttony' victim is set in the police gym as he spars with the older detective, instead of in the car; the two cops are also together when the story returns to the 'Gluttony' crime scene and Doe's message 'Long is the way and hard that out of Hell leads to the light' comes via their pagers, not a note on the wall. Somerset's intelligence is also downplayed in this draft; instead of being able to draw the conclusions about Doe's motives from the library and his own knowledge, he visits McCracken, an old friend and modern artist who provides the 'seven deadly sins' connection – in fact, in this version, it's Mills who searches the library records to track down Doe.

The scenes with Somerset and McCracken also touch on the unnamed woman in the older cop's life (again referred to in conversation with Tracey in the final draft). A second information source is Father Bleeker, a priest who gives more detail on the sins, including an element colour coding each one that only appears briefly in the finished film. Bleeker leads Somerset to Father Stone, an elderly man who was once the overseer of a now-derelict orphanage, hinting that the senile Stone violently abused the children in his care for their sinning – it's only when the library records are cross-checked against Stone's orphans that Doe's name appears.

This version also contains more cuts away to Doe as he moves around the city, setting up his killings. Walker admits he preferred to keep the killer off-screen as much as possible, and even planned in the early stages of writing never to have Doe utter a word throughout the script. In this version, Doe is seen casing the brothel for the 'Lust' murder (after spitting in the face of a street preacher), later carrying food and supplies into the apartment of the 'Sloth' victim (in this draft a black man named Zero) and invading Mills' home. While Walker wanted to keep the killer an enigma, the 1992 draft explains his motivations more clearly, blaming Doe's psychosis on being a victim of Father Stone's mistreatment during his orphanage childhood.

Towards the conclusion, Doe takes the two detectives not to the desert, but to a riverside junkyard where he escapes into the sewers; Mills gives chase only to be shot and captured by Doe, and Somerset races to the church orphanage to head off the killer. In the climactic scene, as Doe prepares to burn the injured Mills alive, Somerset confronts him but Mills is killed; in turn Somerset shoots Doe and the church burns down. The script concludes with Tracey returning to the country and Somerset returning to work. While the script retains the horror of the early murders, this clearly more conventional ending lacks the clockwork perfection of Doe's final 'act' and the bleak, damning closure that made Seven so outstanding.

Other elements from the handful of drafts that never made the cut included the full on-screen autopsy of the 'Gluttony' victim; a foul-mouthed, diminutive woman from the police forensics unit who trails the two detectives at each of the murder scenes, and references to Parsons, Mills' former partner who'd been shot and paralysed prior to his transfer to the city.

Because of Pitt's commitment to film Twelve Monkeys, filming on Seven literally ran out of time as the Christmas period began, with the actor's crucial close-up for the ending un-shot – but reshoots a few months later when Pitt was available enabled the producers to shift the texture of the closing scene and add the coda, a compromise requested by New Line's executives. Some elements of the final scenes were also missing Morgan Freeman and Kevin Spacey, but careful use of stand-ins and editing masked any discrepancies. Fincher is on record as disliking the Ernest Hemingway quote (from For Whom the Bell Tolls) that closes the movie, and indeed the original ending – a fade to black after Mills makes his fatal shot – has more impact. However, DeLuca felt that Somerset's line 'I'll be around' gave the movie 'a redemptive quality' that the 'too abrupt' gunshot ending denied the audience.

The expensive helicopter scenes during the climax were held back by New Line until the film was test screened, and on the return to the desert location much of the scrubland that had been green in early shots was now a dull yellow; in the final cut, these elements are colour-corrected to mask the inconsistency.

As Seven came to fruition, Fincher pushed to ensure that the producers promoted the movie as what it was – dark and dangerous. 'It's a movie that inspires people to dredge up all their own stuff. It leaves so much in the dark. It's funny, because I never thought it was scary at all. When we first finished it, I turned to [editor Richard Francis-Bruce] and said, "My God, what have we done? We've totally let people down in the terror department. We need to go shoot some dismembered bodies and stuff. Go see if you can't get something from the morgue and chop 'em up..." You get inured to things over two years of constant work, you never know if you've gone too far, or not far enough.'

Referring to a test audience at a 'disaster screening' – an audience led to expect something similar to the two stars' previous films – Fincher said, 'You couldn't molest an audience more than to promise *Legends of the Fall* and *Driving Miss Daisy*, and then unleash this movie on them ... they'd just been gang-raped.' Fincher remained determined not to pull any of *Seven*'s punches. 'Come hell or high water, I was going to make that movie, and make it the way I saw it. I was going to put it up there with all its pessimism and cynicism and not shy away from it. I have no apologies.'

CUTS AND CHANGES

The movie's original opening sequence was longer and edited differently from the final cut. Instead of opening at the shotgun murder scene, the story begins with Somerset walking through a vacant old house – his retirement home to be – and he cuts a piece of flowered wallpaper from the wall with his switchblade; outside, he confirms to an estate agent that he'll be buying the place. (The wallpaper piece is still visible briefly in Somerset's apartment when he is getting dressed.) The scene, which was shot close to a maximum security prison, features two trailers piled high with hay bales in order to obscure the neighbouring razor-wire fences; Fincher described the look of the house interior as a homage to the opening of *Butch Cassidy and the Sundance Kid* and called the scene 'overly poetic'.

A following sequence, where Somerset travels back into the city from the country on the train, was storyboarded but never shot, due to budget restrictions. He then gets in a taxi which takes him home, passing by two altercations on the street. Part of the taxi ride (including Somerset's 'Far away from here' line) was re-used prior to the library scene in the later cut. This section also features a brief cameo by Kevin Hunter, the lead singer of Wire Train, as an angry man on a public telephone; Fincher had previously directed Hunter's band in a music video. Somerset then arrives home and uses the metronome to get to sleep (this too is re-used elsewhere in the final cut). His wake-up and dressing scene lingers on the wallpaper segment before cutting to the shotgun murder, which opens with a different angle on the corpse and slightly more dialogue.

In the car after the discovery of the 'Gluttony' victim, the discussion between Mills and Somerset ('Don't jerk me off') was longer, with Somerset's sarcastic retort to the younger cop; the scene was cut down because the director was unable to match the over-the-shoulder shots with the rain effects on the windscreen.

As Somerset approaches the library at night, an extra moment featured scriptwriter Andrew Kevin Walker as a tramp who asks the detective for some spare change.

At the beginning of the dinner sequence at David and Tracey's apartment, the square of wallpaper in Somerset's pocket falls out and she comments on it;

Somerset describes it as 'his future' and the two share a confidential moment, with Tracey admitting that Mills wouldn't understand the keepsake.

After the dinner, when Mills and Somerset have left to visit Gould's wife, Tracey wakes up from a light sleep to find the apartment empty; the original scene was longer, ending with her closing the curtains and a long shot of the apartment building to emphasise her loneliness in the city. There was also the unspoken implication that she is being watched by Doe from afar.

When Mills and Somerset chase Doe from the killer's apartment, Mills is injured in the fall from the fire escape and spends the rest of the movie wearing a bandage around his wrist; the wound was written in during shooting to cover Brad Pitt's real-life injury from falling though a car windscreen.

The approach to Victor's apartment with the SWAT team was longer, with more dialogue between the Captain and California prior to leaving the station. The scene between Mills and Somerset in the car on the way was also longer, with Mills describing the first time he shot a suspect, talking about his 'weird luck' and how he 'slept like a baby' after the fact.

When Doe calls the police to confess to the 'Pride' murder, the scene originally featured a lone cop in the killer's apartment answering the phone there; in the final cut, the call is made to the 911 emergency operator.

The opening shots at the 'Pride' murder scene began with Somerset in the white tile bathroom, seeing the words 'I did not kill her she was given a choice' written on the wall, and a straight razor in a sink streaked with blood; the shot was cut down to lessen the stark effect of the gore.

During the car journey into the desert, Mills insults Doe by implying he's nothing more than an attention-seeker: 'You're no messiah. You're a movie of the week. You're a fucking T-shirt, at best.' The 'Movie of the Week' is a subtle jibe by the filmmakers directed at cut-for-TV movies, but when *Seven* was later aired as just that on US network television, Pitt's line was redubbed to 'Book of the Month' – a jibe by television executives directed at cash-in publishers. Another moment frequently cut from the film on TV transmissions is the bar scene, where Somerset opines that apathetic people just want 'cheeseburgers, lotto and television'.

The ending of the film went through a number of evolutions, including versions where the box contained the head of one of Mills' dogs, where Somerset shoots Mills to stop him killing Doe in cold blood, and where Mills shoots Doe *and* Somerset. Fincher's first cut of the conclusion has less dialogue, with Doe simply watching Mills as he goes through the shock of realising Tracey's death, then closing his eyes as the detective steps forward and shoots him. A storyboarded alternate ended with Somerset and Mills pointing guns at one another as the elder cop warns the younger to drop his weapon, before pushing into a close-up on Doe; Doe is shot, but it is unclear who fired until the camera pulls back to reveal Somerset with a smoking gun. Mills asks 'What are you doing?' and Somerset replies 'I'm retiring.' At the time, Brad Pitt argued that given all we had seen of Mills, it would be unrealistic to imagine him *not* killing Doe in revenge for Tracey – in the actor's words, the scene was 'everything it's been leading up to'.

Another version of the ending had a different coda, with Somerset in a hospital bed recuperating from being wounded by Mills; he's given a note from the younger detective that reads, 'You were right. You were right about everything.' Originally, the film would have ended with a fade to black after Doe's death, but test screenings and editorial choices led the director to add the coda as Mills is taken away and Somerset affirms that he'll 'be around'.

AFTERMATH

With a $30 million budget, *Seven* reaped the rewards of a massive audience share, with an opening weekend of nearly $14 million and competition comprising *Showgirls*, *To Die For* and *Devil in a Blue Dress*. The takings eventually grew into a global gross figure of more than $316 million; for 1995, the movie ranked at ninth place in the year's top-grossing films, beating *Die Hard With a Vengeance* into last place. Along with the *Die Hard* sequel, *Seven*'s 1995 competitors included the return of the James Bond franchise with *GoldenEye* and blockbusters like *Apollo 13* and *Batman Returns*, but it was the computer-animated antics of *Toy Story* that held the top slot for the year.

The film also opened amid a series of profile-raising hits for its lead cast, with Spacey's excellent star turn in Bryan Singer's *The Usual Suspects* the month before, and Pitt and Freeman in *Twelve Monkeys* and *Outbreak* respectively. *Seven* also beat out a former Fincher alumnus, Sigourney Weaver, to the serial killer movie crown by appearing a month before her film *Copycat*.

After *Alien 3*'s critical mauling, *Seven* reversed the trend somewhat and gained a degree of acclaim for the director, the script, the performances and, most frequently, the unflinching final scene. Ben Mitchell of *Neon* said '*That* ending is what *Seven* will always be known for' and called the film 'quite possibly the best serial killer movie ever,' while *Sight & Sound*'s John Wrathall spoke of 'an astoundingly bleak ending which brilliantly subverts the ingrained Hollywood cliché', comparing *Seven* to *The Vanishing* (1988) and *Manhunter* (1986).

Sigourney Weaver, whose film *Copycat* also covered the serial killer theme, added her own voice even at the expense of her own movie: 'I remember when we made *Copycat*, and they said they were going to release it at the same time as *Seven*. I said please don't ... They said, "Oh, it's just David Fincher and Brad Pitt in a moustache," and I said, "No, believe me, David made one movie that didn't make money and he's really going to be careful with this one." And of course, it was a masterpiece, and everybody saw that one and very few people saw *Copycat*. They should have listened to me.'

However, the critical community was not universally behind the film, and Wrathall touched on a point made by many – that Fincher's treatment of women in the movie was poor, when noting that the character of Tracey Mills is 'just being set up as a victim'. CNN's Carol Buckland described Tracey as 'a sacrificial lamb from the second she turns up on screen'. Indeed, aside from the sympathetic wife, the only other women featured in the film are the prostitute and the vain model from the 'Lust' and 'Pride' killings. Fincher also received negative comments and charges of misogyny for his use of female characters with Ripley in *Alien 3*, Christine in *The Game* and Marla in *Fight Club*.

In addition, several critics continued to insist that the director's use of imagery was all surface and no substance; Buckland said, 'Fincher's work runs the gamut from provocatively inventive to just plain pretentious' and labelled *Seven* 'visually depressing', while Kenneth Turan of the *Los Angeles Times* talked of 'feeble contrivance' in the plot, praising the look of the film ('no shot in the picture is an average one') while damning its content ('grotesque and repulsive ... creepy and distasteful'). Edward Guthman of the *San Francisco Chronicle* felt the film was a poor pretender to the Hannibal Lecter crown: 'Placing style above coherence, *Seven* glosses over plot points and shows a weakness for cheap, lurid effects.' Barbara Shulgasser at the *San Francisco Examiner* called it 'gluey, bumbling and singularly un-thrilling'. *Time*'s review was especially high-handed: 'Murk is also the auteurial hallmark of director David Fincher ... Aiming to be a modern-day Bosch, he ends up doing MTV bosh.'

The director told Amy Taubin that 'I didn't set out to piss off all the people who are upset' and vindicated his vision of *Seven*'s unrelenting horror, taking critics like Michael Medved (who had called the film 'evil') to task: 'I'm sure he slows down when he passes an accident scene like everyone else. Death fascinates people, but they can't deal with it.'

As with his review of *Alien 3*, *Rolling Stone*'s Peter Travers came to *Seven*'s defence, understanding the film's intent to 'abrade, not ingratiate' and supporting Fincher: 'That's what happens when you aim high in Hollywood – you're labelled pretentious.' Roger Ebert joined him in his comments in the *Chicago Sun-Times*, calling *Seven* 'a dark, grisly, horrifying and intelligent thriller' and commending Fincher's 'evocative atmosphere' in creating a 'jungle of gloom'. In the UK, the *Daily Mirror*'s Simon Rose called it 'a gripping, chilling thriller'. Some six years after the film's release, Almar Haflidason at the *BBCi* website spoke of Fincher's 'fiendishly unsettling take on the predictable' and described *Seven* as 'an example of classic horror thrills, up-ended and twisted into a bewildering and claustrophobic web of tension'.

As with *Alien 3*, Fincher had crafted a controversial film that incited polarised viewpoints. But with *Seven*, it was a film that was unquestionably his own creation, a seditious movie that made millions in ticket sales with a message not of uplifting hope, but one that suggested our culture is flawed and irredeemably sinful. That *Seven* succeeded at the box-office is a testament to the skill of the director and his company.

Seven earned numerous accolades for its cast and crew, including an Oscar nomination for editor Richard Francis-Bruce and several MTV movie awards (Best Movie, Best Villain for Spacey and Most Desirable Male for Pitt). Morgan Freeman earned recognition from the Image Award for Outstanding Lead Actor in a Motion Picture and the Actor of the Year from the London Critics Circle. The Academy of Science Fiction, Fantasy & Horror Films awarded *Seven* its Saturn trophy for Jean Ann Black and Rob Bottin's make-up effects, while Walker took the Best Writing honours; Walker's script was also nominated for the BAFTA Best Original Screenplay and won Fantasporto's International Fantasy Film award for Best Writing. Fincher also took a Fantasporto award for Best Film, while composer Howard Shore won the 1996 ASCAP Film and Television Music Award, and cinematographer Darius Khondji took commendations from both the American and British Societies of Cinematographers and the Chicago Film Critics Association.

Fincher found the accomplishment of making *Seven* liberating even as he eschewed the critical turnabout. 'It made money so all of a sudden people are like, "Oh, well, okay." The process was fairly redemptive, and I was allowed to make the movie I wanted to make – and [some] people weren't that happy about it. The first time Arnold Kopelson saw the movie he was not that happy with it. I think that once he got over the shock of how *not* a genre movie it was, he actually said, "You took a perfectly good genre movie and turned it into a foreign film." Redemption in Hollywood doesn't bother me, [because] ultimately, who cares?

'I was telling my agent once over lunch about this movie I'd seen, and how shitty it was and how they'd missed the boat, and he said, "Dave, who cares?" "What do you mean?" "Who cares what you think?"' Fincher laughs. 'Because really, it doesn't matter, you're spending a lot of energy, the movie is made and it's not for you to pass judgment. I'm going to make some bad movies, but I don't think I'm ever going to make a movie as bad as *Alien 3* again because at least I'll be able to complete the process. From soup to nuts, you've got to finish no matter how fucked up [it is], you've got to finish what you set out to do. Movies never survive their initial intent, there's always going to be something, and if the people who are financing it don't want it, there's no way you can change it. You can re-cut the movie until you're blue in the face, it still is what you set out to do. I don't know if you get redemption – and I don't care.'

He continues: 'I don't read much criticism, good or bad, because of the business that we're in. You make a movie as quickly as you can, based on an understanding of the story that you're trying to tell, shot out of sequence with the hope to find this lovely arc to build, this tapestry, then you finish it as quickly as you can and put it in front of an audience. You often don't get the time for the subtleties, the fine brush strokes, so a lot of that kind of criticism is [redundant]. Some of it you share with critics and you go, "Yeah, I should have shot that differently, I should have done this, I should have done that." But we basically build a prototype that has to *fly* and carry

$100 million dollars' worth of passengers every time out, so sometimes you're going to be able to do it, sometimes you're going to make people happy and sometimes you're not. You can't expect perfection, as this is a very imperfect way of working.'

Seven is a film that looked back as well as pointing forward. The serial killer subgenre traces its roots to Fritz Lang's classic *M* (1931), the story of a child murderer in inter-war Germany. Fincher himself denies that serial killers make a genre ('They're just cop movies'), but in *Seven*'s frequent use of low angles and *film noir*-style blocking of shots (also seen in Expressionist cinema) he made reference to Lang's lead. The director previously touched on the look of Lang's *Metropolis* for Madonna's 'Express Yourself' video; some observers even see connections between John Doe and the titular villain of Lang's *Doctor Mabuse der Spieler* (1922).

It would be disingenuous, however, to consider *Seven* a mere knock-off. Just as *Psycho* (1960) and *The Silence of the Lambs* (1990) pushed the serial killer motif up a notch, so *Seven* projected it still further, leaving such an impression on the genre that any film following cannot escape being informed by it in some manner. Fincher explained his take on this modern murder phenomenon thus: 'When you start doing research on serial killers, [you see that] these people don't prey on senators, they pick off the weak and the stragglers and the runaways and the prostitutes and the people hitchhiking, people unfortunate enough to be at a 7-11 at two o'clock in the morning. It takes place in a very dark world, and so it just seemed like the darkness was more in keeping with making a horror movie.'

The dark texture of *Seven* would also be echoed on the small screen in elements of *Millennium*, a television series starring *Alien 3*'s Lance Henriksen as Frank Black, an ex-FBI profiler gifted (or cursed) with a near-psychic ability to 'see' into the minds of serial killers. From the pen of Chris Carter, creator of *The X-Files*, *Millennium* mirrored *Seven* not so much in its greater themes of hunting a murderer, but in the unremitting darkness Black encountered each week, and the recurring motif of his home life as an inviolate haven. Resonances from the film crop up in later serial killer stories, sometimes refreshed by matching them with other elements. *Fallen* (1998) introduces a mystical component, with a John Doe-like murderer whose spirit flits from body to body after his execution, *Resurrection* (1999) plays some of the same religious killer themes while ramping up the gore, and the visually sumptuous but hollow *The Cell* (2000) uses a science fiction gimmick to literally step into the mind of a madman.

Despite the brutal closure of *Seven*'s final act, discussion in June 2002 triggered rumours that a sequel to the film was being considered by New Line Cinema. Originally, Andrew Kevin Walker's *8mm* script had been in the frame. 'I got sent *8mm* when it was a spec, when it was floating around and I think it was before Sony bought it,' says Fincher. 'New Line were thinking of buying it and doing it as a sequel to *Seven*, making the Nicolas Cage character Morgan Freeman. It was an interesting notion, but it didn't make sense to me, because you didn't have the righteous indignation in the character. He needs to be a guy who is particularly unsophisticated in order for him to go, "Oh my God. Snuff movies, how can this be?" You couldn't really have Somerset do that, because he's predisposed to know the depths of depravity that humans are capable of descending to.

'I liked the script, and the original ending was amazing, where he drives his car into the median strip, and I thought, "Wow, that's kind of cool. Interesting, but not particularly *emotionally* satisfying..." It's very Andy!' he jokes, doing an impression of a studio executive.

He continues: 'I read it, I was interested in it, but I wasn't interested in making it a sequel to *Seven*, I wasn't interested in making *that* into a sequel to *Seven*, and so it got made by somebody else.'

But the concept of a continuation of *Seven* was still being considered. *Solace*, a script by Sean Bailey and Ted Griffin, writer of the Soderbergh remake of *Ocean's 11*, was bought by New Line with intent to work the story into a follow-up. Griffin's original script about a precognitive cop tracking a psychic serial killer would apparently be rewritten to accommodate the character of Somerset in the lead role, although Brad Pitt's character Mills would not be reprised.

Fincher considered *Solace* a non-starter. '*Seven* is, I think, a fairly complete exercise, it had a beginning, middle and end; even if you like it or not, it's done. I read *Solace*, and I think it's a silly idea to make Morgan Freeman suddenly psychic. I think that there are so many beats, just structurally, like where things happen in the script that seem like they're aping what Andy was doing. It has all the disadvantages of being a sequel because it seems redundant, and none of the advantages. Their only true revelation is the thing that makes it too absurd, the idea that Somerset has been hit on the head and sees the future.'

Although Fincher will not be involved if *Solace* does go into production – music video director Miguel Sapochnik has been mentioned in connection with the project – the possibility of the film should not be dismissed; similar chains of events have led to other scripts becoming sequels in the same manner, such as the reworking of Jonathan Hensleigh's original script *Simon Says* into the film *Die Hard With a Vengeance* (1995).

Seven exudes a darkness that clings to you like a patina of smoke; it is a film that reeks atmosphere like a contaminant, lingers on you and pervades your mind. I was lucky enough to see one of the rare silver prints at a preview screening, and I went out into the London evening with the overcast texture of it still clinging to me, those rich, hyper-real shades of twilight leaking out into the real world. I've lived in a major city all my life and I found myself seeing the hard edges of the metropolis with the same unease portrayed by the movie. Fincher spoke of this film as something with which he intended to scar his audiences, and he succeeds; *Seven* gouges reaction out of its viewers like a rusty scalpel. Love it or hate it, the movie leaves its imprint on you.

Undoubtedly, it is a film with a lightless narrative, a story of depressive, hopeless ill fortune, and all the more hateful to our sensibilities because we care about these characters even while we know that, as Somerset predicts, the story will not have a happy ending. It's exactly this quality that makes *Seven* liked and disliked in equal measure, as it goes about subverting the cops-and-robbers clichés and turns what seems to be a buddy movie into a thriller, and then a horror film; three narratives in one, and all of them strong enough to lock you to your seat for the duration.

Fincher's visual flourishes make this movie, despite complaints from some critics that the film is more MTV than noir; as Nick Lacey notes in *The Ultimate Film Guide: Seven*, the film subverts the 'sunny world view' of music video culture by turning its tropes against it. Matching Walker's savvy script with strong performances by Pitt and Freeman, *Seven* is just the film it should be.

If there's a weak link in the movie, it comes from Tracey. Not through any fault of Gwyneth Paltrow's, but through the severe and callous way the film sets her up as nothing more than a blood sacrifice. Her most important function comes when she brings Somerset and Mills together at the dinner party, but even here we can read the groundwork being laid for her eventual beheading at Doe's hands. She borders on being a cipher, a mere placeholder for the ideal of a loving wife, weakened so much by city life that she can't even tell her husband she's pregnant and has to go to another man for counsel. If there had been more of her, would the impact of the moment with the box have been lessened? Early drafts (see above) had several scenes that gave Tracey more presence, but in the final cut we see *just enough* of her to elicit the right level of shock when we learn of her murder. In this instance, at least, her character is handled in an economical fashion that best serves the film's narrative; a character, like Mills and Somerset and Doe, on a downward trajectory towards her destiny.

In the end, *Seven* is a shocking, horrifying movie because of the emotions it stirs up in us, not just because of the gut-level disgust that the murder scenes and 'psychic violence' throw up. Especially for anyone who has lived in a city, there's an unpleasant mirror being held up to the attitudes and behaviour that many urban dwellers face every day, the 'apathy solution' that Somerset speaks of writ large across the cinema screen. *Seven* forces us to see the terrible logic in Doe's crimes and the damning idea that the capacity for his kind of evil lurks in all people – that it is something that could be compelled from any one of us, just as we see Doe compel Mills to commit murder. *Seven* offers no true solutions, no sermons or redemption from the darkness at its heart; rather, it stimulates and challenges, and leaves us to find the answers ourselves.

FOUR

A Player

'To what extent can you **torture** a movie star?'

FINCHER'S INVOLVEMENT WITH *The Game* had pre-dated *Seven*, and now, with a major box-office hit under his belt, the director had defined his style for the moviegoing audience. Themes and ideas that had surfaced in the earlier films were touched on again as Fincher's vision matured still further, while elements of *The Game* would resonate in his next picture, *Fight Club*. After the challenges of *Alien 3* and the success of *Seven*, Hollywood demanded another critical victory, but Fincher refused to seek out an easy option, choosing a film that was criticised for its emotional coldness and maze-like narrative. Those who expected a new riff on *Seven* mistook Fincher's intent to go in a different direction, retaining the previous film's motifs of a questionable self and society while constructing a deep puzzle-box of a movie.

On the surface a conventional thriller, *The Game* is a labyrinth that perverts popcorn movie expectations; the film takes a distant and emotionless millionaire on an odyssey through his own past, confronting his father's suicide and facing a mysterious agency seemingly out to destroy him. As he would continue to do for each of his films, Fincher dared his audience to come along for the ride, to play a game where the rules were fluid and the prize ephemeral; in many ways, just like the film industry.

THE GAME

PolyGram Filmed Entertainment, Propaganda Films
Director: *David Fincher*
Writers: *John Brancato & Michael Ferris*
Cast: *Michael Douglas (Nicholas Van Orton), Sean Penn (Conrad Van Orton), Deborah Kara Unger (Christine), James Rebhorn (Jim Feingold), Peter Donat (Samuel Sutherland), Carroll Baker (Ilsa), Anna Katerina (Elizabeth), Armin Mueller-Stahl (Anson Baer), Charles Martinet (Nicholas's father), Scott Hunter McGuire (young Nicholas), Florentine Mocanu (Nicholas's mother), Elizabeth Dennehy (Maria), Caroline Barclay (Maggie), Daniel Schorr*

(himself), John Aprea (power executive), Harrison Young (obsequious executive), Kimberly Russell (Cynthia, CRS receptionist), Joe Frank (CRS Data Collating technician), James Brooks (James the bartender), Gerry Becker (new member Ted), Jarion Monroe (new member Victor), Tommy Flanagan (solicitor/taxi driver), Bill Flannery (tubercular commuter), Kathryn Jean Harris (rattle gatherer), John Cassini (man in airport) Harris Savides (Ankles), Aaron Thomas Luchich (City Club waiter), Victor Talmadge (City Club Maitre d'), Marc Siegler (City Club waiter), André Brazeau (heart attack performer), Keena Turner (Officer Hicks), Carlos Hoy (Paramedic Graves), Edward Campbell (Paramedic Stern), Sean Lanthier (Paramedic Kirkland), Curtis Vanterpool (Ambulance EMT), Jay Gordon (triage doctor), Jeffrey Michael (young Officer Walker), Owen Masterson (pickpocket), Yuji Okumoto (Nikko Hotel manager), Hideo Kimura (Nikko Hotel bellhop), Rachel Schadt (Nikko Hotel maid), Mark Boone Junior (shady private investigator), Joy Ann Ryan (Kaleigh Baer), Pete Davidian (Mr Garcia), Jack Kehoe (Lieutenant Sullivan), Christopher John Fields (Detective Boyle), Linda Manz (Christine's roommate Amy), Victor Ferrerira (Assassin Mobubbi), Duffy Gaver (Assassin Brodi), Robert J Stephenson (Assassin Kartmann), Sean Moloney (Assassin Rankin), John Hammil (U.S. Embassy counselor), Rachel Steinberg (Sheraton desk clerk), George Maguire (Sheraton manager), Trish Summerville (hot waitress), Jason Kristopher (teen thug), Lily Soh Froehlich (New Moon café manager), Tammy Koehler (Tammy Fisher), Michael Lynwood (Michael Fisher), Alex Lynwood (Alex Fisher), Charles Branklyn (CRS guard), Spike Jonze (Airbag EMT Beltran), Michael Massee (Airbag EMT Galliano), Sara Davallou (Rachel), Stephen Cowee (Mel).

Crew: JJohn Brancato (co-producer), Ceán Chaffin (producer), Michael Ferris (co-producer), Steve Golin (producer), Jonathan Mostow (executive producer), Howard Shore (music), Harris Savides (cinematography), James Haygood (editing), Jeffrey Beecroft (production design), Steven Saklad (art direction), Jackie Carr (set decoration), Michael Kaplan (costume design), Eric Roberts, Shawn Roberts, Cliff Wenger (special effects), Richard 'Dr' Baily (digital animation supervisor/producer).

Tagline: *'Players Wanted.'*

SYNOPSIS

Nicholas Van Orton is a wealthy investment banker living alone in his family's San Francisco mansion, coldly going through the motions of his life on the eve of his 48th birthday. A joke message takes him to a lunch date with his younger brother Conrad, who is the very antithesis of Nicholas, reckless and edgy, a wild child. Conrad gives Nicholas a gift from a company called Consumer Recreation Services, who provide their clients with a unique experience – 'the game'. A former player, Conrad insists that his game changed his life. However, Nicholas isn't convinced and instead finds himself dwelling on a traumatic event from his childhood, when his father committed suicide at age 48 by leaping from the roof of the mansion.

Returning home, he eats a modest dinner prepared by his housekeeper Ilsa and takes a call from his ex-wife with studied disinterest. But the following day he arrives by chance in the building where CRS are based and decides to investigate. Van Orton meets with Jim Feingold, who explains in vague terms the service that CRS provides. The game is keyed to each player, a real-life diversion for the super-rich. Nicholas is resistant, but takes the battery of tests required for entry – psychological screenings, physical exams and more. Feingold gives him a pen to sign his waiver and tells him they'll be in touch. At his club, Van Orton overhears two businessmen discussing CRS and engages them in conversation, hoping to learn more, but their responses are cryptic.

During a meeting with his lawyer Sam Sutherland, Van Orton receives a call from CRS, informing him that he has failed the qualification criteria for the game. Irritated, he dismisses the experience, but when he arrives at the mansion that evening, a disturbing sight awaits him. In a sick parody of his father's suicide, a life-size clown mannequin lies where his father's body fell. Inside its mouth, Nicholas finds a gold key embossed with the letters CRS. Van Orton is further surprised when a newsreader on television begins to speak directly to him. His game has now begun, the spokesman tells him, and the object of the game is to find out *what* the object of the game is.

Van Orton, now a little suspicious of everyone around him, travels to meet with Anson Baer, a corporate partner; at the airport he sees a baby rattle with a familiar clown face, and confronts a man staring at him only to find the CRS pen has leaked and ruined his expensive shirt. At the meeting with Baer, Nicholas ruthlessly tells the angry older man that he's being retired from his publishing company – but when Van Orton tries to open his briefcase to give Baer his severance contract, it won't unlock, even with the CRS key. Back in San Francisco, he waits for Conrad at dinner to no avail; to make matters worse, a waitress – Christine – spills drinks all over him and she's fired for her error. Nicholas follows her out into the street when he's passed a note reading 'Don't Let Her Get Away', believing that she's connected to the game, but she wants nothing to do with him.

Suddenly, a man collapses in front of them and Christine performs CPR as Nicholas waves down a police car for help. The policemen refuse to let either of them leave and they are forced to ride to the hospital in an ambulance – but the moment they arrive the lights go out and the place is abandoned – it's a CRS fake. With Christine angrily along for the ride, they find their way to a lift, which Nicholas activates with the key from the clown, but it traps them mid-floor and they are forced to climb out. Nicholas realises that they're in the CRS building, but after

Christine trips an alarm, they run to elude the security guards, escaping through an alley. Van Orton takes Christine to his office where she cleans up in his shower; there's a moment of attraction between them before he sends her home in a cab.

The next morning, Nicholas gets a call from the Hotel Nikko, where his American Express card has been found. At the hotel, the clerk tells him his room is ready; inside he finds the debris from a riotous night of sex, alcohol and drugs, complete with blurry pornographic photos apparently depicting him with Christine, lines of cocaine, the briefcase he'd left in the elevator and the ink-stained shirt. Panicking, he tries to hide the evidence and takes the photos. But as he leaves, a car begins to follow him. Nicholas tricks his tail into stopping and confronts a private investigator, who runs before he can find out whom he works for.

Convinced that Baer is behind the photos, Van Orton takes Sutherland to confront him and accuses him of blackmail. But Baer calmly tells Nicholas that he's agreed to take the severance and is happy to retire. Confused and abashed, Van Orton leaves. Sutherland asks for an explanation and Nicholas tells him about CRS and Conrad's gift, discovering another key – a crank handle – in the briefcase.

Van Orton returns to the mansion and is shocked to find the house has been vandalised. Suddenly, a terrified Conrad appears and implores Nicholas to get out. The brothers drive away and Conrad explains that CRS are behind everything, trying to drive him insane. When a blown tyre stops the car, Conrad finds the glove compart-ment is full of CRS keys and runs away, believing Nicholas is behind everything that's happened. CRS taunt him with a recording of their argument and Nicholas abandons the car, hailing a cab – but the taxi is another CRS plant. With Van Orton locked in, the driver sends the cab crashing into the San Francisco Bay; Nicholas escapes using the crank to open the window and swim out. The next day, Sutherland and Van Orton return to the office building with two detectives, but the CRS floor is now empty and no record exists of the company; without motive, the police cannot prosecute.

Shaken by the events of the past few days, Nicholas asks Ilsa about his father, wondering how much of his parent he has in him; he finds Christine's address and goes to see her, in hopes that she may know something about CRS. In her apartment, Nicholas discovers a price tag on a lamp, false-front books and an empty refrigerator – the house is a fake, and he realises that Christine is with CRS. The company sends armed assassins to kill them, and they barely get away. Nicholas forces Christine to reveal what is going on; she tells him that his accounts have been drained of millions of dollars – it's all a huge con-game, and the tests were just to get the passwords for his bank. They drive to Van Orton's cabin, where Sutherland calls to tell him that his accounts are untouched; but Christine has bluffed Nicholas into giving up the bank information they needed, and drugs him.

Nicholas wakes in a Mexican graveyard, penniless and left for dead. Pawning his father's watch, he buys a ride across the border and makes his way back to San Francisco. At the mansion, he recovers a gun and goes to find Conrad, but at

Conrad's hotel he is told his brother has been taken to a mental institution. With nowhere else to go, Nicholas visits his ex-wife; bordering on manic paranoia, he almost loses it when he sees Feingold appear on a nearby television. But this is no mind-game. Feingold is an actor, and Van Orton tracks him down, confronting the man and forcing him to smuggle him back into the CRS building.

At gunpoint, Nicholas has Feingold take him to the commissary, where all the bit players from the game are revealed – the heart attack man, the cab driver, the businessmen, Christine's flatmate, the two detectives and more. There he confronts Christine; chased by armed guards, they reach the roof and Nicholas demands to know what's *really* going on. Realising that Van Orton has a 'real' gun, a frightened Christine tells him that they are still playing the game, that the whole thing has been a fake, that Conrad is about to arrive with all his birthday partygoers. Nicholas refuses to believe her and shoots blindly as the rooftop doors open – hitting Conrad and killing him, to the shock of Feingold and Christine.

Destroyed by what he has done, Nicholas walks to the edge of the roof and steps off, choosing suicide as his father did. Life flashing before him, he plummets through the glass of the atrium below – to land safely on a vast airbag in the middle of a ballroom, where Conrad, alive and well, is there to meet him. The game is over, and Nicholas has had his life-changing experience, just as CRS promised him. As the party gets into full swing, Nicholas steps out to catch Christine before she leaves. With his eyes opened by the game, he does something he never would before and asks her to dinner. Instead, she invites him to take a cab ride.

DEVELOPMENT

With the success of *Seven*, Fincher had proven his ability as a filmmaker and beaten off the Hollywood stigma of *Alien 3*. His visual style and dark storytelling methods were ready for the next challenge; and that challenge was *The Game*. '[This] is not a big action movie, it is more of an intrigue movie,' he said, 'There are no big plane crashes in this film. If this movie is about anything, it's about loss of control. The purpose of *The Game* is to take your greatest fear, put it *this* close to your face and say "There, you're still alive. It's all right."'

Written by John Brancato and Michael Ferris (who would also co-produce), the script had been in circulation for several years, in turnaround at MGM while Fincher had been making *Alien 3*. Developed by producer George Folsey Jr, *The Game* was briefly attached to Jonathan Mostow, future director of *Breakdown* (1997), *U-571* (2000) and *Terminator 3: Rise of the Machines* (2003), with Kyle MacLachlan and Bridget Fonda tapped for the lead roles. The movie was due to start shooting in February 1993, but by early 1992 the script had shifted over to PolyGram. 'Mostow was going to direct it at MGM,' notes Fincher, 'and he had fallen out or given up on it – then Steve Golin got hold of it, and gave it to me. PolyGram put up the money, and we went away and made it.'

Mostow would remain involved, becoming an executive producer after surrendering the director's chair to Fincher. PolyGram had recently become owners of Propaganda Films, Fincher's video and commercial production company, and they chose *The Game* to launch their first venture into film distribution. It was an ideal match; Propaganda had always been considered as a training ground for pop video and commercial directors to graduate to features, and PolyGram Filmed Entertainment saw the potential the group represented.

Fincher's first exposure to the script came from producer Steve Golin, one of Propaganda's founders. 'Steve gave me the script that MGM had bought years ago, that he had bought from MGM. He said, "I've got this script I want you to read, it's called *The Game*." And I was kind of like, "Oh God, it's going to be like *The Most Dangerous Game* [an RKO horror-thriller from 1932], it's going to be a retelling of that..." [But] I liked the script, and I loved the twists and turns. After I did *Seven*, we did about six weeks of just changing the tone and trying to make the story work,' Fincher added. 'I sat down with Andrew Kevin Walker and made Nick Van Orton into the cynical bastard he is. We wanted to create an experience for the audience that didn't *seem* contrived, even though it *is* quite contrived. What we've come up with is a very different take on the idea of old money and wealth; it definitely ain't *Dynasty*.'

Golin was taken enough with the script to revise it several times. 'I loved the concept of it. Rewrote it, rewrote it, rewrote it,' he recalled. 'Maybe ten drafts.' Golin, who had previously produced *Wild at Heart* and worked with Brad Pitt on *Sleepers* (1996), had been prepared to make *The Game* as David Fincher's second movie, but *Seven* jumped the line when Pitt's availability meant that project took precedence. *Seven*'s success had the knock-on effect of enabling Propaganda to get the higher budget they wanted for *The Game* and in 1995 the project began to move forward.

Securing Michael Douglas to play the part of Nicholas Van Orton was seen as a major victory for PolyGram – *Sight & Sound* called it 'the casting coup of the year' – but the actor was not without his reservations in the early stages. As Golin told *Film Vault*, 'Michael was really concerned initially about PolyGram's ability to distribute the movie, so he's been very involved.' No stranger to the role of executive producer, Douglas' presence helped push the film into production; for Fincher, Douglas was taking on a difficult part, and the director noted the challenge of 'finding an actor who'd be able to play Nicholas, who's so unlikeable.' The director told *Time Out*: 'The thing about Michael is that he gives you an interesting cachet, because his name promises entertainment but it also promises friction. He's incredibly successful and mainstream, and yet he's still the fascist from *Falling Down*, the adulterer from *Fatal Attraction*. He allows himself to get into tough spots and then sort things out.'

But the casting of *The Game*'s female lead would prove to be much more problematic. At the Cannes Film Festival in 1996, PolyGram announced that

Jodie Foster would play alongside Douglas; the actress and Fincher had spoken early in the development process about placing her in the role of Christine, but the director was uncomfortable with putting a star of Foster's stature in a supporting part. 'When she expressed an interest we didn't have Michael or a final script. She just wanted to be in it, and I said, "I think it's a little distracting for the waitress to be played by a two-time Oscar winner."'

The original version of the script played Van Orton's introduction to the game differently, having the mysterious birthday gift given to him by an old friend from his university days; one of the first changes was to make this character the errant younger brother, Conrad. 'So [Foster] called back and said, "What if I play the brother's part? Would you rewrite it for me?" I thought that was very interesting, especially as I have two sisters, so that made sense to me. We talked for a while about the notion of rewriting Sean Penn's character to be Van Orton's daughter, and I like Jodie Foster and I like the notion of Jodie Foster. But Jodie also wanted to make *Contact* and we could never work out the scheduling.'

Fincher was taken with the idea of converting Van Orton's sister into his daughter: 'I liked the idea of this character coming back into this man's life, that she was sort of the red-headed stepchild, the bastard child, and especially as he came from money, there'd be that whole kind of thing with the family really frowning upon his first marriage when he was 17.' But Douglas, though 18 years Foster's senior, wanted the part to remain a sibling. Some commentators observed that the actor was unhappy to be placed in a part that made him seem too old for romantic leads. 'I think Michael didn't particularly like the idea of playing Jodie's father – I don't know that Jodie liked the idea of playing his daughter.'

In fact, Douglas and Foster had previously played father and daughter in the 1972 film *Napoleon and Samantha*, but the end result was that the actress pulled out of *The Game* prior to shooting and filed a $14.5 million lawsuit against PolyGram – despite having a first-look deal in place between the studio and her production company Egg Pictures. The lawsuit was amicably settled out of court for an undisclosed amount and pre-production continued. Foster would later work with Fincher on his fifth film, *Panic Room*.

With Jodie Foster no longer on board, the other Van Orton role reverted to Nicholas's brother Conrad. The part was offered to Jeff Bridges, who declined, before Sean Penn was cast. 'Everyone else, like Michael and Sean and Steve Golin, have brothers,' said Fincher, 'and when Michael and Sean got involved they both asked, "How could you see it any other way? It's definitely a brother battle." So I said, "Okay, I believe you."' As well as the shifting brother/sister/daughter role, other parts of *The Game* were subject to revisions, including the sucker-punch suicide ending. 'Originally, Michael's character kills Christine,' said Fincher in an interview with *Film & Video*, 'and he throws himself off the building – and originally the guy who brings him the game was a college buddy ... those were the two elements we kept saying "There's not a big enough emotional hook here for what has to happen." [The script] had the whole father backstory and the rest, but I didn't see why killing this woman who's lied to you at every turn would make you commit suicide.'

The director was also interested in changing what he called 'the tone of Van Orton's trials'. 'Originally, after Christine's character spills drinks on him, he follows her outside, they get in a horse-drawn carriage and then they go and have dinner. It just seemed wrong – this is a guy who's got $600 million, he's not gonna give a shit about a horse-drawn carriage. So we were always trying to make sure CRS challenged him in a way that he wouldn't normally be challenged. They take him apart on a very intellectual level. That's where he feels most in control, they downgrade his sense of entitlement.'

PRODUCTION

From Ferris and Brancato's 1991 draft through to their rewrites in 1995 as pre-production began, the script continued to evolve. Propaganda brought writers Larry Gross and Fincher favourite Andrew Kevin Walker on board to make further changes in 1996 before the script was finally nailed down. Shooting began on location in San Francisco, but not before the production had gone back and forth on the setting. 'Shooting there added probably $3 million,' Fincher noted. 'There was an enormous pressure to bring the movie back to Los Angeles.' Other alternatives floated included relocating *The Game* to Chicago or Seattle. 'There were no mansions in [Chicago]. They were all too far away, with too much travel to his house, so it didn't seem like it had the same storybook quality. It had the old money, but not the prettiness or magic. Seattle ... just seemed like new money and there wasn't the same financial district.'

The depth of Van Orton's world was best brought to light through the locations in the City by the Bay. 'The script was written for San Francisco,' said Fincher. 'It's a detective town, it's an obsession town because of *Vertigo* and *The Maltese Falcon*, you've got all that history, let's do it there. A lot of people choose not to shoot in San Francisco's financial district because it's difficult; thousands of people move in and out of the area every day, so you can't shut down the streets, and it's very hard to manoeuvre around. I love the district's old money, Wall Street vibe.' The solution was to shoot on weekends, when the crew could better control the locations. For Fincher, the San Francisco 'stage' was part of his storytelling toolkit. 'We had those great hills and cable car tracks. The setting combines beautiful old stone buildings, small streets and the hills; the class system is represented pictorially. To capture even more of that old money world, we set a lot of scenes in restaurants with hardwood panelling and lots of red leather. Michael Douglas' character lives in a mansion on top of a hill, so he has to go *down* into the city; in many ways, the movie is about descent.'

Among the San Francisco locations were Golden Gate park, the Presidio and the sumptuous Filoli Gardens and Mansion in Woodside, San Mateo, which served as the Van Orton family home. The Filoli house remained as is, with some simple cosmetic changes such as the addition of a fountain in the driveway to alter the look of the building. The elegant mansion goes through a shocking transformation in the film's third act – 'a personal affront' in Fincher's words – when Nicholas returns to find the place covered with glowing wall scrawls in ultra-violet paint. Graffiti artist Vince Moisden created the artwork (which included such insulting slogans as 'Welcome Home', 'Don't Cry' and 'Hey Stupid'), giving the impression of ruining the house's interior by painting on foam-core boards which were fixed over the real wood panelling. The location part of the cab crash was shot near the Embarcadero, in the shadow of the Golden Gate Bridge, while the water tank elements for Van Orton's near-drowning took place at a stage on the Sony Pictures studio.

Parts of the Chinatown scenes were actually shot in the Los Angeles Chinese district, and other LA locales included the CRS building and the fake hospital, while bluescreen elements for the flashback to Nicholas's father were filmed in a parking lot opposite the Los Angeles Convention Centre. The Sony backlot in Culver City, meanwhile, provided studio space for interiors like the log cabin and Van Orton's office. The alleys down which Christine and Nicholas are chased by the attack dog were a familiar locale for Fincher, having also been used during the filming of *Seven*.

Jeffrey Beecroft, *The Game*'s production designer, described the alley environment as 'totally manipulated', with several fences placed at strategic points to close in the passageway around the characters; parts of the route were actually built on an open parking lot. Some elements of the alley were also locations for Levis, Taco Bell and Nike commercials. 'It's a very scary environment,' said Beecroft, 'part of the underbelly of Chinatown.' Like several other sites in the film (such as the city streets when Van Orton is being tailed, or the corridors of CRS and the Nikko Hotel), the alley deliberately resembles part of the metaphorical maze the lead character finds himself trapped in.

For the clinical interior of the Consumer Recreation Services office, a setting was built inside the Los Angeles Centre Studios (formerly the Unocal 76 building) to suggest stretches of bright steel, glass and polished black marble. 'We definitely wanted that part of the film to be more slick,' said the director. Beecroft wanted the impression of a maze and he inserted an artful reference to *The Wizard of Oz* (1939) in the layout of the CRS headquarters (a film later referred to in Van Orton's dialogue); like the start of the Yellow Brick Road, the CRS office is built around a spiral shape, so that Michael Douglas' character is led onto the path of the game in the same pattern Dorothy follows her journey toward the Emerald City. Fincher shot a long moving scene of Feingold leading Van Orton around the set but the sequence was later edited down. The director felt that the look and visual texture of CRS was based around the concept 'that they know more than you', to sell the confidence-trick angle of the story.

The final segment of shooting took place on location near the town of Mexicali in Mexico, for the scenes when Nicholas wakes up after CRS have dumped him. For this sequence, as Van Orton metaphorically rises from the dead, the production crew built the entire cemetery set, including the crypt.

'It was a long shoot, over 100 days,' Fincher recalled, 'so it was a matter of keeping everyone's morale up because everyone was exhausted. There were a lot of night shoots, a lot of locations, and it was just gruelling.' The director noted that the film's deceptive, multi-layered narrative sometimes made it tough for the actors to keep their lies straight, calling the process 'intellectually really exhausting. Everyone's playing so many roles in it, so it was a question of keeping it all clear. Is Deborah [Kara Unger, as Christine] playing the first lie of being the bad waitress, or the second lie of being the girl who doesn't know what's going on? There are so many different lies going on it was difficult to keep track. Every scene is filled with three or four different lies ... we had to constantly balance all [of them]. The most difficult thing was trying to keep focused on what the lie you're telling at any given moment is; what's the one out front? What's the one people are supposed to be concentrating on?'

Fincher saw the complexity as a necessary challenge for his skills. 'It was really difficult for me; but probably for someone who knows what the hell they're doing, it wouldn't have been so hard. The storytelling ability I've shown so far is questionable – it's certainly true of *Alien 3* – on top of that, a lot of people thought *Seven* was just a simple story all dressed up. I went at *The Game* as if it was my next test, you know, let's see if I can actually do something complicated.'

In a film where so much of the reality presented to the viewer is artificial, the deftness and subtlety of the visual and special effects in *The Game* are all the more cunning. One of the most striking moments comes when Van Orton, rattled by an emotional confrontation with his brother, his car crippled by a blowout, hails a taxi to take him home. Too late, he's trapped in a CRS-driven runaway that takes him straight off the road and into the waters of the San Francisco Bay. The incident had real-life resonance for Douglas, who recalled an incident from his past: 'I almost drowned once, thought I was going to die.'

Fincher had the scene closely plotted through storyboards. 'We laid out the things we needed to see, but it's pretty straightforward. Stunts and action sequences in movies ... you kind of send out for that stuff like pizza.' Placing Van Orton in such a scene appealed to the director. 'What I liked was the idea of, instead of a guy who's a man of action, there's the accountant with a gun trapped in the back seat – and trying to figure out how this can be part of [the game]. This is going too far.' The cab crash also highlights the false 'movie' world that Van Orton is thrown into by CRS. 'This is not a movie about real life, this is a movie about movies,' said Fincher with a smile. 'They're putting this guy in a movie, and he's not acting like a movie star. He runs away, he flips out, he goes in and curses little old men. He knows exactly what's going on and he has *no* idea what's going on.' To simulate the taxi sinking

Dillon (Charles S Dutton) and Ripley (Sigourney Weaver) in *Alien 3*.

David Fincher directs Charles S Dutton and Sigourney Weaver on the lead foundry set of *Alien 3*.

Ripley (Sigourney Weaver) prepares to face the inevitable in the concluding scenes of *Alien 3*.

A British preview advertisement for *Alien 3*.

Teaser advertisement for the British video release of *Seven*.

Brad Pitt as Detective David Mills and Morgan Freeman as Detective William Somerset in *Seven*.

Detective David Mills (Brad Pitt) pursues the killer in *Seven*.

Tracey and David Mills (Gwyneth Paltrow and Brad Pitt) share an awkward dinner with Somerset (Morgan Freeman) in *Seven*.

Nicholas Van Orton (Michael Douglas) is left for dead in the final act of *The Game*.

Nicholas Van Orton (Michael Douglas) confronts Christine (Deborah Kara Unger), the agent behind the chaos, at the climax of *The Game*.

Marla Singer (Helena Bonham Carter) and Jack (Edward Norton) face off in *Fight Club*.

The tragic Bob, played by rock singer Meat Loaf Aday, shares an intimate moment with Jack (Edward Norton) in *Fight Club*.

Helena Bonham Carter and David Fincher take a break during *Fight Club*'s shoot in downtown Los Angeles.

Sarah and Meg Altman (Kristen Stewart and Jodie Foster) try to contact the outside world in *Panic Room*.

Jared Leto, Dwight Yoakham (masked) and Forest Whitaker play
the trio of criminals intent on entering the *Panic Room*.

into the bay, the rear half of a cab was mounted on a rotating rig that would turn on an axis to let water flow in as Douglas wound down the window.

The summit of *The Game*'s effects magic comes in the final moments of the film, as Van Orton steps off the roof of a skyscraper, mirroring the actions of his father. The high-fall climax from the top of the CRS building was actually shot three weeks into the production. 'At least that gave us a couple of weeks to get up and running,' noted the director. Visual effects supervisor Kevin Haug called upon his team to simulate the suicidal dive, from the roof of the Bush Street skyscraper and down through the glass atrium of the historic Sheraton Palace Hotel below (which was actually several blocks away). Only one panel of the actual glass ceiling above the opulent hotel ballroom could be removed for the shoot; just enough to let a stuntman drop through. To create the shattering roof for the film, Haug's team created a computer-generated layer of virtual glass. Other effects technicians used CG tools to digitally remove wires and rigs to make the scene appear seamless, as shots of Michael Douglas and stunt doubles against bluescreen were composited into background 'plates' of the actual locations.

The fall shifts through several angles as the scene unfolds, and these were first plotted out for reference points. To get an idea of how quickly Van Orton's body would fall, at the director's suggestion the effects crew rigged up disposable markers they nicknamed 'Fincher Balls'. Each 'ball' was a water jug filled with milk and glow sticks, which would pick up the scene's lighting as it was hurled over the lip of the roof to fall into the street. Footage of the plunging markers would then be covered with an image of the suicidal character in post-production. Together, shots mingling the actual skyscraper, street footage from Los Angeles, a false roof on a soundstage, miniature models of the building and atrium, a matte painting of the vertiginous drop, composites of the actor/stunt double and the CG glass came together to create this breathtaking sequence.

As well as being difficult in a practical sense, this scene was also one of the hardest to sell to nervous studio executives. 'People were very frightened about the ending, and wether anyone would buy Michael Douglas finally jumping,' said writer Michael Ferris, '[but] it's something that the director and the actor sold beautifully.'

Some of the film's other outstanding – and somewhat eerie – effects moments include the manipulation of real-life television correspondent Daniel Schorr by CRS and Richard 'Dr' Bailey's work on *The Game*'s striking 'marionette' trailer and the ethereal jigsaw puzzle titles. When *The Game* was remastered for laserdisc release, a few effects (such as the removal of bullet squib flashes) were 'sweetened'. Other work by Haug and his staff created more subtle effects, such as darkening patches of sky to make footage shot in the early morning seem like dead of night; in an interview with *American Cinematographer*, Fincher said he wanted 'the idea of a night where things go into deep blacks and shadows.' Whereas the darkness in *Alien 3* and *Seven* had been a function of the unreality of the environment, *The Game* had a night-time that Fincher felt was realistic. 'In some scenes, people run out of little pools of light and just disappear ... we wanted to create the type of feeling you get when you park your car three blocks from your house, and then have to walk down the street. In that situation, you invariably look over your shoulder, because it's dark.'

Some observers compared *The Game* to Hitchcock thrillers like *North by Northwest; Empire* labelled it 'a post-modern remake of *Vertigo*' and *Sight & Sound* drew the same parallel. Fincher begged to differ. 'It's a kind of Hitchcock movie; it's supposed to be plausible but it's not really a lesson in how to live. I never understood what the Van Orton background was, but when I saw the scene where Jimmy Stewart gets hired by his college chum to watch his wife, there's just a feel to it. I was never conscious of it [but] there's probably something of *Vertigo* in there, but I think it's more of a *Twilight Zone* episode, except there's nothing supernatural. It's like you find out they were shooting an episode of *The Twilight Zone* down the street and they thought you were an extra.'

In relation to the lead character, however, Fincher made a different correlation: 'It's more *A Christmas Carol*. That is what it was intended to be, but *Christmas Carol* also has Tiny Tim and it's a love story, and it shows how Scrooge ended up not being a miser. There are emotional signposts throughout it, but *The Game* is a different kind of redemption. It's not particularly smart but it is very intellectual – if you're going to be engaged by it, then you're going to be engaged on a watching, processing level. Nicholas was more of a Gordon Gekko type, more of a player [in early drafts] and I liked the idea of him being more like Scrooge, this emotional miser cut off from the world. He's just dead, he doesn't have anybody, and back into his life comes somebody who should mean something to him, but he's holding them off at a distance – and that person gives him this experience. This is a man who found his soul again, this is a man haunted by the fact that his father committed suicide in his 48th year, so he was beginning to have some suicidal thoughts. [He's] out of touch and divorced and living in his family's home, and having a midlife crisis.'

Michael Ferris noted that Van Orton was first written as 'a much nicer guy' but added that Fincher's colder take on the character took the story in new directions. 'It was a smart [choice], a gutsy one, and I don't think every director could have got away with it or would have been given the freedom to do it that way.'

Fincher portrayed much of Van Orton's isolation through the use of modern technology. 'I liked how much communication took place over phones and voice-mail. He's always trying to avoid his brother by leaving messages all the time. I thought that was an interesting way to handle the interpersonal relationships. Van Orton is damaged goods – I like him. He's atrophied in the way that people are when they cut themselves off from each other. He behaves very much like people I know who have $600 million in the bank; you have to be so guarded, because everybody has an agenda. It's especially bad if you're born into it. All of that stuff is part of a much bigger, richer movie than we had time to get into, because we had a chase movie superimposed over it.'

In a number of interviews, Fincher talked about letting his actors propel the direction. 'This isn't about how it looks, it's about whether or not you believe these people are lying to you, so cast the best people you can and present it as simply as possible. It was a matter of creating a stage for these characters to simply tell you their stories, and my job was to say, "I believe that take." Just cast the right guy and get out of the way.' For his part, Michael Douglas told *Empire* that 'It was a great, great script that was really well thought out ... it's a hell of a ride and you're not driving.' The role of a cool and distant corporate man was something Douglas was no stranger to, with Van Orton only shades away from the Gordon Gekko of *Wall Street* (1987) and the titular role of *The American President* (1995); he'd return to a similar role in *A Perfect Murder*. But the actor was also capable of managing the slow disintegration of Van Orton from his icy persona at the opening of the movie to his suicidal-then-redeemed self at the end, after handling characters like D-Fens in *Falling Down* and the beleaguered Tom Sanders in *Disclosure* (1994).

It's interesting to speculate whether the actor and director might have collaborated on *The Game* to take the audience's expectations of the role and play against it. 'He's a classic enabler,' Fincher said of Douglas. 'He gets off on people who have an opinion and point of view and passion for what they do, so when you go in and say, "No, it has to be this way because of that," he likes that. Michael's intimidating when you first meet him because he's powerful and he's a producer, and he's done more than you will ever do – but he gets pretty easy if he feels you have a distinct idea about what you want to do. Through rehearsals he was giving me sidelong glances, but once we started shooting, it was okay. I knew I'd done my research about the material, and I could answer questions in my sleep about it.'

Douglas drew on events in his personal life – at the time he was in the throes of a divorce settlement – to build the Van Orton character. The actor compared Fincher to Milos Forman and Paul Verhoeven, saying: 'I was a big fan of David's. *Seven* was pretty amazing, it was very, very effective; [but] in the early stage you're thinking, yeah, music video, commercials, yeah right, this is one of those 'visual' directors. And just when you think that, you are all of a sudden totally surprised at how well he watches performances. I think David's work is best described as being eerie. His style and the choices of his pictures are not user-friendly, they are *uncomfortable*. He enjoys that edge.'

Christine, Nicholas Van Orton's combination guide and tormentor in the film, was portrayed by Deborah Kara Unger. Her co-star Douglas recalled she was initially 'a long-shot' for the role, but Vancouver native Unger impressed them all when she came in to read: 'She had all the right qualities for the part.' Unger's layered performance shifts gears time and again until we finally learn in the most basic reveal that Christine's real name is actually Claire; by knowing her name, Nicholas scores his final 'points' and the endgame is closed. Like many elements in *The Game*, Christine's true identity is secretly telegraphed when we first meet her in the restaurant – the Debussy composition 'Claire de Lune' is playing in the background. 'I wanted there to always be the risk that she would just walk out of the movie and you'd never see her again, that she didn't matter at all,' said Fincher. 'I wanted [her] to be the extra who steps to the wrong place at the wrong time and fucks something up for the movie star ... She's always trying to leave the movie, she's always walking out of the room, she's always trying to escape and the movie won't allow her to.'

The instigator of Nicholas's game is Conrad Van Orton, his wayward younger brother; Conrad's appearances at the beginning, middle and end of the film are like waypoint markers for his brother's arc through the story. Fincher's first ideas for the character changed when Sean Penn was cast in the part. 'I'd always seen Conrad as the guy who has seen the light, he's totally reborn ... but Sean just brings another current to it.' Penn's edgy and fragile performance as Conrad brings unspoken volumes of backstory to the characters whenever he and Douglas share the screen. Fincher noted that, despite the actor's reputation for being difficult, their work together on *The Game* went smoothly. 'I didn't run into any of that. He's like, "Okay, I'm here. Where do I go?"' Referring to the initial meeting between the Van Orton brothers, Fincher claims that 'It would have been a very different scene with another actor, because Sean gives you the feeling that he's fucked up and he's trying to ingratiate himself.'

The Game features a number of other notable actors in supporting roles, including Peter Donat as Samuel Sutherland and Armin Mueller-Stahl as Van Orton's associate Anson Baer. 'The thing about Armin that's interesting is that he's a guy who seems both little and big on the screen at the same time,' said Fincher, who had originally conceived Baer as a much older character, a frail and doddering fellow in his nineties. 'There's a compassion and a kind of small grandfatherly thing about him ... there's also this kind of gruffness.' James Rebhorn also plays an important part as Jim Feingold. As the human face of CRS, Rebhorn's character is a key component in the game. 'If he came across like James Mason in *North by Northwest*, you wouldn't want to get involved [with him],' Fincher notes, highlighting Feingold's disarming manner. 'He's the only person who could present this idea to you. If some *smoothy* did that to you, you'd be instantly on your heels.'

Once again, a few familiar faces from the Finch Mob appear. The film's cinematographer Harris Savides appears as 'Ankles', the unlucky guy lost for toilet paper in the airport men's room stall, with Rachel Schadt as the maid at the Hotel Nikko; both appeared as 911 operators in *Seven*. Joe Frank, the CRS data technician, was due to play one of the doctors in *Seven* but scheduling problems meant he was unable to take the part, so Fincher cast him here instead. Other *Seven* alumni include John Cassini, the 'leaking pen' man, Mark Boone Jr. as the private investigator and Michael Massee as one of the paramedics in the airbag scene; the other medical technician in that sequence is played by director Spike Jonze, one of Fincher's Indelible Films cohorts. Fincher would later return the favour by playing an uncredited role as Christopher Bing, an art editor from the *New York Times*, in Jonze's film *Being John Malkovich* (1999).

The performances in *The Game* flow not just from the triptych of Douglas, Unger and Penn, but also from the numerous supporting cast members, many of whom are 'players' in the CRS programme. More than other conventional thrillers, this is an ensemble movie in an atypical sense of the word, as the last scenes reveal the extra layer of actors within the narrative of the 'reel' world. Fincher enjoyed the idea of a secret 'sect' in the acting community who would only work for CRS. 'You have movie stars, you have television actors and you have commercial actors and models – and then you have the CRS guys, who are hardcore, and they're on call 24 hours a day. They might get a call for no reason at all, "Okay, you're a paramedic today, put this on, here's some bullshit speak you can say on an index card, now go be that." And they don't get paid quite as much ... I'm sure the Screen Actor's Guild has a whole department that handles all the billing and stuff for the CRS actors. I loved that idea that there was this weird, secret counterculture.'

The commissary sequence at the film's conclusion where the 'cast' of Van Orton's game are assembled was what Fincher called 'the Mel Brooks scene', referring to the movie *Blazing Saddles* (1974). 'We had to have a guy in Trojan armour, a circus strongman, a couple of women in Vegas showgirl outfits riding elephants, you just needed to throw everything in ... [but] I do think that scene should have been shot with nine people in the room, just the ones you knew, with the idea that everyone you've just humiliated yourself in front of is sitting there talking about *you*.'

On *Seven*, Fincher had worked with Harris Savides to create the intricate lighting and visual mood of the film, and for *The Game* he had Savides step up from the second unit post to be his cinematographer. The two men had worked together since the early 1990s on videos and commercials, and Fincher had nothing but praise for him. 'He's incredibly in demand – probably the most sought-after commercial cameraman in the world. He's very collaborative and always has great ideas.' Fincher, who prides himself on knowing the technical aspects of his craft, knew that Savides would share his vision without needing to be 'steered' to it. 'I knew I wasn't going to have a lot of time to get involved in the lighting, which is something I normally love to meddle in. Harris is one of a handful of people in the world to whom I could say, "Well, you know what to do, so just do what *you'd* do..." I have that much faith in him. He's incredibly responsible, when he tells you how long it's going to take to light a shot, that's how long it's going to take. I needed someone that I could trust, so I could walk away, come back later and say, "Wow, that's beautiful, let's shoot it".'

For his part, Savides notes Fincher's 'great eye' for film. 'David is very clear about what he wants. I've learned a lot from him. He's not like a lot of other directors, who sometimes let their cinematographers run away with things. He has very definite ideas about camerawork.' Fincher credits the cinematographer with what he calls the 'richness of the movie' and adds: 'I'd love for people to see this movie and appreciate how much work went into making it look as if *very little* work went into it.'

The mechanics of lighting the scenes, the palette of colour and shade, were crucial to Fincher's handling of the plot. 'There are infinite choices you can make and with today's technology you can do anything, so the question is deciding what it is you're going to do. What helps the psychology of the storytelling?' The answer was to colour each aspect of the film with a very realistic look, beginning with a 'rich and supple' feel for Van Orton's world of wealth and casual power. Fincher and Savides took references from films where attractive settings masked menacing underbellies, such as *The Godfather* (1971) and *Being There* (1979). 'In our film, things start to get out of control when Van Orton leaves his pristine world. We would let fluorescents, neon signs and other lights in the background be overexposed … we let things get a bit wilder out in the real world.'

The lighting of the characters was equally important, and Savides worked to keep Van Orton darker in the opening sequences. '[He] undergoes a metamorphosis during the course of the film, so we kept him a bit hidden while showing everyone else. We gave him more light later in the story, as he became a new person.' In *Seven*, Fincher had used an atypical film stock and a silver retention process called CCE to bring out the depth of black on the screen; for *The Game*, a Technicolor printing process called ENR was employed. 'It tends to lend a smoother look to things. There are a lot of night sequences and I didn't want them to be milky.'

Seven had also allowed the director to play with unusual approaches in sequences like the freakish opening titles, and in *The Game* the scratchy home movies that represent Nicholas Van Orton's childhood memories gave him that opportunity again. Shot on 16mm, the negatives were scratched, subjected to bleaching, and left to over-expose in sunlight to age them, in order to make the sequence 'look like archival footage' according to Fincher. 'Ferris and Brancato had this idea that you could set the film up with these home movies, and then the home movies would become the flashbacks.'

The clockwork precision of *The Game*, its narrative of boxes-within-boxes made the film an exercise in moviemaking exactitude for the director. 'It's kind of a cinematic 12-step programme!' he joked. 'It's a tricky movie because on a certain level you want to fool people, but on another level you have to be aware of the fact that you're making a movie. People know you can do anything you want, so it is a cheat. You're walking a tightrope between what the movie can show that is believable and yet still compels the movie forward in the right way; but you have to make sure that people don't just shout "Bogus!" at the end and think, "Of course he could do that, it's a movie!" This film, for me, was an interesting study – not in human behaviour or how people relate to each other or what they want from life or any of that … it was what does an audience want or expect or need from a film?

'My question was, "How much will they put up with? Will they go for 45 minutes of red herrings?" You have control over everything that somebody sees and hears for two hours, the audience knows you can show them anything – you've got computers, you can make a Tyrannosaurus Rex eat a car – so the question is what *don't* you do? Every time you go to a close-up, the audience knows subconsciously that you've made an editorial decision, that you've said, "Look at this, this is important." In a movie like this, where everyone is lying, you can run an audience ragged by showing them things that are supposedly important, but every time you underline something, every time you do that the audience become aware of it and they start to catalogue it, because they know this movie will have suspense and mystery – but you don't want to exhaust that. You have to be very cautious about *when* you want to do that.'

The director did his best to shoot the majority of *The Game* with a single camera in broad, open scenes or 'moving master' shots. 'When you use multiple cameras, everybody becomes focused on co-ordinating things rather than achieving a point of view. Co-ordination is the most difficult and time-consuming aspect of filmmaking. We tried to stage scenes as simply as possible – if we shot a conversation at a table, we wanted the scene to be about what the characters were saying, not about the camera. When you shoot a scene like that with multiple cameras, you run the risk of boring people with coverage.' Fincher felt that breaking out of commonplace editing patterns forces the viewer to pay attention. 'It can create an interesting tension. By not cutting away, you can make them feel a certain type of anxiety. In a movie where you're trying to subvert people's expectations, ideas like that are key.'

Early on, Fincher had considered shooting *The Game* 'in continuity', filming the scenes in the chronological order in which they appear in the final movie, but admitted 'There wasn't a chance.' He continues: 'One question we kept asking ourselves was, "What is the expectation here?" I didn't want it to feel like it was being engineered cinematically, with a close-up of the keys or whatever. I didn't want to underline stuff and have the ominous music cue come in.'

The director points to the scene where Van Orton is trapped in the runaway taxi cab, and his attempts to obscure the line between the real and the 'reel'. 'We thought, if we put music on this, will it make this a movie? And if it's a movie, is it too safe? Maybe the thing to do is not put music on it, just use sound effects, because then you don't get the thrilling strings telling you *Dah! Dah! This is the part where the cab runs away!* It's not that. Does that make you think, "Shit, this could end really badly?" I mean, to what extent can you *torture* a movie star? To what extent can you humiliate them? How far can you take them?' Fincher also kept the audio clear of musical overtones in the film's most potent moment, Van Orton's suicide dive. 'In the final scene there's no music. That was a very conscious decision because you expect music when it's a big moment in a film, so when there isn't does that make it a movie, or make it real?'

During the scenes in Chinatown, the presence/absence of the orchestral track is used to underline another event. 'There's another music cue that goes all the way through as Michael's character goes to his hotel, and then to see his wife and finally ends up in Chinatown.' At this point in the story, Nicholas Van Orton is 'very fragile' and, when a car thief attempts to assault him, Van Orton pulls a gun and scares him off, perhaps believing that the thief is another CRS 'actor'. The music, Fincher said, 'literally disappears on the frame where the car-jacker comes in, so it's as if the car-jacker also car-jacks the movie and interrupts everything that's going on. We were playing with all those ideas.'

Despite his sparing use of soundtrack in *The Game*, Fincher retained a sense of mood via the music of Howard Shore, who had previously scored *Seven*'s uniquely grim emotional landscape with a similar series of rising and falling rhythms. Sound designer Ren Klyce, who brought *Seven*'s nameless city to life, also worked on *The Game*'s aural picture. Other music cues in the movie serve to underline certain story moments, such as Jefferson Airplane's suitably trippy 'White Rabbit' over the graffiti scene and closing credits, or the songs played by the big band ('Life Goes to a Party' and 'The Best is Yet to Come') during the birthday bash.

'I was never tempted to pay any kind of homage to specific movies, but I was always aware that the game they create for [Van Orton] deals with movie stakes,' said the director. '[It's] the big heist, the big con ... it's kind of dealing with movie set-pieces, things that don't happen in real life. In real life, when people steal from other people, they don't drug them and leave, they shoot them and go on about their business. It's only in movies that it's important to rub somebody's nose in it. He is trapped in a movie, that's what CRS offer him, that's his personal adventure.'

The development of *The Game*'s script involved refined shifts rather than large-scale alterations. 'It was more of a tone thing for me,' Fincher noted, 'a lot of little changes. The original script was a little sweeter, a little more of a "stop and smell the roses" kind of thing, it wasn't quite as mean. The character of Nicholas, for example, was much more a well-loved corporate raider type, much more of a man's man, a kind of a Richard Branson character. I preferred the idea of a guy who was more of a vampire, the kind of creature who stayed in the dark and the fire had gone out. Instead of him being a physical miser, he was an emotional miser – but everybody thought that was too sinister. My attitude was, "Let's make a popcorn movie that's more sadistic than anyone can imagine."'

According to John Brancato: 'This is a one-joke movie, really. There is this game and it's supposed to change your life, and it will have a happy ending. They pretty much tell him from the beginning what it is he's going to get, it's going to be an entertainment, it's going to be a distraction – but the way entertainment works is that you have to forget you're being entertained. That's a lot of what we attempted to do to the audience.'

There were many more jokes and lighter touches in the initial script, conceived with Van Orton as a younger man in his mid-twenties who would take on the challenges of the game with verve and a sense of adventure – and, indeed, Douglas petitioned Fincher to add some comedic moments to the film. The director jokingly referred to the escape-and-chase sequence from the restaurant to the hospital as Douglas' 'Jerry Lewis homage', but he also credited the actor with bringing warmth to an otherwise cold character: 'That's all Michael Douglas.'

'We always though that with a character who is pushing 50, it starts to become pure sadism,' noted Brancato. Ferris felt that casting the role as an older man turned the story into one about a character dealing with his mortality. Part of the through-line of the story involved the suicide of Van Orton's father and the causes behind it; in the finished film, the father's death is left veiled in hints, but the first take on this thread had Van Orton gradually uncovering the truth. From his early impression that his father killed himself as a cowardly escape from a financial crisis, he learns through the CRS machinations that his parent was in fact suffering from depression – something that Nicholas is on the verge of as he reaches the same age.

To take Van Orton apart for his eventual 'reconstruction' at the film's end, Fincher wanted CRS to attack the sense of security and power the banker's wealth gave him. 'They're relinquishing him of all control. He never gets to do it his way. It's all about, "You have no control over your life. All the control you thought you had is now gone."'

Two sequences in particular hooked the director during his first reading of the script. 'I loved the scene where Christine drugs him. I thought, "Wow, that's really genius," because you're just so worked up by that point and you hate the moment. You go, "Oh God, why didn't I see that?" And I loved the shoot-out at the house.' The latter sold Fincher with the description of Christine's apartment. 'The scene in the house with the price tag, when he discovers that the whole house has been set-decorated – that for me was when I said, "I've gotta see this, I've gotta make this movie." I was not expecting to have the rug pulled out from under me in that respect. I kept thinking, "Okay, I think she's in on it, which means she *isn't* in on it..." And then to find out that she *is*. And it's done in such a ham-fisted way, I loved that. It's very rare that you find a movie where the middle section of it works. I just didn't buy the set up or the [original] ending where he shoots Christine.'

But the sequential switchbacks in *The Game*'s narrative were the biggest draw for him. 'There are a couple of good gimmicks in the [script]. Christine says, "Don't you get it, it's all about fucking money, you idiot!" And you're thinking that can't be it – but then what did they do for the first 18 pages? They just told me how rich this guy is, they kept telling me what they were going to do, but they sold me that [the game] was this other experience, that it was bigger and more profound than just getting his money – and then she brings it back around and goes, "No, that's not it at all, it's *just* about money." When I read the script I just got giddy. You get all the way around the bend with the thing, and it gets back to

"Remember page one, when we told you how fucking rich this guy is? *That's* what it's all about." I loved that. And then I loved the fact that it *wasn't* about that, that there *was* something else. That's what *The Game* is for me.'

He continues: 'There are lots of red herrings that your brain naturally catalogues because you don't know what will turn out to be relevant. Movies usually make a pact with the audience that says, "We're going to play it straight, what we show you is going to add up." But we don't do that. In that respect, it's about movies and how movies dole out information. Certainly with the last two scripts, I've been drawn to things that begin to dismantle the architecture, not of movies, but of the pact that a movie that is responsible entertainment makes with an audience.'

Conrad's appearances in the story propel Nicholas through the key points of the game, but the script had first called upon the character to appear in another scene, just before the finale. 'He goes to see Conrad in hospital and Conrad is hopelessly insane,' Fincher recalled. 'He says, "Don't leave me, don't leave me" and [Nicholas] just can't deal with him and he leaves.' The director felt the scene lengthened the third act unnecessarily and put Van Orton in a poor light. 'It gave Conrad a great scene to just be a psycho, but we couldn't figure out what it would mean. It was just another *asshole* beat.'

Up until late 1995, the Ferris and Brancato drafts were still centred on a younger hero in his late thirties, and the character of Van Orton was less morose and more engaged by the antics of CRS. Key elements that were withdrawn during the development process included a confrontation with a mugger on the subway and a recurring CRS agent masquerading as a Rastafarian (later the driver of the runaway cab). The humour present in the 1995 script was also cut down, losing jokes like CRS staging a fake earthquake warning and one of the actors fixing a 'Kick Me' sign to Nicholas's back.

Gross and Walker's collaboration with Ferris and Brancato added an important supporting character in the form of Van Orton's housekeeper Ilsa; her presence in later drafts provides an important link to Nicholas's father and a sounding board for his questions about the suicide. The later script also brought in a biblical reference (shades of Walker's *Seven*) when Van Orton asks a former player what the secret is and his oblique reply is 'John. Chapter Nine. Verse 25. "Whereas once I was blind, now I can see."' Despite their input on the script, Gross and Walker were not credited for their work on the final production, although the inclusion of a police officer named Walker is possibly a nod towards one of the writers; Fincher would later give Walker a similar name-check for his uncredited work on *Fight Club*.

Perhaps the most significant alteration in *The Game*'s script came in character-ising the person who brings the game to Nicholas. In the original draft, the Conrad character (then named David) was a prep school chum rather than Van Orton's blood relation, as the writers had always assumed that Van Orton would have been an only child. '[He had] grown up in that kind of isolation,' said Ferris. 'Once we had the connection of the younger brother, the jump [into the game] became a lot easier to swallow, because there's so much emotional bonding that goes on, even between antagonistic brothers like this, that suddenly you accept him doing this thing to appease his brother, just to work off some baggage from childhood.'

Brancato credits Fincher with the inspiration for the change. 'It's a really clean, workable idea. As soon as we heard it, we realised how it would create a domino effect through the story and really help strengthen the character relationship.' The writer noted that the 'emotional chilliness' of the script was thawed somewhat by this simple yet important change in the plot dynamic: 'The brother helped give us a much more visceral, emotional core to the story.'

Fincher mentions a romantic subplot that was trimmed between Van Orton and Christine, which remains as a small hint at the film's close. 'There was a love story early on ... but that's not the way to interest [Van Orton], he's incapable of stopping to smell the roses, no matter how many roses you present to him – that's what the movie is about, in a way. There was kind of a honeymoon period where they got him together with the waitress, and I said, "I just don't buy it, I don't buy this guy getting in a car with *anybody*." If you've got $600 million in the bank, you live your life a little bit more cautiously than ordinary people.'

Ferris felt cutting the romance was a good idea. 'I think it's something we put in as a sop to traditional filmmaking, that there has to be a love story somewhere in the centre of this because it's a movie. The movie didn't really need it, and I think the relationship between (Christine and Nicholas) plays a lot more credibly by giving her a harder edge and not trying to introduce some sappy romance.'

CUTS AND CHANGES

Nicholas Van Orton's first name in the early drafts of *The Game* was Schyuler (pronounced Skyler); coincidentally, Michael Douglas also played characters named Nicholas in *Black Rain* (1989) and *Basic Instinct* (1991).

The part of the television anchor played by real-life National Public Radio spokesman Daniel Schorr, who also appears in Ferris and Brancato's *The Net* (1995) and *The Siege* (1998), was originally written for CNN reporter Bernard Shaw. At the time, CNN refused to let any of their newspeople appear in 'fake' roles, although this policy was dropped after *The Game* and Shaw went on to appear in several feature films as himself.

After the lights go out in the hospital, Nicholas and Christine were originally to have found their way out using a pair of special glasses which would show up a path in 'invisible' paint; Fincher initially planned to take the characters inside the scenery to reveal the false frontage within. The Mercy Hospital set remains standing and has appeared in several other films and television shows.

Parts of the 'red bra' scene between Nicholas and Christine in his office were cut; in extra dialogue, Christine asks Van Orton about his life, looking out at the impressive view from his window and remarking on his wealth. Fincher was unhappy with the scene and shot it three times; he felt the conversation was too obviously setting up the relationship between the two characters and excised it.

One of the last scenes to be cut from the script followed directly after Nicholas escapes from the sinking taxicab. Rescued by a voluptuous girl on a nearby boat, he rejects her advances and decides he's had enough of the game, realising she's an obvious CRS operative. In the final cut of the movie, when the cab goes off the edge of the wharf into the water, the boat can be seen out in the bay.

The character that became Christine's roommate Amy was first conceived as her father, reflecting the younger age of the leads in the early drafts.

In the original version of the script, Nicholas woke up in a rubbish heap after being drugged – symbolically putting him as far away from his riches as possible. Instead, he wakes in a crypt, which is illustrative of the character's 'death' and 'rebirth' and one of several moments of Christian imagery in the story.

An element cut from the Mexico sequence featured Van Orton being hit by a local cop before he finds his way to the American Embassy, which explains his facial injuries.

Van Orton's watch, the gift from his parents that is the last tie to his old self, is sold to buy a trip across the border. Fincher considered – but ultimately rejected – the idea that the watch would be recovered by CRS agents and returned to Nicholas by Conrad in a scene at the end of the game. The inscription on the case reads "On Your 18th Birthday, Your Father's Watch, Love Mother."

In the scene where Van Orton asks for a lift in the diner, Michael Douglas accidentally dropped the money he was holding during the second take, and, despite shooting the scene another ten times, Fincher chose to use that shot because it seemed more realistic.

A line explaining the car-jacker in Chinatown was discussed but never shot; at the post-game party, Nicholas would have mentioned the car thief off-handedly to Feingold, only to be told by the CRS executive that "he wasn't one of ours", meaning that part of Van Orton's experiences was actually real.

Nicholas's confrontation with Feingold at the zoo was written to be at an elephant enclosure, but production designer Jeffrey Beecroft instead chose an indoor location, a tiger cage, where the bars and the prowling big cats better reflected the emotions of the moment between the characters.

An element missing from the rooftop scene came just as Van Orton jumps, when Christine (who was originally shot instead of Conrad) suddenly reveals she isn't dead and tells Nicholas he's making a terrible mistake. Thus, whereas he falls with intent to commit suicide in the final film, this line would have changed Nicholas's mindset and made his survival the 'prize' for finishing the game rather than a final trick on the part of CRS.

After getting up from the airbag, there was more dialogue with Feingold explaining the last phase of the game to Van Orton, but reactions from test audiences led Fincher to cut what he felt was 'over-explaining after the point'.

Deborah Unger mis-read a line of dialogue during the kerbside conversation between Christine and Nicholas, when answering his question about where she's from. Fincher felt the moment worked well for the character – that she'd lied so often she wasn't even sure of her own truth – and left it in the movie.

An alternate ending had Nicholas exiting the hotel, where he declines a cab ride and walks off alone down the street as two repairmen carry replacement panes of glass into the atrium. Another variation on the ending would have had the camera panning around to reveal a piece of graffiti with an upward-pointing arrow and the words 'Level Two', intimating that the game is not over.

AFTERMATH

PolyGram's investment in *The Game* proved fruitful when it opened at the top of the box-office chart on 12 September 1997, beating *GI Jane* and *Fire Down Below* into second and third places. The company's first attempt at theatrical distribution grossed $14.3 million in its opening weekend, soothing frayed nerves in the upper hierarchy. PolyGram executive Andrew Fogelson told the *Los Angeles Times* that he was as 'skittish as a cat, but it turned out to be a truly wonderful weekend.' *The Game* stayed a strong performer, but at the end of a year marked by colossal blockbusters – *Titanic, Men in Black* and the *Jurassic Park* sequel *The Lost World* – the film's $48 million US box-office total was less than half the 100 million plus earned by *Seven*.

Critics were frequently hard on *The Game*, coming as it did after *Seven* and forced to compete with the earlier movie's incredible box-office impact. Adam Smith of *Empire* declared that *The Game* had none of the 'coruscating visual originality and devastating emotional wallop' of Fincher's other work, calling it nonsensical and 'a major disappointment'. Charles Taylor of *Salon.com* said that 'for a movie being sold as a box of surprises, *The Game* is, at heart, about as conventional as it gets.' When some critics called the film farfetched, Fincher retorted: 'Is it any more implausible than *Con Air*?'

Other observers saw *The Game* differently. Roger Ebert at the *Chicago Sun-Times* said 'the movie is like a control freak's worst nightmare' and Marc Savlov of the *Austin Chronicle* praised 'the effortless ease with which Fincher creates palpable disquiet and overwhelming anxiety.' *Sight & Sound*'s Philip Strick drew genre parallels with the modern techno-intrigue of television's *The X-Files, VR.5* and *Dark Skies,* and films like *Conspiracy Theory* (1997), calling Van Orton's trials 'rewarding spectator sport' and praising Fincher's panache and his 'eye for the potent single shot'. Andrew Male of *Neon* looked further back for The *Game*'s roots, to films like *The Parallax View* and *The Conversation* (both 1974), each a product of the post-Watergate cinema that the young David Fincher grew up with. 'Don't expect answers,' wrote Male. 'The Game is a film that seeks neither truth nor likelihood but sheer, bloody astonishment. It succeeds on every level.'

Fincher addressed the movie's 'middle-child' stigma so: 'I don't know if it's being overlooked; movies are kind of like kids. You have five kids, and certain kids the teachers are going to like, certain kids are going to be good in sports, there's going to be the one kid who's the life of the party and the one who spends time in their room, so it's kind of like that.

'The people that love this movie are analytical. Whenever I meet accountants or lawyers they go, "You did The Game? I loved that!" I think it has to do with the analytical mind, people who like mind games, people who want to sit and go "Okay, now..." There's an aspect of letting go to it that a lot of the Friday night date movie crowd are just not that interested in. They like being ahead of it. There's a vast part of the movie-going audience that likes being smarter than their movies. Not to say that The Game is a particularly smart movie, but it requires a certain suspension of disbelief and you kind of have to like the puzzle of it, you have to enjoy that sort of thing. I like Sleuth, I like The Last of Sheila, I like those kind of movies. I liked The Stunt Man, those kind of movies that are poking you [intellectually].

'It's not a particularly emotional movie and ultimately, I think for a movie to be successful on a wide scale there has to be some kind of vicarious, cathartic experience and emotion that people can tap into. I certainly think that The Game is a movie with a lead character that's hard to relate to as well as like. People have said, "So you made a really good movie last time. Why would you go and make a movie like this?" People who don't like to be tricked by the films they watch tend to hate The Game.'

Once again, Fincher brought audiences a film, and an ending, that caused discord. He told Neon's Damon Wise of a test screening outside Los Angeles: 'Three people left at a critical point before the end. They said, "I can't deal with this, I hate this movie," and they got up and left – so they have no idea how it really ends.' In a way, Fincher compares The Game to the psychological test film Van Orton watches – 'You're not done until the movie is done with you.'

The roots of The Game lie in what John Brancato calls 'paranoid, controlled environment stories' from such 1960s television series as The Prisoner and The Avengers. David Mamet's House of Games (1987) is another antecedent, sharing The Game's narrative of privileged intellectual characters moving from their antiseptic world into a shady landscape of double-crosses and stings. Elements of the film are suggested by F/X: Murder by Illusion (1985) and echoed in Antitrust (2000). On a broader level the film recalls the whole skein of 'human prey' stories from 1932's seminal The Most Dangerous Game to The Wicker Man (1972) and more recent action fare like The Running Man (1987), Hard Target (1993) and Surviving the Game (1994), while the manipulated world aspects of the story surface again in comedic clothing for The Truman Show (1998) and in Gothic dress for Dark City (1997).

There's also a strong component of actual game design philosophy present in the film's plotting, as Michael Ferris explains. 'We always imagined that CRS had a backup contingency plan – A lot of people took the film to task by saying they couldn't possibly have anticipated [Van Orton] would do all the things that he did to lead him to the next stage of the game, but the idea was always that they haven't, they've anticipated any number of possible things that he might do and they have a different set of circumstances in place in case he does that.'

Since the writers had chosen not to take the viewer 'backstage' at CRS to show the inner workings of the agency, the unfolding plot was told solely from the player's perspective. 'CRS is like a computer game,' said Brancato, 'you can see it as a series of decision trees. If you turn to the left you'll get one set of experiences, if you turn to the right you'll get a different one. A lot of [the film's] logic isn't traditional narrative but rather decision trees and game theory. If you do one thing, the next thing will happen, then you have this branching experience – and then you can bring him back into the main line at different points.'

New York Times critic Janet Maslin used this similarity in a negative context, saying 'the film has the steady momentum and flat trajectory of a video game.' The sequential structure of computer gameplay is employed in a different fashion in films like *Run Lola Run* (1998) and *Cube* (1997). A real-life (and far less dangerous) team version of the game takes place annually; with a $25,000 entry fee, ten teams of up to six players take part in a complex scavenger hunt, solving puzzles to find clues which lead to other puzzles. Just like the CRS game, the real version often employs actors as part of the mechanics. As recently as November 2002, a television producer cited the movie as the inspiration for a faked 'reality' show similar to *Big Brother*.

An interactive CD-ROM of the film was briefly mooted, while Ferris and Brancato admitted that plans had developed for a possible television series based on *The Game*, just as their feature script *The Net* had been turned into a weekly serial; however, any TV version would have found it well nigh impossible to maintain the structure and mythos set up in the film, and it's likely that this was what caused the project to evaporate.

Only David Fincher could convince a film company making their first movie to swallow an ending where one of Hollywood's best-known leading men leaps off a roof after murdering his own brother. In every film he directs, Fincher finds ways to confound expectation, to reverse endings with a flourish and sneak up on you with that sucker-punch you never saw coming. In microcosm, this is the very matter of *The Game* itself – the ability of a storyteller to whom you've trusted a couple of hours of your life to turn your safe world into one of uncertainty and doubt.

As the force behind the game, the shady corporation Consumer Recreation Services seems horrifically omnipresent in Van Orton's world, their presence often telegraphed to the unwitting game-player through the appearance of the acronym

CRS – on the side of the patrol car that shadows Nicholas and Christine after they escape the stalled lift; the cab company ('California Regal Sedans') whose runaway taxi swan-dives into the bay; the television repair service van ('Cable Repair Specialists') which hides the armed surveillance team outside Christine's apartment. In a subtle visual joke, the CRS corporate logo is the optical illusion of the 'impossible triangle', a hint that nothing the company shows us is actually real. 'I liked how much CRS got their logo around,' said the director. 'I think corporations are the enemy,' he explained in the pages of the *Guardian Guide*. 'Corporate thinking is dangerous because it's mediocre, pigeonholing and simplistic. I don't have to go to a board of directors to get money for a movie, but when you're working on any kind of scale, you are a victim [of it] to a certain extent.'

Like all Fincher's films, *The Game* rewards successive viewings even after the central hoax has been revealed, if only to study the story for clues that speed by the first time around. Moments like Christine's real name telegraphed through the title of the music playing as she enters the film, the chess set scattering across the floor as Nicholas's world – and his game – falls apart, the gun hidden inside a copy of *To Kill a Mockingbird*, and the blink-and-you'll-miss-it appearance of a photo of actress Linda Manz (who plays Christine's flatmate Amy) hanging on the wall of the New Moon Café, showing her in her role in the film *Days of Heaven* (1978). A far more obscure visual gag is the occasional appearance of a can of haggis in certain scenes. 'Haggis' was a nickname for Harris Savides, and the crew attempted to sneak it into the background of several shots in the film.

Perhaps what makes *The Game* work so well are the reversals of expectation that wrongfoot the viewer over and over again in both the original script and the final film. At first the game is presented as a quasi-mystic unknown quantity, a self-improving and life-changing experience, until we enter the world of CRS. Then, we suspect that Consumer Recreation Services are up to something else, that it is a con game – what else *could* it be, when presented in such a slick, clean manner? – and our fears are confirmed by Christine's double-cross. But we travel right to the edge with Nicholas and to the next revelation: it *was* just a game and now it has gone too far. And then the climactic turn of the screw as he takes the fall and lives, the final lie exposed.

'Hopefully the psychology of it will have some kind of resonance,' says the director. 'I don't want Van Orton to seem like a hockey puck; he makes certain choices and he responds to certain things.' At the film's conclusion, Fincher wanted moviegoers to be engaged by what he calls *The Game*'s 'fairly sadistic fun'. 'I hope the audience walk out of the theatre and go, "What would my game be?" Or go next door to eat and go, "I know what yours would be – it involves some kind of crashing jet liner..." I like to subvert expectations. I hope *The Game* is entertaining, but it's also a little prurient, a little sadistic, because you enjoy the suffering and anxiety of the central character. You want to see him learn a lesson.'

It's no wonder that Fincher was attracted to the feature, and we can be sure that, in another director's hands, *The Game* would not have found the same razor-edge resonance it did with him. It's not hard to imagine that Van Orton's predicament – being stripped of any control over his life – directly spoke to the director's experiences years earlier working on *Alien 3*. Critics argued that the film's 'movie logic' and game-like progression were its weaknesses, but in fact these are its strengths; as Fincher himself said, *The Game* runs on the rules of a feature film because Van Orton's game is exactly that, a thriller where he has become the unwilling protagonist, a live roleplaying adventure where the world is the board and his life supplies the pieces. It's a clever conceit, to take what in other stories would seem like contrivance and invert it to make a sound framework for the plot. *The Game* flips through reality like a hand of cards, from our viewpoint as an audience in the real world to Van Orton's life and the mythology of CRS's false game environment. And Fincher delights in blurring the lines.

It isn't easy to like Nicholas Van Orton, with his aloof and indifferent manner; we view the early phases of his game with quiet amusement as he's taken down a peg or three, but soon enough we become as trapped in the narrative as he is, and from there it's a winding course to the very edge – and then over. In many ways, *The Game* is Fincher's 'forgotten classic', overlooked in later, post-*Fight Club* years; it is the intelligent but sullen sibling overshadowed by the brighter light shone on the films that bracketed it, and unfairly so. This is a movie that shows Fincher's love for the narrative twist by pinning its audience to a chair for two hours of switchbacks, turnabouts and spins.

The Game is a film about perception, about the unpleasant concept of just how malleable our personal realities are. Each of us at some time in our lives will wonder if we are the centre of things, entertaining the solipsistic notion that we're the star of our own movie. And for Nicholas Van Orton, he's exactly that, except it's a film that he doesn't want to be in. The conceit of *The Game* leaves you wondering if your reality is as fragile as Van Orton's, if you – like him – could be propelled towards suicide by someone who knew *exactly* what psychological buttons to push. It's the same tension that underlines the character of David Mills in *Seven*, and to a degree that of *Fight Club*'s narrator Jack.

On the morning of my meeting with David Fincher, I took time out to stop at a coffee shop and review my notes. As I waited to cross the street, a van halted across from me and I matched gazes with the indifferent driver. On the door beneath his window were three large letters – CRS. And for that brief moment I caught my breath, wondering about a game of my very own. In an age of reality television like *Big Brother* and streets filled with CCTV cameras, *The Game* seems not so fictional after all. It is the triumph of this movie that you walk away from it without being able to shrug it off.

FIVE

Hit Me

'I just didn't think it was violent enough.'

THE GAME HAD examined the falseness of consumer society through the constant double-crossing of its lead character and played with ideas of identity and power. But now David Fincher was ready for the main event, for a movie that would do the same and then more, accelerating him way past the accolades and reproaches garnered by *Seven*.

With *Fight Club*, the director's first take on adapting a novel for the screen, Fincher would make his most contentious, most talked-about and most dangerous film to date. It was a teeth-rattling haymaker that defined him as one of the boldest directors of the decade, a challenging picture that once more divided his audience. As another collaboration with Brad Pitt, some observers suspected Fincher's new film would be *Seven* in a different guise. But *Fight Club* would be nothing of the sort, being drawn from a controversial book and touching on subjects that many found uncomfortable – and, in some cases, downright objectionable.

Fight Club is a story about paths, following the life of an unnamed narrator as he finds himself directionless and overcome by the ennui of modern living – only to have that bland existence ripped away by the charismatic Tyler Durden, a reckless anarchist who preaches self-improvement through self-destruction. But as with Fincher's previous films, beneath the surface lies the dark undercurrent of a far more twisted reality.

—————— FIGHT CLUB ——————

Fox 2000 Pictures, Art Linson Productions, Regency Enterprises
Director: *David Fincher*
Writers: *Jim Uhls*
Cast: *Edward Norton (the narrator, aka Jack), Brad Pitt (Tyler Durden), Helena Bonham Carter (Marla Singer), Meat Loaf Aday (Robert 'Bob' Paulson), Zach Grenier (Richard Chesler), Richmond Arquette (intern), David Andrews (Thomas), George Maguire (group leader), Eugenie Bondurant (weeping woman), Christina Cabot (group leader), Sydney 'Big Dawg' Colston*

(speaker), Rachel Singer (Chloe), Christie Cronenweth (airline attendant), Tim De Zarn (Inspector Bird), Ezra Buzzington (Inspector Dent), Dierdre Downing-Jackson (woman), Robert J Stephenson (airport security officer), Charlie Dell (doorman), Rob Lanza (man in suit), David Lee Smith (Walter), Holt McCallany (the mechanic), Joel Bissonnette (Food Court Maitre d'), Eion Bailey (Ricky), Evan Mirand (Steph), Robby Robinson (next month's opponent), Lou Beatty Jr (cop at Marla's building), Thom Gossom Jr (Detective Stern), Valerie Bickford (cosmetics buyer), Jared Leto (Angel Face), Peter Iacangelo (Lou), Carl N Ciarfalio (Lou's bodyguard), Stuart Blumberg (car salesman), Todd Peirce (first man at auto shop), Mark Fite (second man at auto shop), Matt Winston (seminary student), Joon B. Kim (Raymond K. Hessel), Bennie E Moore Jr (bus driver with broken nose), W. Lauren Sanchez (Channel 4 reporter), Pat McNamara (Commissioner Jacobs), Tyrone R. Livingston (banquet speaker), Owen Masterson (airport valet), David Jean-Thomas (policeman), Paul Carafotes (Salvator, winking bartender), Christopher John Fields (proprietor of dry cleaners), Anderson Bourell (bruised bar patron #1), Scotch Ellis Loring (bruised bar patron #2), Michael Shamus Wiles (bartender in halo), Andi Carnick (hotel desk clerk), Edward Kowalczyk (waiter at Clifton's), Leonard Termo (desk sergeant), Van Quattro (Detective Andrew), Markus Redmond (Detective Kevin), Michael Girardin (Detective Walker).

Crew: Ross Grayson Bell (producer), Cean Chaffin (producer), John S. Dorsey (associate producer), Art Linson (producer), Arnon Milchan (executive producer), The Dust Brothers (music), Jeff Cronenweth (cinematography), James Haygood (editing), Alex McDowell (production design), Chris Gorak (art direction), Jay R Hart (set decoration), Michael Kaplan (costume design), Rob Bottin (special makeup effects supervisor), Cliff Wenger (special effects co-ordinator), Robin D'Arcy (visual effects producer), Ren Klyce (sound designer), Kevin Haug (Visual Effects Supervisor), Richard 'Dr' Baily (Digital Animation Supervisor/Producer).

Tagline: *'Mischief. Mayhem. Soap.'*

SYNOPSIS

On the upper floors of a skyscraper, Jack contemplates the imminent destruction of several office buildings and the gun jammed in his mouth, thinking back to his first association with a person called Tyler Durden...

Jack is a 30-something corporate drone whose life has stalled into a dull, hopeless, insomniac nightmare. Unable to connect to anyone else, failing to fill his vacant self with pointless material possessions, he finds himself drawn to a series of support groups for the victims of terminal illness and becomes addicted to the experience. But Jack's 'misery tourism' is spoiled by the arrival of Marla, another faker; Marla's presence ruins Jack's comfortable lie and he confronts her. The two of them find a curious, twisted connection in their mutual compulsion for the groups, but they can't relax in each other's presence and they divide up the support group meetings between them.

Jack continues his job; he's a recall co-ordinator, examining the wrecks of crashed cars that are secretly manufactured with substandard components, flying from place to place across the country in a jet-lagged daze. And it's on one such trip that he finds himself seated next to Tyler Durden, a sharp, good-looking guy who hand-makes soap for expensive boutiques. Tyler notes offhandedly how easy it is to turn soap into explosives if you have the right chemicals. On landing, Jack discovers his luggage has been lost, mistaken for a bomb, and finally returns home to discover his apartment gutted by a catastrophic gas explosion; all his carefully purchased furniture has been catapulted into the street. Unsure what to do, he calls Marla – but hangs up. Instead, he dials Tyler's number and the two men meet at a bar.

Over a few pitchers of beer, Jack and Tyler discuss their life and Jack's situation. The charismatic Tyler has an anarchist, nihilistic view of the world; he's a freelance consumer terrorist, working night jobs as a projectionist (where he splices single frames of pornography into family films) or a waiter (where he taints the food of rich diners). Tyler agrees to let Jack stay at his place on one condition – that he hits him as hard as he can. How can anyone ever know anything about themselves if they've never been in a fight?, he reasons. The meeting degenerates into a flailing punch-up and the two men, enlivened and happy, end the evening by heading back to Tyler's place – a rotting, decrepit Victorian house in the middle of an industrial estate. Over the following weeks, Tyler and Jack's fights become a regular thing, and soon other men are joining in, other men who feel just as numbed and hopeless as Jack did; and Fight Club is born in the basement of Lou's Tavern, a seedy bar.

Marla calls Jack after taking an overdose of sleeping pills, but he's not interested in saving her life; however, the next day he wakes from an erotic dream about her to find Marla in the house. After she leaves in a huff, Tyler appears and describes how he rescued Marla from her suicide attempt and took her home for sex. Jack bottles up his anger – not only has she invaded his support groups but now Marla is invading his friendship with Tyler. Tyler makes Jack promise never to speak about him to Marla and, as the two continually make love while Jack sits alone, Jack nurses his rejection and lets his job slide, little by little.

A telephone call from the police detective investigating the destruction of his apartment tells Jack that the blast was caused not by a gas leak, but by home-made dynamite ... which someone such as Tyler might be capable of creating. Meanwhile, Marla continues to orbit around Jack, apparently interested in making a sexual conquest of him as well. That night, Tyler instructs Jack in soap-making, beginning with the theft of a key ingredient – human fat from a liposuction clinic – and ending with a terrible chemical burn that signifies Jack's 'initiation' into Tyler's way of life.

After grudgingly helping Marla perform a breast examination, Jack bumps into Bob – a former support group member – and discovers the existence of other Fight Clubs he knew nothing about. Meanwhile, Tyler proves his strength of character by facing down the owner of Lou's Tavern, and he sets the Fight Club members a 'homework assignment' – pick a fight with a stranger and *lose*.

In the meantime, Jack confronts his boss and blackmails him over the faulty cars, adding injury to insult by beating *himself* up to make his boss appear guilty. With the extortion money, he and Tyler can now afford to have Fight Club every night of the week. Tyler's assignments become more innovative and anarchic, tasking the members to destroy TV antennas, erase video rental stores' stocks of cassettes and wreck other icons of corporate power. As a shocked Jack watches, Tyler takes a 'human sacrifice', forcing a convenience store clerk at gunpoint to quit his pointless job and make something of his life. Jack speaks to Marla, trying to make sense of her relationship with Tyler, but only succeeds in making her annoyed, and she stalks out of the house.

In the basement, he discovers that Tyler has constructed a makeshift barracks – and outside is the first of his new 'recruits'. Over the next few weeks, more and more men from Fight Club – including Bob – arrive to become 'Space Monkeys' and join Tyler's new endeavour, Project Mayhem. Tyler slowly builds an army of followers, committing acts of sabotage and vandalism across the city – but Jack is increasingly being left out of Tyler's plans. His rejection finally boils over in a fight with one of Tyler's men – the pretty boy Angel Face – and he viciously beats him into semi-consciousness. Later, during a rainy drive, Jack and Tyler argue about Project Mayhem, and Tyler crashes the car to give Jack 'a near-life experience'. The next day, Tyler is gone and Project Mayhem has seemingly become a self-supporting entity. The Space Monkeys are carrying out Tyler's commands and Jack seems unable to stop them; he tells an unhappy Marla that 'Tyler went away' and returns to the house to discover that Bob has been killed during a Project Mayhem mission. Despite his attempts to make the Space Monkeys realise what they have done, they misinterpret his words and make Bob's death a rallying cry for Tyler's cult of personality.

Jack sets out to track down Tyler with clues from a set of airline ticket stubs, racing from city to city, finding evidence of Fight Clubs all over the nation and meeting nothing but silence from dozens of men who all bear the same fighting scars – until finally one member addresses Jack as 'Mr Durden'. Frantically, Jack calls Marla and demands to know if they have ever slept together; the answer is yes and suddenly Jack finds himself face to face with the elusive Tyler. With growing unease, Jack realises why everyone is confusing him with Tyler – *they are both the same person* ... Tyler is the personality that Jack wants to be, his alter ego made manifest and free. Suddenly, Marla's behaviour towards him becomes clear and Tyler threatens that now she knows too much about 'them'.

Jack returns to the house to find it empty and abandoned, with evidence that the Space Monkeys intend to blow up a series of credit card companies as their next targets. He tries and fails to apologise to Marla and finally puts her on a bus out of town, in hopes of saving her from the Space Monkeys, before giving himself up to the police. But even here, Project Mayhem has members, and he narrowly avoids being castrated by a trio of cops. Escaping into the night, Jack breaks into one of the buildings and tries to disarm Tyler's bombs – but his alter ego is waiting for him and knocks him out...

On the upper floors of a skyscraper, Jack contemplates the imminent destruction of several office buildings and the gun jammed in his mouth. With nothing left to lose and no way to stop his other self, he fires the gun – 'killing' Tyler. The Space Monkeys arrive with an angry Marla, but despite his injuries he manages to apologise to her and they share a moment of honest attachment, just seconds before the office blocks explode and collapse. And, as the last moments of the film flicker past, a single frame of pornography flashes by...

DEVELOPMENT

Fight Club followed a steep arc into feature film production. Even before its publication, the original novel by Chuck Palahniuk had found its way, still in galley form, into the hands of Laura Ziskin and Kevin McCormick at Fox 2000 Pictures. A common occurrence in an industry hungry for fresh ideas, the book had been quietly slipped by its publisher into the sights of Fox's creative fire-watchers.

But from the beginning, it had been the dream of another production executive, Raymond Bongiovanni, to get *Fight Club* made into a feature. The movie ends with a dedication to Bongiovanni, who died before production began, and it was his initial interest in Palahniuk's book that set the ball rolling. 'God bless Raymond,' noted the novelist, remembering their first phone conversation about the project in 1995, when Bongiovanni called 'just to see if I wasn't insane.' Around the same time, the producer had been introduced to a script called *Hard Hearts* by Jim Uhls, who was subsequently chosen to adapt the book. The script Uhls would create was a remix version of Palahniuk's slim 1996 novel, shifting key scenes and dialogue passages into a narrative better suited to the big screen.

When Bongiovanni died, his obituary in *Variety* ended by affirming his last wish – to get *Fight Club* filmed – and Palahniuk describes how his agent telephoned him after the producer's funeral. 'He said, "Your name was mentioned eight times during the eulogy. You can't buy better press than that."' Although he would never see it, Bongiovanni would posthumously get what he wanted. Ziskin recalled that, within 36 hours of hearing about the novel, 'I was sitting on the edge of my bed in the middle of the night, reading passages to my husband.' In turn, McCormick recruited partners Joshua Donen and Ross Grayson Bell to be *Fight Club*'s 'cheerleaders' at Fox. 'The studio's internal coverage condemned the material as being exceedingly disturbing,' said Bell. 'I read the manuscript and all the reasons the studio reader cited for *not* making the book into a movie were exactly the reasons *to* make the movie.'

In turn, Donen and Bell passed the novel to David Fincher and began to woo him for the directing job. At the time, Fincher was contemplating an unproduced script called *The Sky is Falling*, about two priests who discover proof of the non-existence of God and go on a commandment-busting crime spree.

McCormick was certain that Fincher was the best choice to helm *Fight Club*. 'I got chills,' he said. 'David is one of the only directors who can tell you two years before he's shot a scene exactly what you'll get when he's through.' Donen was instrumental in getting Fincher on board, performing the 'Human Sacrifice' scene down the telephone when the director initially resisted reading the book. At the time, Fincher was busy working 12-hour days as he completed his cut of *The Game*.

'Josh Donen, who is my agent now, was the lead producer on *Fight Club*,' Fincher recalls. 'He called me and he said, "I have this book, and you have to read it tonight," and I said, "Ah, Josh, I'm not going to read a book tonight." "You gotta read this. It's really fast." "I can't, I've got a dub tomorrow..." "Look, take three hours and finish this book, just sit down and read it." "Well, give me one reason why." "Okay, there's this scene where there's this guy called Raymond K Hessel..." and he goes into the Raymond K Hessel scene and explains all this to me. I said, "Okay. I have to read this book, all right, you've got to send it over. I have to read this." So I read it that night and I flipped out. I was laughing so hard that I just said to myself, I've got to be involved in this. If anyone should make this movie, I should at least give it my best shot.'

Fincher had acted quickly but, it seemed, not quickly enough – he called Donen the next day only to learn that Fox had already bought the feature rights. The director was wary of working with 20th Century Fox again after his experiences with them during the production of *Alien 3*. 'I was not happy. I said, "Well, there goes that idea." But Josh said, "No, no. Joe Roth is not there any more, Tom Jacobsen's not there..." The one good thing about these multi-national corporations is that once you decide you loathe the people that are there, they're usually gone so quickly that it doesn't really matter.'

With monumental understatement, the director told *Digital Bits*: 'I didn't have a very good time with Fox the first time – but Josh called and told me to just go in and talk with Laura Ziskin, and tell her that I wanted to make it.' He continues: 'I read the book and knew that you couldn't make this movie in 2003, this movie had to be 1999, you had to make it before the next millennium, because a lot of things the book talked about in such a startling way would be silly today, they wouldn't have the same sort of visceral impact.'

Fincher was energised by the material, citing features of the story in which he identified with the narrator Jack. 'At some points in my life, I've said, "I could get that sofa and then I'll have the sofa problem handled." As I was reading Chuck's book, I was blushing and feeling horrible. How did this guy know what everybody was thinking?'

He adds: 'It seemed kind of a coming of age story for people who are coming of age in their thirties instead of in their late teens or early twenties. In our society, kids are much more sophisticated at an earlier age and much less emotionally capable at a later age. Those two things are sort of moving against each other. There's an idea that on the path to enlightenment you have to kill your parents, your god, and your teacher. So the story begins at the moment when the Edward Norton character is 29 years old. He's tried to do everything he was taught to do, tried to fit into the world by becoming the thing that he isn't. He's been told, "If you do this, get an education, get a good job, be responsible, present yourself in a certain way, your furniture and your car and your clothes, you'll find happiness." And he hasn't.

'And so the movie introduces him at the point when he's killed off his parents and he realises that they're wrong. But he's still caught up, trapped in this world he's created for himself. And then he meets Tyler Durden, and they fly in the face of God – they do all these things that they're not supposed to do, all the things that you do in your twenties when you're no longer being watched over by your parents, and end up being, in hindsight, very dangerous. And then finally, he has to kill off this teacher, Tyler Durden. So the movie is really about that process of maturing. It is talking about very simple concepts. We're designed to be hunters and we're in a society of gatherers. There's nothing to kill any more, there's nothing to fight, nothing to over-come, nothing to explore. In that societal emasculation, this everyman is created.'

With its story of a protagonist placed before conflicting life paths, Fincher compared the movie to *The Graduate*. 'It was talking about that moment in time when you have this world of possibilities, all these expectations, and you don't know who it is you're supposed to be. And you choose this one path – Mrs Robinson – and it turns out to be bleak, but it's part of your initiation, your trial by fire. And then, by choosing the wrong path, you find your way onto the right path, but you've created this mess. *Fight Club* is the nineties inverse of that, a guy who does not have a world of possibilities in front of him, he had no possibilities, he literally cannot imagine a way to change his life.' Edward Norton agreed: 'My grandfather was very uncomfortable with *The Graduate*. He thought it was negative and inappropriate. But my father loved it, thought it was a great metaphoric black comedy that dealt with his generation's feeling of disjointedness, and that's exactly what *Fight Club* is. My character is sort of like Benjamin, and Brad's character is like a postmodern Mrs Robinson.'

Fincher reflects on one of *Fight Club*'s simple truths. 'There's something about getting hit in the face that gives you an adrenalised vision of life that's very profound, it's like nothing else you experience.' It was just that experience that inspired Palahniuk to write the novel. After getting into a fist-fight that left his face bruised and discoloured for weeks, the author realised that people around him were afraid to ask him how he'd got that way. 'It was like, if you looked bad enough, no one would dare ask you what you did with your free time.'

Given *Fight Club*'s edgy material, it would have been easy for Fox to take the route of least resistance, casting unknowns and avoiding the pitfalls a big budget would create; but the director wanted to go full tilt to do the book justice. 'I told [Ziskin], "Here's the movie I'm interested in making and I'm not interested in watering any of this shit down. I have no interest in making this anything other than what this book is, which is kind of a sharp stick in the eye." She was very cool with it. We could have made it a $3 million *Trainspotting* version, or we could do the balls-out version where planes explode and it's just a dream and buildings explode and it's for real, which is the version I preferred to do – and she backed it. The real act of sedition is not to do the $3 million version, it's to do the big version.'

Fincher demanded – and got – the autonomy that he needed to do the film right, telling the producers, 'When I come back to you, I'm coming back with a script and it's going to be the script I want to shoot. Instead of coming back and saying, "What do you think? Oh, yeah, I can change that," I'm coming back with a script I'm willing to kill for. But I'm also coming back with a budget and I'm coming back with a schedule and a cast.' With the fierce content of *Fight Club*, part of the wonder of it is just how Fox agreed to make it in the first place. 'Movies don't get made at major studios because people say, "Well, this is a major political topic and we should jump all over this." They look at it and go, "Will kids like it? Can we get the 18-to-24 demographic?" I didn't have any kind of mission,' says Fincher. 'I just knew that I liked the story, I liked the journey and I thought it was incredibly cinematic.'

Producer Art Linson told *AICN*: 'It's very simple. You've got Brad Pitt and David Fincher together for the first time since *Seven*. You've got me as a producer. The last time those guys worked together, the movie did $300 million worldwide. They're looking at the cost of this thing and thinking, "We're not going to get killed on this thing, no matter what." They're not thinking, "We have to put this on screen. I was born to make this movie." No executive thinks like that. They're looking at Fincher and Brad and thinking, "Maybe it will be *Seven* in another costume." Of course, it can't be. And if we'd told them, "Brad's going to play it with a shaved head and part of his teeth knocked out," they might not have been as receptive to it. It was courage on the part of Fincher and courage on the part of Brad. They had more to lose.'

The director felt that Fox knew what they were letting themselves in for. 'There's nothing about any of our pasts that would lead them to believe we were gonna go off and make *Runaway Bride*. I think there was always a worry that it was going to be sinister and seditious. And we always said, "No, it's gonna be funny and seditious." The sinister element is the context for the understanding. The things we talk about in the film are dark fantasies or stewing rages that come out in unexpected ways. We always wanted to temper it with humour.'

The evolution of themes from *The Game* was clear to him early on. He called the films 'cousins'. '*The Game* is a *Twilight Zone* episode. That's all it's supposed to be. In *Fight Club* it's even worse, having to contend with somebody who is powerful and you look up to them and his ideas become all too questionable, but then to find out that they are indeed your ideas, that this is your mess, that you are the leader.'

Pitt was on board almost from the beginning, while Sean Penn had passed after being briefly considered for the roles of both the dour Jack and the charismatic Tyler. 'I sent Brad the book and he turned up on my doorstep the next day ,' Fincher jokes. 'And I live in a gated community. I don't know how he got past security.' Pitt's desire for the part raised eyebrows in the Hollywood community. 'People who don't know Brad think he's a strange choice for the role, but people who do know him, who know the Brad Pitt who hangs out at his house with his five dogs, who chain-smokes, who lives under an inch of dust, they think he's perfect.'

Fincher had been instrumental in getting the actor on board, to the extent of flying to Pitt's home in New York City while the actor was working on *Meet Joe Black* and waiting for hours on his doorstep until he returned in the morning. At the time, Pitt wasn't interested in looking at new projects, so Fincher took him out for a pizza and convinced him to read *Fight Club* on the strength of his excitement about the project.

In *Fight Club*, Pitt shook off any pretence at the pretty-boy mantle he'd gathered from *Legends of the Fall* and *Seven Years in Tibet*, amping up the trend-bucking courage he'd shown in *Seven* to maximum. 'His work in *Fight Club* was stellar,' said Linson. 'He never showed any evidence of an actor who was out there trying to protect his 'Brad Pitt-ness'. Without a shred of false vanity or the use of old tricks to win over an audience, Pitt proved to be a formidable actor of enormous talent. Can anyone imagine, 30 years ago, Robert Redford or Warren Beatty shaving his head or working without caps on his teeth or exposing himself so raw and ruthless as Brad had done and just let the chips fall?'

Pitt himself saw the risk as a logical one. 'It didn't seem gutsy to me at all. It seemed like it would be foolish not to do it.' The actor was effusive about Fincher and the movie. 'It's a pummelling of information. It's Mr Fincher's Opus. It's provocative, but thank God it's provocative. People are hungry for films like this, films that make them think.' And from the start, Pitt saw the explosive nature of *Fight Club* before it hit. 'Fincher is piloting the *Enola Gay* on this one. He's got the A-bomb.'

Then it was on to Edward Norton, taking the role of the film's narrator, named as Jack in the script, although he's never actually called that in the dialogue. But this was not without a delay courtesy of Norton's previous employers at Paramount Pictures. In 1995, Norton had made his feature debut in Paramount's *Primal Fear* on a contract that locked him in to making two more films for the studio; the role got him an Oscar nomination and a Golden Globe award, followed by parts in three other features at three other studios. Norton considered by 1997 that Paramount's option on him had lapsed, but as he went into contractual negotiations for *Fight Club*, Paramount demanded he fulfil his obligation with a part in an unmade feature, *Twenty Billion*, which would prevent him appearing in Fincher's movie.

Fox refused to go head-to-head with Paramount and left Norton to sort out the situation, which he did by extending the option. However, the revised deal would have ramifications for the actor when Paramount exercised their rights in 2002 and cast him in their remake of *The Italian Job*. Norton had offered to take roles in a handful of other Paramount projects, including *Mission: Impossible 3* (which at the time Fincher was set to direct), but the studio had reportedly refused.

Norton called *Fight Club* a film that was 'off the charts'. 'It's not a photograph, it's an El Greco, lurid and crazy. For me it's always about, have I seen this before? And I'd definitely never seen this before. Nobody's ever seen this before. Fincher sent me the novel, and I read it in one sitting. It's obviously a surreal piece that operates at an almost allegorical level within someone's madness, and I felt immediately that it was on the pulse of a zeitgeist I recognised. It speaks to my generation's conflict with the American material values system at its worst. I guess I've felt for a long time that a lot of the films that were aimed at my generation were some baby-boomer perception of what Gen-X was about. They seemed to be tailored to a kind of reductive image of us as slackers and to have a banal, glib, low-energy, angst-ridden realism, none of which I or anyone I know relates to. They didn't speak to the deeper and darker underlying sense of despair and paralysis and numbness in the face of the overwhelming onslaught of media information that we've received from the cradle.'

Norton's everyman appeal and dour, measured ennui as the film's narrator brings a realistic feel to his performance in *Fight Club*, instantly selling the concept of a man adrift in his own life. 'His contribution is that he's exactly that guy,' Fincher told the *Guardian*. 'You can believe that he's over-thinking the whole situation and creating this whole problem for himself.'

The *Fight Club* triumvirate was now almost complete, with only the role of Goth queen Marla Singer to be cast. An early contender was singer-actress Courtney Love, co-star with former boyfriend Norton in *The People Vs Larry Flynt* (1996). But the part went to British actress Helena Bonham Carter in April 1998, a casting choice that blew holes in her earlier Merchant Ivory-type profile. Initially, the actress had reservations about the script, but she was wooed to the part after discussing *Fight Club* with Pitt at a post-Oscar party. One week later, she met with Fincher and agreed to join the production.

Bonham Carter's first impression of the script had been a strong one. 'I thought, "In the wrong hands, this could be abominable." I was the last one on board. I wanted to meet Fincher just to ascertain that he wasn't a complete misogynist. The script was awfully dark ... it could have been immature or possibly even irresponsible. But after meeting him, I could tell that it wasn't going to be a concern. He's not just an all-out testosterone package. He's got a healthy feminist streak.'

The director's initial meeting with her involved showing the actress a rough outline of the 'brain ride' title sequence. '[It was] a glimpse inside the mind of Fincher,' she noted. 'Then I sort of knew that I could trust him, that I was in good hands. He has such a specific vision that I knew he'd be doing half the work for me.' *Fight Club*'s author Chuck Palahniuk later spoke of her performance in the film as a perfect 'Audrey Hepburn on heroin', and Fincher has nothing but praise for a woman he calls 'a very gifted, very specific actress', commenting on her ability to play against type as Marla and handle the blackly comic character. 'She just cracks me up, she was very caustic and funny.'

For her part, Bonham Carter admitted she modelled the character partly on Fincher: 'He thinks he's Marla,' she noted. On set, the character was nicknamed Judy, after costume designer Michael Kaplan had described her as 'Judy Garland close to the end.' 'Helena would listen to her records while she was in her trailer,' said Kaplan.

The evolution of *Fight Club*'s script saw Jim Uhls and Fincher working together closely from the earliest drafts. After the scriptwriter and director combed through an initial outline with Ross Bell, Uhls created a new draft that formed the basis for their collaboration. Art Linson joined the development process as the writer shifted the pitch and movement of the novel to make it more cinematic. 'The challenges of the adaptation were finding a structure for the film in terms of cause and effect and building momentum, and exploring the characters deeper and further in dialogue and behaviour,' the writer noted. In addition, Fincher's writer on *Seven*, Andrew Kevin Walker, took a pass over the script in a series of uncredited rewrites. As a nod to his hidden work, the three police detectives who attempt to cut off Jack's scrotum near the end of the film were named Detective Andrew, Detective Kevin and Detective Walker.

One of the earlier drafts cut the narration completely, but the look of the story without Jack's dry stream-of-consciousness ramblings made the script suffer. '[Jim] had written a version that eliminated the voiceover because Ross Bell told him it was a crutch,' Fincher noted. 'It was like taking the voice out of Dashiell Hammett. The interior monologue is what gives you some sort of context, some sort of humour. Without the narration the story is just sad and pathetic.' Uhls agreed that the film should always have had a narration attached.

After five drafts over eight months – many of which Uhls wrote for free – Fincher and Linson took the Fox executives to dinner and presented them with the finished, ready-to-shoot script. 'We dropped this huge pile of stuff,' says Fincher. 'They came in and we gave them something like three bibles' worth, a huge package. I said, "This is the movie. $67 million, here's the cast, we have this many days of shooting, this is why, these are the stages we want at Fox. We're going to start inside Edward Norton's brain and pull out. We're going to blow up a plane. We don't know who's going to play Marla, but we think it's going to be this person. Give us your answer tomorrow." They called back and said, "Okay."'

For the writers, one of the more difficult scenes to craft was the bar-room conversation between Tyler and Jack that serves to introduce the viewer to Durden's anarchist worldview. Fincher, a director known for his tendency to shoot and shoot, set up two cameras for the scene and filmed nearly 40 takes, a weighty 40,000 feet of film, to get things right. In the end, the scene was allowed to evolve organically through Norton and Pitt's half-scripted, half-improvised dialogue. 'It was a collective effort,' notes Norton, and the director added that making the scene work involved a lot of time spent 'playing Nerf basketball.' Both Uhls and Palahniuk were more than happy with the director's translation of their storyline to the screen: '[I felt] a combination of being blown away by the finished product,' said the scriptwriter, 'and at the same time it matched [my] expectations in the sense that it looked exactly right to me – this is the way I saw it.' The novelist concurs: 'There is not one shot in this movie that is not a beauty shot.'

PRODUCTION

Filming began in July 1998 and ran for 138 days to early 1999 at Fox Studios and nearby Los Angeles locations. In order to set up many of the film's shots ahead of time, Fincher used pre-visualisation to plan his camera set-ups. Known as 'pre-vis', the process creates a virtual computer-generated model of locations and allows the director to manipulate angles, sets and actors without the need to physically be on site. As well as complex greenscreen and effects shots like the airliner collision, Fincher also used pre-vis on comparatively mundane scenes, such as Jack's return to his ruined apartment.

'[This] is something I favour whenever possible,' Fincher said, 'just as a means of problem solving before getting to the stage. I do this because I've found that the shortcomings in your technique are often among the key factors that define the moviegoing experience for the audience, so eliminating these problems before-hand is always preferable. Aspects of reality can intrude during the shoot, especially on location. But by learning about them in advance through pre-vis, I can avoid those problems, working cheaper, faster and without a lot of unnecessary coverage.' Production designer Alex McDowell noted that Fincher's use of the process allowed planning to take place 'down to the tiniest degree, within inches,' for shots like the mid-air collision.

Alien 3 had shown Fincher that working with Fox and without the safety net of a producer in tune with his vision was hellish. To cover him, Fincher relied on Art Linson, who had worked on *The Untouchables* (1987), *Heat* (1995) and *The Edge* (1997). The director said, 'I was like, "Dude, the first three weeks of shooting, they're gonna see the daily footage of skinny women in support groups with veins painted all over their faces, saying how they would like to get fucked one more time before they die. It's not gonna have the voiceover yet. Studio people are gonna be looking at that. You've gotta be there to watch my back, so they can understand that this is not just cynicism. The cynicism of Ed's character at the beginning of the film is not the attitude of the film."

'I don't know how sharp they were [at Fox] but I do know that there are people – to this day – who were working with this movie and had no idea that it's funny. There were people at the studio that said, "This is evil and nihilistic." And I said, "No, it's not." Because it's talking about frustration, about an inability to find an answer. It's about a guy struggling to make sense of something, as opposed to a guy giving in to the fucked way things are. So there were definitely people who didn't get it.' He continues: 'I think it's funny. But I don't know, maybe I have a different take on funny. I want people to understand that they should laugh. We're not saying, "Okay, everybody, you're done seeing the movie – get out in the parking lot and start fighting." I do think it is a darkly comic tale of maturity ... I loved the idea, for instance, that Tyler is a man who makes soap for a living and he makes the soap from human fat stolen from lipsuction clinics. That's funny.'

The director had placed a clause in his contract guaranteeing him final cut on the film – but only if it came in under $50 million. 'When the budget went over, Bill Mechanic said, 'I can't do this to my shareholders. I can't give this to you because then I have no recourse when this movie goes over budget." I said okay, I understand that. But we had some little contractual loopholes – the title sequence was about $800,000. We could have done the sequence with white titles over black and then cut to Edward's face. So they held that out for the first six months. If we were going rampagedly over budget, and were getting careless about spending money, then they weren't going to give us the title sequence. But we stayed pretty much on schedule and pretty much on budget, and by the end, 12 weeks into the shooting, they finally said, "Okay, you can start the title sequence." Ultimately, when Bill said, "I can't give you final edit over $50 million. If you can do it for $49.9 then you can have final cut," I said, "I couldn't do it for that, but I trust you and you trust me so let's do it."'

Mechanic had been another of the champions of *Fight Club* from his lofty position as the chairman and CEO of Fox Studios. But months later he would leave, in a move that some industry observers attributed to his involvement in this controversial but less-than-blockbusting film. Linson recalls a conversation after the first screening of the film in his book *What Just Happened?* '[Mechanic] had stood up for *Fight Club* as boldly as he could, but after this screening he knew that if this baby didn't fly, there might be a huge career price to pay. Then Mechanic addressed me with one of those fateful lines: "I don't care what anyone says, I'm proud of it, really, really proud of it."' However, Fincher was pleased by the support he got across the board from *Fight Club*'s executive cheering section and said of them, 'Not one of them backed off about the movie.' Mechanic would later go on record as saying: 'This is one of the best movies ever made at 20th Century Fox.'

Fight Club had been set to wrap production in December 1998, but changes to the ending (see below) led to a few re-shoots and the production slipped back, shifting the release to October 1999 after Fox cited the 'combination of a hurried post-production and a crowded summer schedule.' Some observers considered the reasons for the delay to be Fox's squeamishness about releasing so strong a film after the shooting incident at a high school in Columbine, where two teenagers gunned down several students – but Fincher maintains that it was the studio's desire to let him improve the film, granting the director an additional $700,000 for re-shoots. 'It just wasn't ready. There was a lot of concern about the length of the movie. I had it down to two and a half hours, but we wanted to get it down to two-nineteen. I needed more time.'

Much of *Fight Club*'s look comes from the tension between the bland, washed-out nature of the 'outside' world and the heavy darkness of Tyler Durden's secret society; like the black depths of *Seven* and the night shoots of *The Game*, Fincher and Jeff Cronenweth (now his director of photography) pushed their film stock and equipment to the limits, shooting through spherical lenses instead of the more typical anamorphic ones to hold the low levels of light that populate much of the movie. 'Lurid was definitely one of the things we wanted to do,' the director noted, explaining his ideal for the coloration of the *Fight Club* world. 'We wanted to control the colour palette. You go into a 7-11 in the middle of the night and there's all that green-fluorescent, and like what green light does to cellophane packages, we wanted to make people sort of shiny. Helena wears this opalescent makeup so she always has this smack-fiend patina, like a corpse, because she is a truly romantic nihilist.'

The influence of films like *Blade Runner* comes through in scenes like the interiors of Tyler's house on Paper Street, with the rain slicking through the rooms as Fincher's self-confessed homage to that movie. The night shots from George Lucas' *American Graffiti* (1973) were also an inspiration for Fincher and Cronenweth. '[They] have this sort of mundane look, but it still has a lot of different colours and they all seem very true. We talked about making it a dirty-looking movie, kind of grainy. When we processed it, we stretched the contrast to make it kind of ugly, a little bit of underexposure, a little bit of re-silvering, and using new high-contrast print stocks and stepping all over it, so it has a dirty patina.' Fincher had previously used the re-silvering process to darken the blacks and shadows in *Seven*.

The movie's locations were a mixture of nondescript, any-city exteriors around Los Angeles and Long Beach, and interiors built at the Fox lot. 'We wanted to present things fairly realistically, except obviously the Paper Street house. There are no Victorians with 18-foot ceilings in LA county.' The house was constructed in a vacant lot in San Pedro, on land set to be redeveloped as a port, surrounded – as the film shows – by nothing but warehouses and scrap metal dealers. Built from the ground up, Tyler's three-storey home even had a backstory of its own, sketched in by production designer Alex McDowell to account for the overlapping décor, the falling-down state and the remote, solitary site. The isolated location gave Fincher control over exterior shoots at night, with no other residents for miles; however, the production did attract the interest of the local police, after distant neighbours had called in UFO sightings, caused by the self-illuminating helium balloons used to light some of the scenes.

Fincher and McDowell examined the work of photographer Philip-Lorca diCorcia as a source of inspiration for what the director called 'the motel-life world.' 'Marla's apartment, which was a set, was literally like photographs of a room at the Rosalind Apartments in downtown LA. We just went in and took pictures of it and said, "This is it, build this."'

For all the violence in the film and the subsequent accusations of incitement to violence that it stirred up, there was just one incident of real disorder on set, when Jeff Cronenweth was struck by a beer bottle thrown by a local resident. 'We all experienced our own little *Fight Club*,' he said, 'and I have the scars to prove it.' Irritated by the noise of the film crew as they shot in the scenes outside Marla's hotel, the man who threw the bottle was subsequently arrested, while Cronenweth was not seriously injured.

The first weeks of filming concentrated on the office scenes with Jack and his boss, played by Zach Grenier. 'As much as possible we tried to incorporate real office buildings, [we] just went down and said, "All right, put some cubicles in and we'll shoot." Kind of a low-budget approach.' Scenes such as the attempted castration in the police station were shot at the Los Angeles Centre Studios, where Fincher had previously shot interiors for *The Game*. Jack's bland apartment was based 'almost exactly' on a similar place in Westwood, rented by Fincher during his early years in Los Angeles; the buildings and interiors chosen for the movie were picked because of their prosaic, commonplace nature, so that the storyline didn't appear to be tied to any one place – something Fincher had done before in *Seven*. McDowell did his best to ensure that locations like the airliner interior, the hotel rooms, the office and Jack's apartment all used the same palette of colours and fabrics, suggesting the 'sameness' of life outside the Fight Club.

As with Fincher's previous movies, sound design played an important part in *Fight Club*, with Ren Klyce returning to the fold after his work on Fincher's last two features. 'We had such a hard time getting the timbre of Edward's voiceover, because it has to sound like a thought,' Fincher recalled. 'We ended up using five different microphones trying to get this sound. You listen to it and it doesn't sound like a thought, it sounds like a guy talking to you. The voiceover in *Blade Runner*, if you listen to it, sounds like a guy reading prose while he's sitting on the john. How do you avoid that?'

Music in the film also added a layer of subtext; as with the hard industrial themes of 'Closer' that open *Seven* and the surreal 'White Rabbit' over the end titles of *The Game*, Fincher chose to close *Fight Club* with the aptly named 'Where is My Mind?' by The Pixies, segueing out of the strident techno-sampled themes of Michael Simpson and John King, The Dust Brothers. Pitt and Norton had a mutual admiration for the band Radiohead and had briefly pushed for them to score the film in the earliest stages of development.

In *Fight Club*, for the first time the director was adapting a work from one medium into another. Fincher noted, 'Chuck Palahniuk is a pinball machine of ideas, there were things bouncing around, and stuff lighting up. His novel is written in a funny but clinical style, in which the narrator provides various recipes for disaster – this is how you make nitro-glycerine, here is the formula for napalm ... I needed to zip right through the narrator's verbal diarrhoea; and to do this, I decided to illustrate his asides in a way that brought out the menace of these everyday, found objects. This approach used camera moves and effects to complement his voiceover, taking hold of the audience by their eyeballs, providing a frantic, slightly otherworldly quality.'

The director wanted early elements of the film to look like 'a stylised version of our Ikea present' and to reflect the world inside Jack's head. 'I remember having a conversation early on when we were discussing what the feel of the first act should be. It's not a movie, it's not even TV, it's not even channel changing, it's like pull-down windows. It's like, take a look at it, pull the next thing down – it's gotta be downloaded, it's gotta move quick as you can think. It doesn't wait for you. If you don't keep up, you're lost. It's like you've tripped and sprained your ankle. You have to tell the rest of the audience, "Go on, go ahead without me." We had to come up with a way that the camera can illustrate things at the speed of thought.'

Fincher talked about the idea of *Fight Club* as a 'random access' movie, capable of shifting quickly in time and place, but without leaving the viewer baffled. 'At the beginning of the book, there's a great speech about how the gelignite is wired together and set to go off. How do you show that? Wouldn't it be great if you could see Edward looking at Brad and then just drop 30 storeys, right though to the inside of this van, see what he's talking about and then go back?' The single, vertiginous fast-pass down the side of the building was constructed with a mix of computer-generated frameworks overlaid by actual photographic images; the process is called photogrammetry. 'We mapped them on to simple geometric shapes and did an incredibly fast camera movement over them, and it just drops – I can make them go as fast or as slowly as I want, I can make it go through the wall. If you look at it frame by frame, the camera goes into a janitor's room that has a calendar with naked girls ... they literally went in and photographed these little rooms the maintenance staff would have used. It goes by so quickly.'

Visual effects supervisor Kevin Haug noted that miles of film had to be shot to get the thousands of 35mm stills needed to construct the scene. The jump-cut opening of the film shows Fincher's intent perfectly. 'That's one of the things that was interesting to me, how much can you jump around in time and go – wait, let me back up a little bit more, okay, no, no, this is where this started, this is how I met this person ... So there you are in the present and then leaping back to go,

"Let me tell you about this other thing" ... It's almost conversational. It's as erratic in its presentation as the narrator is in his thinking.'

The window-dive is just one of several computer-generated or computer-assisted sequences in the movie that allowed the director to accomplish physics-defying shots that would be unworkable with a conventional camera. 'To me it was a selfish means to an end. It wasn't about, oh it would be cool to try something like this.' The photogrammetry process became part of the film relatively late in the production process, initially planned just for use in the high-speed fly-through of the apartment in the gas explosion flashback. But Fincher saw the potential to use it to illustrate story points elsewhere in the movie, including the slow journey through the contents of the waste bin in Jack's office (nicknamed 'the Galaxy of Trash'). The trash sequence was so detailed that to render just one frame of footage took an entire day of computer processing.

Fincher describes the explosion scene: 'In voiceover, Jack muses about what arson investigators will determine about the blast, and in his imagination he sees the stove left on while gas leaks out and fills his apartment, and then the moment when a refrigerator compressor clicks on and everything blows up. At 50,000 frames per second, you'd see gas molecules catching fire, which would be a lot more interesting than cutting outside to see furniture flying into the trees.' Fincher told *Cinefex* how these elements construct Jack's worldview. 'Demonstrating the narrator's thought processes became an important part of my set-up, those first 40 minutes when audiences are taught how to watch the film. Providing a 'mind's-eye' view would help audiences understand the way this story was being told. We wanted an incredibly myopic framework, one that was valid given our intent to tell the story from the viewpoint of this particular guy, who turns out to be crazy. We wanted to leap out-of-body, moving the camera in a very free way to visualise his all-over-the-place thoughts as he tries to work things out for himself.'

The technique was also used in the surreal sex sequence with Marla, which combined motion blur, images of the location, actors and body doubles; for Fincher, it was a way to avoid directing a conventional sex scene. 'We had two cameras, one shooting one-second exposures and one shooting at 250th of a second. We had this idea of [looking like] a kind of Francis Bacon version of Mount Rushmore. I can't ask people to simulate fucking, it's too embarrassing. It would be easier for me to shoot pornography than the love scene from *Top Gun*,' he notes. 'I'm scared of [directing] sex scenes – "You've got to moan, but moan lovingly..."'

Another innovative effects sequence comes as Jack finds himself walking through his apartment as if it were a page from a home-furnishing catalogue. 'In the book he constantly lists his possessions. How do we show that, how do we convey the culmination of his collecting things, and show how hollow and flat and two-dimensional it is? So we were just like, "Let's put it in a catalogue." We brought in a motion-controlled camera and filmed Edward walking through the set, then filmed the camera pan across the set, then filmed every single set dressing and just slipped them all back together, then used this programme so that it would all pan. It was just the idea of living in this fraudulent idea of happiness. There's this guy who's literally living in this Ikea catalogue. We didn't have the money, but I would have loved to have done a whole sequence of it.'

In shooting the scene, the changes in illumination and radiosity as items of furniture were removed and replaced created a unique challenge for the effects crew. After Fincher's experience of making real commercials, the Furni scene is perhaps a little bit of payback. 'I never took advertising seriously enough to wonder if there was any moral ambiguity about it,' he adds. Fincher later made a joke at the expense of Ikea on the liner notes for the *Fight Club* soundtrack, and staff at Fox were concerned enough about corporate disparagement that they pulled them from the release; the director recalls asking them, 'Have you actually *seen* the movie?'

But it was the film's opening that trumped any effects shots Fincher had ever done before; lessons learnt from the emotive scene-setting of *Seven*'s titles were writ large with *Fight Club*'s 'brain ride'. 'We wanted a title sequence that started in the fear centre of the brain,' Fincher told *Film Comment*. 'The sound of a gun being cocked that's in your mouth, the part of your brain that gets everything going, that realises that you are fucked – we see all the thought processes, we see the synapses firing, we see the chemical electrical impulses that are the call to arms. And we wanted to sort of follow that out. Because the movie is about thought, it's about how this guy thinks. And it's from his point of view, solely. So I liked the idea of starting a movie from thought, from the beginning of the first fear impulse that went *Oh shit, I'm fucked, how did I get here?*'

The director's initial concept for the titles was to have them reminiscent of a night-time dive in the ocean; dark, wet and scary. Digital Domain's visual effects supervisor Kevin Mack, a self-confessed 'amateur neurologist', defined the sequence in the same fashion as a theme park ride, with no immediately visible cuts throughout the lengthy pull-back. In order to create the titles, a medical illustrator was employed to concave the journey through Jack's cerebellum while Mack broke the ride into 'rooms', with hidden 'doors' to conceal movement from one to the next.

Then there are the comic-shock moments when Jack fights with himself in the basement car park. 'That was sort of a total afterthought,' notes the director. 'We knew we wanted a kind of Peter Sellers-*Dr Strangelove* battle at the end, and we wanted to heighten the absurdity. Originally, he gets the gun away and starts shooting at himself, but it was just too much money and too much work. So we thought, "What if Tyler really was scary at the end?" He needs to reach a point where he's saying, "Okay, if you're not going to go along with the programme, I can't make you – but if you're gonna get in the way, I will break your ankles and throw you down the stairs."'

In the dramatic final moments, when the grand plan of Tyler's Project Mayhem lays waste a dozen skyscrapers, the effects crew were once again challenged to match live action elements with multiple CGI constructs. Practical flash bulbs on the set illuminated Norton and Bonham Carter in time with digital explosions and layered footage of real scaled-down detonations; matched with virtual buildings, the demolition is dazzling. Although it's never exactly clear what city *Fight Club* is set in (there is anecdotal evidence that it's supposed to be Wilmington, Delaware, where the headquarters of several credit card companies are located), the collapsing blocks were all based on real buildings in Century City, close to the Fox studio lot; in fact, the skyscraper to the far left of the frame is the head office of 20th Century Fox, also seen in *Die Hard* (1988).

A less destructive scene comes in Jack's subconscious 'ice cave' where he encounters a penguin as his 'power animal' – something that Chuck Palahniuk copied from his personal experience of guided meditation. Created by Blue Sky Studios, this sequence also features a more indirect effect, with clouds of CG breath giving the impression of a cold environment. The breath effects were originally created for the finale of *Titanic*. In a very subtle connection to this moment, the production designers ensured that the character's wardrobe contained boxer shorts and ties with tiny penguins on them.

Some effects were of a more conventional nature, and two notable elements ended up on the cutting room floor. 'There was a prosthetic piece in the scene where Angel Face gets beaten up. You actually see his nose split and the skull underneath, then this kind of jelly-like bubble of blood gushes out like a volcano. We had to cut that, and I'm okay with that. The scene still makes people understand that things have gone horribly awry.' The second practical prosthetic was more complicated and eventually dropped in favour of a computer-assisted replacement; in the moment when Jack shoots himself in the mouth to kill Tyler, Fincher had used make-up effects expert Rob Bottin to create an animatronic replica of Edward Norton. Bottin, whose work includes *Seven* and the *Robocop* films, built a fully articulated head, but the director was unhappy with test footage. Instead, a multiple-camera rig filmed Norton as he was blasted with compressed air, and this footage was enhanced by BUF, one of the film's visual effects crews, once again using the photogrammetry technique.

Another practical effect that was later enhanced by computer comes in the 'Operation Latte Thunder' flashback, when the Space Monkeys blow up a piece of corporate art and trash a coffee shop. Because of difficulty with the physical location, there were concerns that the lightweight version of the rolling brass sphere would not perform as needed. As a real metal ball that size would have crashed straight through the concrete pavement, the hollow plastic prop was covered with a slightly larger CG duplicate in post-production, which allowed the effects crew to add tertiary effects and the impression of a much larger mass.

In his supporting role, rock star turned actor Meat Loaf cuts an imposing figure as Bob, the bodybuilder whose steroid addiction has turned him into a wobbly parody of his former self. 'Bob was a favourite character of mine from the book,'

Fincher recalls, and it was a chance viewing of an episode of *Behind the Music* on VH1 that inspired the director to offer the role to the singer. Meat Loaf impressed Fincher and Norton so much with his audition that 'we offered him the job right there.' To become Bob, with his trademark "bitch tits", the actor wore a multi-layered 'fat suit' made of burlap bags, each filled with birdseed, adding hundreds of pounds to Meat Loaf's frame. In addition, like the 5'3" Helena Bonham Carter, the actor had to wear eight-inch elevator shoes to make him bigger than Norton and Pitt.

Fincher had originally wanted to have make-up artist Rob Bottin create a prosthetic chest for the actor so that he could go topless in Bob's fist-fight with Jack, but costs meant that Meat Loaf simply kept his shirt on in the scene as shot. Art Linson remembers that '[Laura] Ziskin ... was concerned about the giant nipples on the giant breasts and wanted them removed from the fat suit, or at least not have them appear so erect. Fincher denied the request; the nipples remained vast and hard.' Allegedly, the Planet Hollywood franchise had asked to have the fat suit prop to display in one of their restaurants, but it was so soaked with sweat after production that Fincher feared it would violate too many health and safety codes. The director instead offered the restaurant the fake Bob corpse, on condition that guacamole be served out of its blown-off head ... but Planet Hollywood declined.

The Finch Mob also appear in force throughout *Fight Club*. Holt McCallany, the 'mechanic', was a former Fury 161 inmate in *Alien 3*; Christopher John Fields, the dry cleaner, was Detective Boyle in *The Game* and Rains in *Alien 3*; the valet driver was played by Owen Masterson, a pickpocket in *The Game*; Robert J Stephenson as the airport security officer was also a SWAT team cop in *Seven* and a CRS assassins in *The Game*, and Richmond Arquette, the intern who suggests Jack visit the support groups, was the delivery van driver in *Seven*. Other cameos include Jeff Cronenweth's sister Christie as the airline check-in attendant, visual effects supervisor Kevin Scott Mack as one of the doomed jet passengers in Jack's dream sequence and Ed Kowalczyk of group Live, as the waiter who serves Jack and Marla.

The gut-wrenching last act twist has become something of a Fincher trademark, and *Fight Club*'s reveal of Tyler's true nature is no exception. 'How could you possibly know?' he asks. 'We spent tons of money to get two different people to make sure that you wouldn't know. The point is not whether you're stupid or smart because you didn't see it coming, the point is that that's the realisation that this guy comes to. But if you trick people, it's an affront, and you really better be careful about what you're doing. I've had this argument with a couple of people we've shown the movie to. Like, "Fuck you man, this is like *The Game*, you're just looking for some way to dick with me." It's not about tricking you, it's a metaphor, it's not about a real guy who really blows up buildings, it's about a guy who's led to feel this might be the answer based on all the confusion and rage that he's feeling – and it's from that frustration and bottled rage that he creates Tyler.'

Palahniuk's book is a lean and spare work, with a first-person narrative that cries out to be spoken dialogue; small wonder then that Jim Uhls carried off a slick transition to script that holds the audience just as tightly at the novel. The Tyler and Jack duality is coolly threaded into the visual retelling, and Uhls' work in re-ordering Palahniuk's punchy sentences allows them to drop easily from Jack's mouth without appearing forcibly relocated.

For readers who have come via Fincher's movie, the number of noticeable cuts made in the novel is intriguing. Crucial among these is the all-important meeting between Jack and Tyler Durden; for the movie, the moment is etched into the montage of the hellish tedium of transcontinental air travel, loaded with meaning even as he first remarks, "Hey, we have the exact same briefcase." On the page, there's even more meaning to be read into things when the two men meet alone on a nudist beach, as Tyler builds a driftwood sculpture; it is the homoerotic charge that plays across the later fight scenes made manifest.

'I wanted to play with that, so people would be squirming, thinking, "Oh God, am I reading a queer novel? Oh God, I'm reading a queer novel!",' the author told *Flowers Wild*. 'Then they get to the end and they think, "Oh yeah, they're not queer, they're just insane. Yes!" There would be that huge rush of relief. I also wanted to play with the idea that we have all these buddy movies, where we're never supposed to broach the idea, "What is it that keeps Butch Cassidy and the Sundance Kid together for so many years?" We're never supposed to broach that aspect of those relationships, of what's innate in every buddy movie. Fincher just went crazy with it, ramping it up even more.'

The director noted that the beach would have been 'an uncomfortable place for an audience to meet characters' and concludes of *Fight Club*: '[It's] more of a self-love story, which is a product of our times, than a homosexual love story.' The airliner meeting works in the structure of the film by introducing Tyler, underlining Jack's morose worldview one more time, and giving the viewer a capsule of their characters and relationship-to-come in just a few lines.

We're also treated to an additional Tyler story in the novel, a spiky moment that adds another legend to his consumer terrorist background. From the movie, we learn about his culinary sabotage as a waiter, but the novel provides a flashback to a time when he is working a private dinner party at the home of a rich couple. The wife approaches, clutching a note she's discovered in her perfume cabinet that reads, in true Project Mayhem style, "I have passed an amount of urine into at least one of your many elegant fragrances." The scene ends with the distraught wife littering the bathroom with smashed perfume bottles, her hands bloody and stinging from the cut glass and spilled, stinking scents – Tyler's revenge for all those dead whales.

One of the most contentious *Fight Club* moments – and it's hard to isolate just one in a film that's top-heavy with them – is the stealing of the human fat from the liposuction clinic to make soap. Critics slammed the scene for its echoes of

Nazi atrocities, but for post-World War II generations the resonance of that sequence is firmly rooted in contemporary cosmetic surgery culture. In the novel, the fat comes from Marla's mother, as her so-called "collagen trust fund". Palahniuk explains Marla's desire for 'Paris Lips', and to that end she's been gleaning fat from her own mother's trips to the clinic for later collagen injections – the theory being that fat from a related donor will last longer.

Another element that brings a slightly different charge to a scene altered for the movie comes when Tyler gives Jack his chemical burn kiss; perhaps sowing the seed of Project Mayhem, as Jack struggles to deal with the pain of the lye burn, he remembers a visit to Ireland where he joined a group of locals in urinating on the Blarney Stone so many Americans come over just to kiss. Other changes are smaller – the target of Tyler's bomb is a museum, not a credit card agency; both Jack and Tyler fight their bosses before getting fired; and Jack is the one who alone performs the 'Human Sacrifice' routine on the hapless Raymond K Hessel.

But perhaps the most significant alteration from page to screen comes at the end. The film's literally explosive finale sees the office towers crashing down as Project Mayhem's ultimate mischief comes to fruition, even as Tyler Durden himself 'dies'. But this is a massive change from the conclusion of the novel, which ends with the bombs failing to go off – Jack blames the Space Monkeys for using untrustworthy paraffin in the explosive mixture – and Jack's capture by the authorities. Instead of Marla arriving in the custody of the Space Monkeys, she willingly comes to save Jack with a posse of people from the support group, but too late to stop him shooting himself. The last chapter of the *Fight Club* novel finds Jack in a mental institution, with the ghost of Tyler departed but the work of Project Mayhem still going on, in the hands of untold numbers of disciples around the nation. This fundamentally changes the end of the *Fight Club* narrative, as Tyler wins (or may win) in the movie, but loses (or may lose) in the book.

Fincher addresses the decision behind the change. 'Jim Uhls and I got to this point where we were sitting there saying, "Okay, why don't the bombs explode at the end?" "Well, because they would destroy all these great public buildings." I was like, "And why don't we wanna do this? They're credit card companies, right? So why don't we do it?" Originally we were going to have Ed and Helena in this van with the Space Monkeys, driving away while all the buildings collapse, but it was a little long. But I never thought the mental institution thing with Tyler worked. I always felt, and I said this to Chuck, that the book seemed to fall in love, totally in love, with Tyler Durden. It couldn't stand to let him go. I wanted people to love Tyler, but I also wanted them to be okay with his vanquishing.'

It's also worth noting that for all his anarchistic bent, in the film Tyler Durden never actually kills anyone. In the book, he coolly shoots dead the mayor's special envoy on recycling, who was compiling a list of Fight Clubs, at a murder mystery party, while the only on-screen killing in the movie is by a police officer.

CUTS AND CHANGES

Jack's visit to the 'Partners in Passivity' support group featured extra moments where terminal cancer victim Chloe makes a pass at him, and he remarks (in a line from the novel) that she 'looks like a pirate'.

An element shot but cut from the support groups montage showed Marla crying in Bob's arms, much to Jack's chagrin. Another shot cut from this sequence, where Jack thinks of Marla as he lies in bed, would have shown him trying – and failing – to masturbate.

The airport scene where Jack is forced to wait for his vibrating suitcase to be cleared by the bomb squad was longer, with the clerk informing him it has been accidentally destroyed (explaining why he has no luggage when he returns to his apartment). The clerk also makes a quip about 'Air Mattresses', a derogatory industry slang nickname for airline flight attendants. A moment storyboarded but never shot would have shown a cut away to the case exploding on the airport tarmac.

The bathroom scene where Tyler and Jack discuss their fathers was a last-minute re-shoot, filmed in an afternoon on the Paper Street house set at the studio, the day before the scenery was dismantled. Fincher's first version of the scene was shot on location in the house's back garden, with the two men drinking beer on a rusted set of swings, but the director was unhappy with the finished sequence.

An element that was considered but never shot would have shown the immediate after-effect of the gas explosion in Jack's apartment, with his 'nice, neat, flaming little shit' flying through the air and landing in the trees; for cost reasons, the production used the cheaper alternative of just showing the resulting wreckage.

In the novel, Jack is dogged by the doorman at his apartment as he walks to the telephone booth after arriving home, the doorman making vague, threatening comments about Jack's collusion in the gas blast; a similar scene was shot but discarded in favour of the different version used in the final cut.

Marla's comment on Tyler's lovemaking – 'I haven't been fucked like that since grade school' – was originally written as 'I want to have your abortion,' and, despite earning laughs at preview screenings, Fox's Laura Ziskin demanded a less objectionable replacement. Fincher agreed on condition that the replacement line be the final change. However, when the 'grade school' line was inserted, Ziskin was even more concerned and tried without success to convince Fincher to put the 'abortion' line back in. The re-shoot of the line took place inside the rectory of a church, with the cast and crew crowded amid various items of religious paraphernalia.

The office scene where Jack's boss Chesler reprimands him about abusing the photocopier was edited differently, with a slightly darker tone as Jack makes his oblique threats; but post-Columbine, the dark take on the scene suddenly lost all humour and was dropped.

After evaluation by members of the Los Angeles Police Department's bomb squad, Tyler's practical lesson in how to manufacture homemade plastic explosives was carefully altered – but not too much – "in the interest of public safety", so that moviegoers could not copy the recipe. Fincher noted, 'It's out there anyway. It's in *The Anarchist's Cookbook*. It can be found.'

The boardroom presentation scene was longer in earlier versions, featuring a slightly different narration from Jack without the comments about 'swallowing a pint of blood'. The moment where he shows his bloody teeth to the camera was an out-take in which Fincher had asked Norton to show him his make-up, and the director left it in.

Two scenes that appeared either side of Jack's self-mutilation in Chesler's office were cut when that sequence was moved in editing. In the first, as Jack leaves for work, he discovers Tyler has quit smoking and then considers how Durden has now quit all his night jobs in order to make soap. After the scene in Chesler's office, the second missing moment comes as a happy Jack returns to the house with a shopping cart full of computer gear. He starts to tell Tyler that he's quit his job and has extorted money from the company, but Tyler cuts him off with the line, 'We have to take Fight Club up a notch or shut it down for good.'

An early draft of the script had Jack joining Bob and the Space Monkeys for 'Operation Latte Thunder', rather than showing it in flashback; this draft also made less of Bob's death, without the 'His name is Robert Paulson' chant.

The UK release of the film lost four seconds at the demand of the British Board of Film Censors, in moments where Lou punches Tyler in the basement and where Jack pummels Angel Face over and over. The BBFC's director, Robin Duval, considered these scenes to feature 'an indulgence in the excitement of beating a defenceless man's face into a pulp. The board required that cuts be made in each case.' In fact, the beating of Angel Face had already been altered from an earlier cut, which dwelt more on the assault instead of cutting away to the men watching the fight. Ironically, the cut version is nastier, as it leaves more to the imagination of the viewer.

Jack's conversation with Marla in the café was re-shot later in production to alter some elements of Norton's performance, which both the actor and director felt were too whiny and ingratiating for the character.

Fincher edited together a version of the scene where Tyler gives his farewell speech ('Feel better, champ') to the sleepy Jack, but later decided to use a series of fades instead of simple cuts; the version used in the final cut of the film lends the scene a more dreamy and unreal quality.

AFTERMATH

When the finished movie premiered at the Venice Film Festival in 1999 it incited harsh commentary that left the director reeling at the press conference, held the following day at the Excelsior Hotel. 'That Venice screening ... I was ready to take my own life after that,' he recalls wearily. 'I never thought that we'd be carried out on their shoulders, [but] it was too serious an environment [for the film].' Brad Pitt, who was also on the panel, described the experience thus: 'We were on the firing squad.' Fincher memorably dealt with one German reporter who ranted about the movie with the sarcastic reply, 'You're absolutely right, and I'm sorry.' Jeff Cronenweth jokes that Fincher preferred to wander around the city than face the press again, feeling that it would be a better use of his time to photograph Venice with a digital camera, 'so that long after it sank, he could shoot a movie there.'

The film's mediocre opening weekend was blamed by many on a marketing campaign that Art Linson called 'ill-conceived' and 'one-dimensional', that 'only sold the titillation of young guys beating the shit out of each other without letting the audience know of the much smarter and wittier ironic purpose to the whole journey.' Fincher, who has always had issues with the marketing of his movies, attempted to take the Project Mayhem ethos into the ads for *Fight Club* by having Pitt and Norton record two seditious Public Service Announcements in character as Tyler and Jack. 'I wanted to set the stage for the idea of disseminating misinformation, and I knew there was gonna be enough misinformation about this movie without any help from me.'

Fight Club was released in the wake of *Godzilla*, which used a marketing campaign based around the size of the monster – poster panels read "His Foot is as Big as This Bus", for example – and one lost bit of *Fight Club* marketing spoofed the Sony Pictures campaign with an ad that claimed Tyler Durden's penis was "as Big as This Billboard". Box-office takes increased in markets outside the USA, but it wasn't until the DVD release – complete with a new marketing campaign – that the film achieved the cult status it deserved, becoming one of the best-selling Fox discs to date.

On its original theatrical run, *Fight Club* earned over $107 million for 20th Century Fox at box-offices around the world, opening with an $11 million hit against two strong entries in the horror genre, *Stigmata* and *Stir of Echoes*, both of which rode the wave of interest generated earlier in the year by *The Sixth Sense*. The film also found itself up against *American Beauty*, a movie that some observers considered to be an alternate view on many of the themes highlighted by *Fight Club*. Against stiff blockbuster competition like *The Matrix* and *Star Wars Episode 1: The Phantom Menace*, the film nevertheless made an indelible impact on 1999's moviegoing public and polarised the critical community for and against David Fincher – yet again.

The director had irritated fans when he broke the mould of the *Alien* saga, pushed audiences with their own attraction-repulsion in *Seven* and played with their heads in *The Game*. Now *Fight Club* brought all that together and the critics lined up either to lionise or pillory him.

Roger Ebert of the *Chicago Sun Times* called it 'the most frankly and cheerfully fascist big-star movie since *Death Wish*', going on to bandy phrases like 'macho porn' and 'numbing', and Kenneth Turan of the *Los Angeles Times* once more tore into a Fincher movie, describing *Fight Club* as 'a witless mishmash of whiny, infantile philosophising and bone-crunching violence'. Alternatively, *New York Times* critic Janet Maslin, who had condemned *The Game*, felt that the director 'for the first time finds subject matter audacious enough to suit his lightning-fast visual sophistication, and puts that style to stunningly effective use.' Ed Gonzalez of *Slant Magazine* spoke of the film as '... a mind-bending, nihilistic experience that, like Herman Hesse's brilliant novella *Damien*, explores the dialectical grey between the id and the super-ego.' Others were more to the point, like *BBCi*'s Almar Haflidason, who simply said, '*Fight Club* rocks.'

Coming in the wake of 1999's schoolyard shootings at Columbine and elsewhere, *Fight Club* was accused, along with films like *The Matrix*, of promoting violence. In the *Hollywood Reporter*, Anita M Busch declared Fincher to be 'socially irresponsible' and suggested that the film should 'become Washington's poster child for what's wrong with Hollywood.' 20th Century Fox found Busch's comments so objectionable that they withdrew their advertising from the *Reporter* in protest. Fincher noted at the time, 'Making movies is a crapshoot. This movie was written five years ago. Nobody saw Columbine coming, nobody saw any of that shit happening. Nobody knew there would be a new shooting every three weeks in the United States. To say that because we have Columbine then we have to be very careful about the ideas we put out there is inane, ludicrous. I think we have to be responsible for ideas that we present in a prurient or a glamorised way, but I don't think that the violence in this movie is portrayed in a glamorous way. I think the anarchic elements of it are properly dealt with and put in their moral place.'

The arguments lined up against Kubrick's *A Clockwork Orange* (1971) were called out of retirement and re-applied. 'This dangerous Hollywood head-trip could inspire similar machismo among distraught males convinced they have nothing to lose,' said Bob Smithouser of *Focus on the Family*. 'That's just rhetoric from the unimaginative,' said the director. 'I did not think people would be as offended as they turned out to be with the movie.'

He describes overhearing the comments of two women who work for CAA – the agency that represents Fincher – leaving an advance screening: they were 'going off saying, "This shouldn't have been made, who do these people think they are? This is socially irresponsible, this is exactly what's wrong." It reminded me of the moment in *The Rocky Horror Picture Show* when Susan Sarandon is looking at the monster and says, "Too many muscles." Tim Curry turns to her and says "We didn't make it for *you*." [But] after the initial onslaught of derogatory comments about how offended they were, I could just not give a fuck. I've gone beyond it pretty quickly. People say this movie advocates violence, but did *M*A*S*H* advocate alcoholism? That's how the characters in that movie dealt with their circumstances in Korea. And this is how the characters in this movie deal with their circumstances. This isn't *A Clockwork Orange*, it was never intended to be. It's a fairy tale, a coming-of-age story about choosing a path to maturity.'

Fincher was again attacked for his handling of female roles. 'I like working with women and like working with men,' Fincher protests. 'It never has been an issue for me. *Fight Club* was something that I related to as a man; on a masculine, 1999-era level, it was something that I really understood. I understood the anger behind it and I understood the frustration behind it, but it wasn't like I was getting even with women.'

'I always saw the violence in this movie as a metaphor for drug use,' said Fincher. 'What you're trying to show in [Jack] is that he has a need. There's sensuality to this need and there's sensuality in this need being fulfilled. So maybe that's wrong, but the only way to help is to talk about it. The violence gives him the pain he feels. You're talking about a character that's ostensibly dead. You're talking about a guy who's been completely numb. And he finally feels something and he becomes addicted to that feeling. He has a need to feel, and that need is fulfilled by the Fight Club, so there's a kind of parallel in a weird way to people who disappear into drugs.'

The drug culture parallel also appears in what the director calls 'The secret society, the people who congregate there, the lingo, the code and all that stuff. The drug metaphor I felt was clearly obvious, but I never thought the violence was glamorised. I think there's much more glamorisation of violence in the kinetics of chaos and the ballet of chaos in *The Matrix* then there is in this film – but it didn't offend me in *The Matrix*. I thought *Raging Bull* was beautiful and I know it was talking about something that was ugly, but I thought that the way it made that ugliness fascinating was by making it beautiful.'

For his part, Edward Norton asked: 'Is it any darker than *Dr Strangelove*? There's more carnage in *End of Days* than there is in *Fight Club*.' But even before the film was finished, it was coming under fire from commentators and even Fox employees; one extra, who appeared in the 'Remaining Men Together' support group scene, was so incensed by what he considered a sick joke about cancer sufferers that he walked out and refused to accept his wages – but later returned to demand full Screen Actor's Guild pay. Others found *Fight Club* inspirational, including fashion designer Donatella Versace, who based a Fall Collection on Tyler's outlandish thrift-shop outfits and Project Mayhem sensibilities; a less well-reasoned idea for a product based on the film – a *Fight Club* beat-em-up video game – was nixed early on by an incredulous Fincher, and no one dared consider the sales potential of Paper Street brand soap bars...

In the critical community, those who loved the film lined up not only to laud it, but also to scorn their counterparts. 'How good is *Fight Club*?' asked *Rolling Stone*'s Peter Travers. 'It's so fired up with explosive ideas and killing humour that the guardians of morality are yelling *Danger – Keep Out*!' At *Reel.com*, Jim Emerson said: 'Those who felt less enthusiastic about the picture didn't just dislike it – they loathed it, reviled it, demonised it.'

But rather than shy away from the negativity showered on the movie, Fincher subverted the vitriol of the critics and made it part of the appeal; the special edition of *Fight Club*'s DVD release reprints the sharpest barbs, including Alexander Walker's notable comment from the *London Evening Standard*: 'It is an inadmissible assault on personal decency.' Walker also compared the movie to Nazi propaganda and said: 'this film is anti-capitalist, anti-society, and indeed, anti-God.' Fincher replied: 'I'd like to put that on a one-sheet. I would! I'd go see that movie in a heartbeat.', and added: 'There's a bizarre Puritanism that you find in the strangest places.'

Indeed, when the film made its premiere on British network television, BBC2 followed Fincher's advice and boldly ran the negative comments in their promotional trailers. 'I don't know if *Fight Club* is anti-God,' the director said. 'These [critics] are so sad, I think there's really only a handful of people who mean anything in that business. I don't know why [Walker] had such a bug up his ass, but I'm glad that the movie affected people in that way. I think a lot of people took it a little *too* seriously and I think a lot of that had to do with the way that it was promoted. I do think that this movie, promoted as a lark, is something that would freak people out, because it's not. If you make something that is talking about things that make you feel uncomfortable, like the notion of disenfranchised men creating vats of nitroglycerine in their houses and wanting to destroy public buildings, those are things that, even pre-9/11, made people uncomfortable, just the notion that there are certainly enough Dylan Klebolds and Timothy McVeighs out there.

'That's what Chuck Palahniuk was talking about, and sometimes to be properly satirical you need to exaggerate grossly and I think that's what the book did. There are people who are uncomfortable with the notion of even speaking those things out loud, there are people who are uncomfortable in movies when they see even the most tame inference to homosexuality, and it's going to make them feel like they're seeing a recruiting film. I don't see the movie as a condemnation of capitalism, although I'm perfectly comfortable condemning capitalism myself. But I do think it's a definite condemnation of the lifestyle seekers, the lifestyle sellers and the lifestyle packagers. People misread a lot of what happened in *Fight Club* as some sort of anarchist recruiting film, and really, I don't think the movie really promotes any specific answers, it just says, "This is a frustration and it's part of the maturation of the male creature." Fuck them if they can't take a joke. *Fight Club* is what it is, you're either in on it, or you're not gonna buy it.'

Brad Pitt saw the negative reaction to the film as symptomatic of critics unable to accept *Fight Club*'s intention. 'It attacks a status quo that these men have given 40 years of their lives to.' The actor, like so many people involved in the production, was willing to stand by the quality of his work, and critics be damned. 'This was one of the first times I did not care what anyone thought – it was just dead on.'

Fight Club would – and still does – divide critics, but while it never earned the accolades of its tamer box-office neighbours, the film still pulled in a number of awards. The unmissable technical expertise earned it an Oscar nomination for Best Sound Effects Editing and a Golden Reel nomination from the Motion Picture Sound Editors of America; the Blockbuster Entertainment Awards gave Pitt and Norton the Favourite Action Team category, while Bonham Carter took *Empire's* Best British Actress. Norton also scored with the MTV Movie Awards for Best Fight, for beating himself up at the film's climax. The movie even garnered a nomination from the American Political Film Society, but did not win.

As with *The Game*, despite the fact that *Fight Club's* twist ending makes it a one-joke story, the film continues to yield up new discoveries to viewers who return to it. In the car park outside Lou's Tavern when Tyler and Jack have their first punch-up, for example, *Fight Club* refers to Fincher's previous film with a sight gag – Jack bounces off a brown station wagon during his fight with Tyler, the same car driven by the Jim Feingold character in *The Game*, with its CRS parking permit still visible on the windscreen. It isn't difficult to imagine that Jack and Tyler's world might also be Nicholas Van Orton's; but rather than being a clever bit of self-reference, the appearance of the car was actually an ironic coincidence that was as much of a surprise to the director.

Perhaps as a nod towards his work in commercials, Fincher parodies Ridley Scott's famous 1984 advert for Apple when the Space Monkeys blow up a set of Macintosh Computers. The scene takes place 84 minutes into the movie and Fincher ensured that the ticking digital timer on the bomb at the movie's end is actually showing the correct time until detonation. Another visual joke, which plays with the movie/reality breach that runs all through the film, comes when Jack forces Marla onto a bus to escape – on the street nearby are cinema hoardings advertising *The People Vs Larry Flynt*, *Seven Years in Tibet* and *The Wings of the Dove*, movies starring Norton, Pitt and Bonham Carter respectively. Although it's not very clear in the final shot, as the bus pulls away a group of men stand up to surround Marla – the Space Monkeys sent to capture her; this scene also made an impact on Edward Norton, who was hit by the bus in one failed take.

As well as less direct references to films like *Blade Runner*, *The Graduate* (1967) and *American Graffiti*, there are subtle in-jokes like Jack's procession of false names at the support groups, each one the name of a movie role played by Robert DeNiro in the 1970s or a character from *Planet of the Apes*. Norton's friend Drew Barrymore is glimpsed on the cover of a movie magazine and even *Star Trek* is obliquely referred to when Jack suggests he'd like to fight William Shatner – a layered gag when you consider that Shatner as Captain Kirk once found himself fighting a violent doppelgänger in the television series episode 'The Enemy Within'.

Although they're not obvious on your first pass through the film, *Fight Club* is staged very carefully with small 'tells' about the relationship between Jack and Tyler. 'We had tons of little rules about Tyler,' notes Fincher. 'Tyler is not seen in a two-shot within a group of people. We don't play it over the shoulder when Tyler gives

Jack an idea about something that's very specific, that's going to lead him, it's always Tyler by himself. There's five or six shots in the first two reels of Tyler, where he appears in one frame, waiting for Edward Norton's character. When the doctor says to him, "You wanna see pain, swing by First Methodist Tuesday night and see the guys with testicular cancer, that's pain," and, *boop*, Brad appears over the guy's shoulder for one frame. We shot him in the environment with the people, and then we matted him in, so that Tyler literally appears like his spliced-in penis shot, just *dink, dink*. We did a lot of that stuff.'

Fincher jokes that these are 'DVD moments', while Richard Bailey nicknamed them 'the most expensive piece of dirt on the film ever'. Another example comes during a close-up on a TV screen. 'That little promotional Marriott Hotel television loop, when they're showing all their banquet facilities, there's this shot of all these waiters going "Welcome" and Brad's in the middle of those waiters.' Sharp-eyed viewers will also notice moments such as the change in seating between Tyler and Jack before and after the car crash, all telegraphing the character's inter-relationship. Fincher felt that it was important to maintain the conceit that *Fight Club* is a film happening in a world where Tyler Durden is a real person, letting the character warp in and out of the 'reel' world; one notable example comes when Tyler's speech in the basement is delivered with such force that it seems to distort the very film strip out of its sprockets.

The final, two-frame shot of a penis just before the end credits also serves to warn us that it's Tyler up there in the projection booth, feeding us this film. 'There was, if you'll pardon the phrase, a bone of contention about that,' jokes Fincher. 'That was our way of saying, not that it isn't over, just that the spirit of Tyler Durden is kind of still out there. Tyler Durden is alive and well and in the theatre while you're actually watching this movie.' Both Fincher and Palahniuk had jobs as projectionists in high school, but they deny splicing frames of porn into any movies that *they* handled. The scene also explains the 'cigarette burns' that mark the change-over for film reels, and Jeff Cronenweth noted that he was always afraid a real projectionist would mistake them for the real thing, and cut off the end of *Fight Club*'s second reel.

The director kept up the 'Tyler Lives On' theme with the DVD release of *Fight Club*, substituting the usual FBI copyright warning with a Project Mayhem version that demands you 'Get out of your apartment. Meet a member of the opposite sex. Stop the excessive shopping and masturbation. Quit your job. Start a fight. Prove you're alive.' Fincher also wanted to tamper with the 20th Century Fox and Regency Pictures logos that open the film, but both companies refused to have them 'Tylerised'.

Fight Club is a virus. It's not a film you can just *watch*; it's a contagious set of ideas sheathed in blacker-than-black comedy, a set of extremes that you will love or you will hate. And either way, it will make you feel *something*. Fincher said before and after *Fight Club* that marketing has always been a concern of his, and it isn't hard to imagine the shock on the faces of Fox's advertising staff as the director handed them this movie, coiled like an angry cobra inside the film can.

I almost missed *Fight Club* myself for this reason. The book had shot past my radar, and the trailers I saw didn't make my interest needles twitch. Brad Pitt? Something about bare-knuckle boxing and soap? If I wanted to see guys beating seven bells out of one another, I was just going to watch *Raging Bull* again. But like Tyler's Fight Club, like his Project Mayhem, the movie snuck up on me. A friend called me and said, 'Go and see it. Don't ask why, just go.' But what's so good about it? Without a trace of glibness or artifice, he replied, 'The first rule of Fight Club is, you do not talk about Fight Club.'

And he was right. The film's matter became its own marketing, a subversive meme spreading from like-mind to like-mind. Tyler's cardinal rule applies just as much to the movie in the real world as it does to the reality in the 'reel' world. To explain the plot of the film robs it of its power – the viewer must come to the movie as uninformed as possible to best experience Jack's odyssey. I came to *Fight Club* expecting to see a few good punch-ups and came out the other end punch-drunk. It's fierce, it's sharp, and it's a *trip*.

There seems to be no middle ground with this film. Fincher's work prior to *Fight Club* divided his audience into camps of pro and con, but with *Fight Club* rant or rave are apparently the only two responses. Jack's wasted life, his emasculated nowhere existence, speaks to an entire generation, and not just to men. But it also alienates another through its disturbing imagery and the questions it raises. Some people will only ever look at this movie and see the violence, the nihilism and the self-absorbed revenge fantasy. Others can navigate past this and pick up on the subtexts lurking beneath, on what *Fight Club* really has to say about life at the end of the Millennium.

We can equate the film's viewers with three characters from it. There are the Jacks, who see the seductive in the destructive but ultimately look beyond it to the real path forward. Then there are the Tylers, in love with the thrill of chaos but nothing more. And lastly there are the Richard Cheslers, who can't connect in any way with the messages the movie has to offer. It sounds facile and trite but, as Fincher notes above, you either get *Fight Club* or you don't. If it doesn't speak to you, then it was never meant to. In the end, this is a movie about metaphor, about connection to what is real in your life and understanding what isn't. It is, as Tyler Durden tells Jack, an experience where 'You choose your own level of involvement.'

SIX

House Arrest

'You can't overcome chaos.'

AFTER THE RADICAL *Fight Club*, any film that followed would have seemed conventional. But Fincher's next choice of project was deliberately chosen by him as a return to the thriller territory he had mapped out in *The Game*. And, despite its outward appearance as a simple locked-room narrative, the director's visual flourishes and his eye for mood made *Panic Room* a cut above the ordinary.

In this concise, totally constructed setting, Fincher hoped to apply the full range of his creative and technical expertise to a film environment that was completely under his control. Starting with intensive pre-production design and computer-assisted planning for scenes and shots, Fincher's scheme for *Panic Room* was to build a picture that would be uncomplicated and easy to film. But the director would discover that the best-laid plans could not match the random misfortunes that would plague the set almost from the start of filming.

In this, his fifth studio feature film, Fincher created a highly charged thriller set during a single night in a New York townhouse. On this stage, a mother and daughter confront three criminals intent on looting the house's hidden safe, turning a home invasion into a complex game of hunter and hunted. On the surface, *Panic Room* appears to be the most conformist of the director's works to date, but lurking below it is the trademark Fincher tone – brooding, dark and intimidating.

PANIC ROOM

Columbia Pictures Corporation, Indelible Films
Director: *David Fincher*
Writer: *David Koepp*
Cast: *Jodie Foster (Meg Altman), Kristen Stewart (Sarah Altman), Forest Whitaker (Burnham), Dwight Yoakam (Raoul), Jared Leto (Junior), Patrick Bauchau (Stephen Altman), Ann Magnuson (Lydia Lynch), Ian Buchanan*

(Evan Kurlander), Andrew Kevin Walker (sleepy neighbour), Paul Schulze (Officer Keeney), Mel Rodriguez (Officer Morales), Richard Conant (SWAT cop), Paul Simon (SWAT cop), Victor Thrash (SWAT cop), Ken Turner (SWAT cop).

Crew: *Ceán Chaffin (producer), John S. Dorsey (associate producer), Judy Hofflund (producer), David Koepp (producer), Gavin Polone (producer), Howard Shore (music), Conrad W Hall & Darius Khondji (cinematography), James Haygood & Angus Wall (editing), Arthur Max (production design), Keith Neely & James E Tocci (art direction), Michael Kaplan (costume design), Joseph Viskocil (special effects supervisor), Nicolas Bonnell (visual effects producer: BUF), Raymond Gieringer (visual effects supervisor: Toybox).*

Tagline: *'It was supposed to be the safest room in the house.'*

SYNOPSIS

Newly divorced single mother Meg Altman and her daughter Sarah are searching for a new home in New York City, and by chance they manage to view an elegant townhouse new to the market. The former home of a rich industrialist who recently died, the five-storey house is perfect for the Altmans – and among its amenities is a unique feature called a panic room. A hi-tech bolt-hole designed to protect householders from home invasion, the panic room is an impregnable safe haven with food supplies, air, an independent telephone line and a bank of surveillance monitors that cover the house; and with an automated hydraulic door made of thick steel, anyone inside is effectively invulnerable to assault. But, with Meg's fear of confined spaces, she takes an instant dislike to the room.

Despite Meg's misgivings, mother and daughter move into the house and, as night falls, they share a moment of connection over Meg's divorce ordeal. After putting Sarah to bed, Meg tries and fails to shut down the panic room's systems, resolving to deal with it in the morning.

Later that night, as Meg sleeps fitfully, two men – Burnham and Junior – approach the house. Burnham knows the layout of the building and quickly breaks in, but he's shocked to discover that the vacant house now has two residents. As he argues with Junior over their plan to unlock a hidden safe, a third burglar arrives, a dangerous thug named Raoul. At first, Burnham wants to abort their scheme to get to the former owner's secret fortune, but Junior reminds him of his own desperate circumstances – a difficult divorce – and Burnham reluctantly agrees to proceed.

Meanwhile, Meg awakens to discover the trio of burglars and races to rouse Sarah; the men chase them around the house until they escape into the temporary respite of the panic room. Over the public address system, Meg orders them to leave, threatening them with the imminent arrival of the police – despite the fact that the panic room's phone line has yet to be connected. Burnham, who works for the house's security company, knows she is bluffing, and Junior ominously tells the Altmans that "what we want is in that room." With Meg and Sarah unwilling to leave the panic room, Burnham sets about locking them all into the house, while Raoul and Junior try – and fail – to break into the room with a sledgehammer.

In order to flush out the women, Burnham taps the panic room's ventilation duct and uses a propane gas canister to foul the air; but Raoul and Junior favour a quicker approach and turn up the gas to maximum, choking Meg and Sarah. With only moments to go before they suffocate, Meg uses a fire-lighter to ignite the gas, blowing up the canister and severely burning Junior in the process.

As Raoul and Junior argue over the plan and Burnham's unwillingness to injure the women, Sarah uses a torch to shine through the air vent and into a sleepy neighbour's window, sending an SOS message – but the mayday goes ignored. While the criminals argue, Meg ducks out of the panic room and returns with her cellphone, just seconds from being caught. However, the phone can't pick up a signal inside the concrete vault of the panic room; instead, Meg pulls the main telephone cables from the wall and hooks up the inert panic room handset. Her emergency call to the police is fruitless, but she manages to reach her husband Stephen just seconds before the burglars cut her off. And, to make matters worse, Sarah's blood-sugar level is falling, a potentially fatal problem for the diabetic girl.

Junior decides to quit the house and give up on the break-in, but not before inadvertently revealing that the safe in the panic room contains not just $3 million but at least five times that amount. Rather than let him go and chance police intervention, Raoul shocks Burnham by killing Junior in cold blood. Moments later, Stephen Altman arrives to investigate Meg's phone call. Raoul threatens both men with his gun, and orders Burnham to come up with a plan to get the woman out of the room. To Meg and Sarah's horror, Raoul brings Stephen to the door of the panic room and savagely beats him, threatening to kill him unless they come out. Burnham blocks off the camera outside the panic room, but Meg's attention is elsewhere as Sarah has a sudden seizure – her blood-sugar level is now so low she's bordering on a coma. Without a vital injection, Sarah will die.

On the monitors, Meg sees Burnham dragging an unconscious Raoul downstairs, leaving Stephen in the bedroom. Meg takes the opportunity to leave the panic room to recover Sarah's medicine. But Raoul, who has actually switched places with Stephen, enters the panic room with Burnham, shutting Meg out – but not before she throws the medical kit in after them. Trapped outside, Meg has Raoul's pistol but no way to save Sarah's life. Raoul, meanwhile, has his hand caught in the door mechanism but Burnham refuses to open it while Meg is close by. Burnham agrees to give Sarah her injection if Meg goes downstairs, and she complies. On the lower floor, Meg gives Stephen the gun and waits. As Burnham starts work on opening the safe, Raoul threatens to kill Sarah if any police enter the house.

But Stephen has already called them, and Meg is forced to lie to two police officers who ask to check out the house; despite the questioning of one suspicious beat cop, Meg gets them to leave, realising that is up to her to deal with the invaders. She knocks out the security cameras, blinding the monitors, and sets up an exit route for the criminals. Inside the panic room, Burnham cracks the safe to discover $22 million in bonds. Leaving the room with Sarah as a hostage, Burnham and Raoul unwittingly follow the path through the house that Meg has planned for them, leading them into an ambush.

Meg attacks Raoul and Burnham takes the opportunity to escape as police sirens approach, but the vicious Raoul turns the tables on the Altmans and hits back, disarming Stephen, punching Sarah and beating Meg. Raising the sledgehammer to kill Meg, Raoul is shot dead by Burnham – unable to leave the Altmans to their deaths, Burnham has risked his freedom to return and dispatch the murderer. Meg, Sarah and Stephen are safe, at last. As the police burst in, Burnham runs. He is captured, however, and the wind catches the bonds, scattering them into the air.

Later, a new day finds Meg and Sarah alone in Central Park, poring over the classified advertisements in search of a new home...

DEVELOPMENT

With *Fight Club*, David Fincher affirmed his credentials as one of the most outstanding directors of the 1990s, but the film's involved shooting and composition left him with a desire to take on something different for his next project, something more straightforward. His fifth picture would be *Panic Room*, a drama with a small cast set in a single location, scripted by writer-producer David Koepp. 'I liked the discipline of it, the limitations,' Fincher noted, 'I thought there was something scary about it; that it'd really be something to tackle. I wanted to make what Francis Ford Coppola called "a composed movie" ... After *Fight Club*, which had nearly 400 scenes and almost 100 locations, the idea of doing an entire story inside one house appealed to me.'

The director recalls his original thoughts on the project: 'I thought it would be a fun movie to make, and I was wrong. *Panic Room* was a bit of a Rubik's Cube. I never would have thought it would end up being as complicated as it was. It's supposed to be a popcorn movie, there are no great, overriding implications, it's just about survival. Unlike *The Game*, where we had a very difficult story that we tried to tell in a simple fashion, *Panic Room* was a very simple story that we chose to tell in the most difficult fashion.' Unforeseen changes in cast and crew, problems with footage, faulty equipment, power failures and even flooding later led Fincher to comment, '[This] movie was cursed.'

The script was inspired by Koepp's interest in real-life panic rooms, the modern-day equivalent of medieval 'priest holes' and castle keeps. In the early 2000s, the dangers of home invasion – both real and perceived – remain a growing concern for the urban populace, and the development of these safe havens for the wealthy in New York City caught Koepp's eye. The writer-director of movies like *Stir of Echoes* and *The Trigger Effect* (1996), David Koepp also worked on *Snake Eyes* (1998), *Mission: Impossible* (1996), *Spider-Man* (2002) and the first two *Jurassic Park* films (1993 and 1997). The *Panic Room* script sold to Sony Pictures for a reported $4 million in February 2000, briefly connecting with Ridley Scott as a possible director prior to Fincher's involvement.

'I got sent this piece of material from Josh Donen, who said, "This is a movie that you probably don't want to see, because as a director it's not got a lot going on, in terms of changing scenery ... however, as a director from the other side of it, it will be really difficult to make this interesting. It all takes place in one house, in one night." I read it and I liked the notion. I liked the idea of the [puzzle] of the house, that was attractive to me – the only production value you really had was the narrative tension – because it's always the same background, it's the same rooms over and over.'

Koepp would also be involved in the feature as a producer, teamed with Gavin Polone and Judy Hofflund, who had worked with him on *Stir of Echoes*. Fincher, meanwhile, brought a regular collaborator to the project in the form of Cean Chaffin, whose association with the director stretched back to his days in commercials and pop videos. A staff of key creatives was assembled as pre-production started in earnest, including Fincher veterans Darius Khondji as director of photography, production designer Arthur Max, costume designer Michael Kaplan and editors James Haygood and Angus Wall.

'I liked David Koepp's trip,' said Fincher. 'He has a sort of unique flair, he loves what audiences love about movies. He loves the inherent movie-ness of a movie, and he writes that stuff, he's completely unabashed about it. I read the script and I thought, "Nah..." Then I read it again and I thought, "Well, you know, if you could do something with the omniscience of this, that's not unlike the specific subjectivity of *Rear Window*." If you could take one step back, so you're presenting this [story] that all takes place in this one place, you're presenting it in such a way that you build this sort of dread through distance, as opposed to putting you in these people's shoes. It's like you're going to be telling the audience watching this: "You can't do anything about it, they can't hear you, you can't help them, as loud as you scream they're not gonna hear."

'I thought there was an interesting element of tension in that, and I liked the notion of making [something like this]. I'd never made a *movie* movie, I'd never made a "Friday night, let's go to a movie" movie. *The Game* wasn't that, it was never designed to be that and probably should have been that, but certainly *Fight Club*, *Seven* and *Alien 3* can't even count as that. I've never had to be in lock-step with the audience as you take them through the movie, I have always been able to play it as, "When they catch up, this is what we're going to do." And so I thought it was a good skill to hone and a good skill to see if I have, a good skill to develop.'

Fincher recalls his first principles in studying the script for *Panic Room*. 'I read a script, going, "A: Is it a movie I'd want to see? B: are there a lot of movies like it already out? C: and do I think I can do something with it?" That's my criteria. This movie's been a challenge for me because it's all in one night, all in one place. It's like the high-school play. It's like eight people and that's it, that's all you got.' He notes that the story was fully developed prior to his involvement. 'I mean, the script was finished when it came to me, let's not pretend I'm Ingmar Bergman here. I just like that it does what movies do best.' The lean and spare nature of *The Panic Room* (as it was originally called) appealed to him. 'It's a pretty terse script, there's not a lot there. The whole time, it was like, an hour-and-45-minute movie, that's what it's gotta be. It's got to feel like one night. Is it going to feel like that or is it going to feel like three nights? That was the key to making it.'

Fincher and Koepp, both creatives with a fine eye for detail, were in accord from the start, and the director cited the writer's exacting style. 'David's a real stickler for telling you what you need to know at the last possible minute. This is a *movie* movie, it's about what the expectations are about movies as much as our expectations about people. In that sense, it is a true genre picture, it exists to either deliver or subvert your expectations of what's going to happen in a given situation. It's a crime thriller, but it's also in the *Treasure of the Sierra Madre* vein. These people are going in to look for what they perceive as the quick solution to their problems. Money is never the quick solution to anyone's problems. It's just an object that everyone's after for the wrong reasons. It's a cinematic study in how you use or abuse the one setting for maximum effect. I was drawn to it because I loved the idea – They've gotta get in, they've gotta get in, now how are they going to get out? A simple reversal.'

Casting began in the summer of 2000, with one of the first roles – that of the thuggish Raoul – offered to singer Maynard James Keenan, whom Fincher had directed in the music video 'Judith' for the band A Perfect Circle. But Keenan's commitment as lead singer for the group Tool meant he could not accept. Instead, another vocal performer took the part, country music star Dwight Yoakam. The two female leads went to Nicole Kidman and the young Hayden Panettiere, with Forest Whitaker (who had already studied the *Panic Room* script before declining to direct it himself) and Jared Leto rounding out the trio of house-breakers. Kidman had briefly been interested in the role of Marla Singer in *Fight Club*, and Fincher saw her as the right choice for Megan Altman. 'When I first read the script I imagined it with Nicole Kidman. I talked to her, she said she'd do it and we put a cast together.'

Production got underway in October in New York and Los Angeles, starting with rehearsals for the cast prior to the January 2001 start-date for principal photography. But by the end of the year, child actress Hayden Panettiere was gone and a quick bout of re-casting took place to find a replacement. 'Nicole is a very glamorous actress, also very vulnerable, so we cast Kristen Stewart to complement that, to be her antithesis, tomboyish, androgynous, dismissive, a teenager at ten years old. It was about the daughter being a parent to her mother.' But events beyond the control of cast and crew would later cause this characterisation to shift when a second actor dropped out of the movie.

The pre-production of *Panic Room* allowed Fincher to utilise a lot of the technology and processes that he had grown into with *Fight Club*, including use of animated storyboarding, or pre-visualisation. Ron Frankel, the film's pre-vis supervisor, told *VFXPro*: 'It is a technical planning tool ... We'll come in using high end computer modelling and animation software, the same stuff they use to do final visual effects like *Shrek* and *Jurassic Park*. We're taking [it] and applying it to pre-production as a design tool. We'll build a model of the production environment, a 3D model of the set on the soundstage. This gives David access to a tool to essentially design this film way beyond what storyboards are capable of doing.

'He could take each of these movies and design it shot by shot, take the individual shots to his editor, they could edit the movie together, put it into sequence. He could evaluate whether the shots are working in sequence or not working in sequence, come back to me and say, "Throw out this shot, that shot and that shot. Let's change this one, tilt that one up a little bit, cut in on this one earlier," and then take it back to the editor. Before he even began filming, he had an edit of about two thirds of the film in his head and on videotape that everyone could watch to understand what it was he was seeing as he described each of these shots.'

Use of this system allowed the director to shave days off the duration of principal photography, enabling Fincher to evaluate and discard potential camera set-ups before actually committing any manpower or hardware. Prior to shooting the film, Fincher showed fellow director Steven Soderbergh the test footage and was rewarded with a dire warning. '[He said,] "You know, you've gone through all this trouble, and I guarantee you this will be your undoing. This will be the reason why none of this goes off the way you have it planned, because you have invested so much time and so much planning. Invariably, the gods frown on this notion." I was like, "Oh, you're such a pessimist. It doesn't always happen that way. " But of course he was right.'

PRODUCTION

With Kristen Stewart on board, *Panic Room*'s cast was set and shooting began early in 2001. But misfortune struck the project less than three weeks into production when Kidman injured herself. 'She was running up steps or down steps. She said, "Ouch!" We thought that maybe she had hyper-extended her knee or something like that,' Fincher noted. 'She started limping and my initial reaction was, "Oh, she wants to leave early." But then her doctor came in and shot some x-rays, and she had a hairline fracture of the bone beneath her knee joint.' The actress had suffered a knee injury while filming *Moulin Rouge!* in 2000, and the bone had not completely healed; it was severe enough that the actress was forced to leave the movie, and suddenly *Panic Room* was without a female lead.

Although filming briefly continued on scenes that didn't feature Meg, the production was effectively derailed. To make matters worse, at the same time the Writer's Guild of America and the Screen Actor's Guild were threatening industrial action over contractual disputes, making it imperative to find a replacement quickly before a possible strike could take effect. 'Nicole had to drop out; at that point I was totally prepared to not do the film, fold the set, send everybody home, thank you very much,' said Fincher. But Columbia Pictures had other ideas and quickly began scouting for a new actress.

Among the stars rumoured to be in the running were Sandra Bullock, Angelina Jolie and Robin Wright-Penn; but it would be Jodie Foster who would step into Kidman's shoes. 'After Nicole got hurt, I told the studio to shut it down and collect the insurance – they would have made a $3 million profit from it – but they wanted this movie, so I told them it would cost like $10 million more to shut down and gear back up. They wanted it, so we sent the script over to Jodie Foster and we met in the bar at the Four Seasons Hotel, and she agreed to do it.'

Foster had previously been occupied with her commitment to direct the movie *Flora Plum*, but that film had also been laid low thanks to an injury; lead actor Russell Crowe had hurt himself and pulled out of the project, leaving Foster free. 'Her movie had fallen apart while we were shooting with Nicole,' said Fincher. 'I called her and said I had a script she might be interested in.'

'My movie was shut down in August and *Panic Room* started in January,' Foster told *DFN*. 'At that point I figured I would jump into a movie as an actor, [but] I thought I wasn't going to find one. The writer's strike was looming, so I figured I would take some time off, I didn't want to jump into a movie that wasn't any good. I hope that Nicole is happy about this, because you hope somewhere out there that there is an understudy that will take over for you if something happens, otherwise the responsibility of the movie going down the drain is on your shoulders and the film would have gone away if I hadn't shown up before the strike.'

At the time, the actress-director had agreed to head the awards jury at the 2001 Cannes Film Festival – a gesture seen by some as an olive branch from the organisers to the Hollywood studios – but she stepped down as soon as she accepted the *Panic Room* lead. Reports later alleged that the Cannes jury were unhappy with Foster's decision and dropped her film *The Dangerous Lives of Altar Boys* from the festival as a result. Foster and Fincher had almost worked together on *The Game* (see Chapter Four), later discussing the script *Mank* (see Chapter Seven) as a project for them to collaborate on. 'We talked about another movie I wanted to do about Herman Mankiewicz, in which I wanted her to play [silent movie star] Marion Davies,' said Fincher; but now the chain of events surrounding *Panic Room* brought them together once more.

'We had a drink and discussed it,' the director told *Empire*. 'I said, "I think you ought to know we started shooting with Nicole Kidman." She said, "Okay, but there's certain things I can do and certain things I can't. I don't think I can play this kind of lost trophy wife." I said, "I don't think you can, either." Nicole Kidman makes you make a different movie, it's like Hitchcock casting Grace Kelly, it's about glamour and physicality. With Jodie Foster, it's more political. Jodie is someone who has spent 35 years making choices that define her as a woman and define women in film. Jodie Foster is nobody's pet. It became very distinct with Jodie, and the relationship with Kristen changed. It became about how they were similar, how they bottled their emotions and found a way to deal with each other's frailty.'

Signing for a reported fee of $12 million, the actress had just over a week to prepare for the role of Meg Altman before *Panic Room*'s production resumed, and Fincher found he had to alter his direction of certain scenes in order to accommodate the new lead. 'There were a lot of things that I wouldn't think I would need to change that I did. We were working on two different sets basically, the panic room and the main floor. You have all the physical stuff that has to happen pretty well set, but when we shot things with Jodie that we had already shot with Nicole, I found a different vibe, not just in what they have to say. Certain lines did have to be rewritten.' Fincher draws attention to the scene where Meg and Sarah share a pizza: 'The scene was already shot with Nicole, [but] when we went to recreate it with Jodie, it just didn't work, it was weird – so we had them switch sides and do different things. People just carry different vibes with them.

'In my opinion, Jodie Foster can play anything,' Fincher adds, 'but *helpless* is asking a lot of the audience to believe, because she just isn't. The character was originally written more helpless.' Foster herself felt the strengthening of her role helped the narrative. 'The somewhat stronger character, in the beginning, decides that she's going back to school. She's spent the last 15 years with a rich older guy who squashed her identity so she's going back to Manhattan. She also feels guilty for dragging her kid out of the suburbs where she had a yard and friends, so she buys a big house her ex-husband will pay for to appease her guilt.

Initially, [for Nicole Kidman] it was a very different character, it was written as someone who probably was a really young model who married a much older man. I'm older than Nicole so I can't play a lot of that stuff.'

Foster took the short lead-time in her stride. 'I like just showing up like that,' she said. 'Everyone else had six weeks of rehearsal and I just showed up, there was nine days between him calling me and me showing up on set. There were no rehearsals but you don't really need preparation for a movie like this. Fincher needs preparation because he has so much blocking and camerawork to do.'

Panic Room's cinematographer Darius Khondji, who had previously teamed with Fincher on *Seven*, added: 'I worked for a long time with Kidman, and it was sad when she had to leave the movie. The studio panicked, but Foster came to the rescue. I had to shoot all the scenes again with Foster, so it was very interesting to get to see the scenes with these two great actresses.'

Although all Nicole Kidman's footage was scrapped, she still managed to make an uncredited contribution to the film, appearing off-camera as the voice of Stephen Altman's nameless 'supermodel' girlfriend. Ironically, Kidman would later star in *The Others* (2001), a spooky tale turning on some of *Panic Room*'s themes. 'Of course at that stage none of us knew what *The Others* was about, it was just a little movie being made in Spain,' joked the director. 'Hmm, woman in peril, in big house ... hot idea. You go through this all the time, though.'

Filming continued for a further five weeks until another concern became apparent. Foster took Fincher and producer Cean Chaffin aside for a private meeting, and the director feared the worst. 'Jodie walks up and says, "I've got some good news and some bad news." And before she says anything more, Cean goes, "You're pregnant! That's so great!" And I'm like, "Great? What do you mean, great?" ... Nothing went like it was supposed to on this movie.'

Foster's pregnancy created a new hurdle for the production as her extra weight began to show, but Fincher was unwilling to rush the filming. To conceal her increasing bulk, the actress suggested the use of a heavy sweater to cover the more revealing tank-top she wears in the early part of the film. 'I would have had there be more changes, but we had to shoot in continuity because of everything that happens to the house. That meant a lot of the way we shot couldn't be changed, so as time went on I just got more and more pregnant. You can see my weight change. There's a certain part of the movie where I go get a sweater and I designed that to cover myself. At a certain point, my stomach and boobs were going to be so huge it would really be ridiculous,' she joked. 'If it took longer, I was going to show up with a tank top that said *"Fuck You!"*'

'That was a problem,' Fincher noted. 'We shot all the wide stuff, then the medium stuff, and then the close-ups. Jodie's stunt double, Jill Stokesberry, who is really amazing, did most of the action stuff, because it would be really irresponsible to throw a woman who is six months pregnant around. Jill would step in for most of it then Jodie would do the close-up and I would yell, "More violent, more violent!"' The director was also able to cover up Foster in scenes that took place inside the panic room, where physical action was less important.

But in addition to the knock-on delay created by Kidman's departure, the film's principal photography was also lengthened by the logistics of the shoot, such as the multiple uses of video monitor footage. In order to shoot both the actual scenes and the security camera versions of the same, many of the sequences with the burglars were filmed twice, with alternate camera positions and lighting rigs required for each one. Fincher's reputation for perfection meant long shoots for each set-up. 'One day, we spent eight hours rehearsing a shot,' he recalls. 'Lighting it, blocking the actors only to find we couldn't do it, so we scrapped the whole day's work.'

The director was not afraid to film takes over and over to get the fine detail required; one five-second shot, where Meg is attacked by Raoul and she drops Sarah's medical kit, was filmed over 100 times. 'The language of that shot is very specific,' Fincher told the *Seattle Times*. 'You have to see in the background that someone is getting attacked, you have to see the thing fly out of their hands, and you have to be able to see what it is when it lands. It has to look like it's been lost, not like it's been tossed, and it has to land in a place where the audience can register what it is. So if it falls out of focus, or if it slides out of the frame, you have to do it again.'

The director felt his methods were justified. 'You don't shoot a lot of takes if you don't need to and I don't shoot a lot of coverage. I shoot very specifically what I want and I know I'm going from this to this, so I'm looking for the overall performance in part A and the overall performance in part B to be right and also where they connect to be right so that it's fluid. I think Jodie understands that. The other thing is Jodie is in literally almost every shot with an 11-year-old. One of the things I said to [Jodie] up front is, "Look, we're getting two-time Academy Award winner Jodie Foster and I'm going to put her right next to Kristen Stewart and she's got to be as good as you. We're going to shoot as many takes as it takes for her to be good. You have to be good all the time because on Take 17 when she's good, that's the one that's going in the movie." She knew that going in and it's tough. Not because Kristen is not skilled, she was incredibly skilled ... but there's a lot of things for an 11-year-old to take in on a movie set.'

Foster told CNN's Larry King: 'It was a very difficult shoot, physically, emotionally, being in a room for that long, being in the same clothes. Also, the director, who is just an extraordinary, visionary guy, is also very meticulous and makes very meticulous movies. So, a lot of takes.'

By July, it was clear that *Panic Room* would not make its February 2002 release date, and the heavily pregnant Foster was suffering from a sprained hip due to distended ligaments caused by her condition. Fincher recalls an irate conversation with studio executives after screening dailies of the movie's opening scene, with Foster hiding her stomach under a coat and purse. 'We were on the phone with Columbia going, "This is bullshit. Jodie looks like a crack whore, all sweaty and strung-out." It was just ridiculous.' The studio decided to suspend production and rescheduled the film for a March release; Foster gave birth in September and then returned to complete a series of re-shoots – including the opening scene – and additional photography two months later.

Fincher was approached at the same time by Columbia, who wanted to discuss shooting a different ending to the film, after the SWAT raid climax and Burnham's capture rated poorly with test audiences. Forest Whitaker noted: 'The studio did request for him to change that ending a little because of audience response. The studio asked if he could change it so the character is in the park at the end ... but he [Burnham] crossed a lot of moral lines; it's tragic and he's got to go to jail.'

'I had final cut, so I was happy to try it,' says Fincher. 'However, they hadn't held on to the original sets because the storage costs were so high. I told them that we would need to rebuild about $3 million of a $6 million dollar set in order to reshoot. In the end, cheaper minds prevailed.' Burnham's fate remained the same, and the budget stayed at $48 million.

Fincher did agree to have editors James Haygood and Angus Wall revisit Burnham's scenes and select takes where the character was less sympathetic for the final cut. 'Everybody had way too much sympathy for him in the test screenings,' said Wall. 'We found other performances where he was more matter-of-fact,' added Haygood. 'It wasn't that he was ever going to be some super-aggressive hard-ass, but we had to make him more straightforward, even eliminate some of his dialogue so that somebody would say something to him and he just goes about his business.'

But concerns with actors, re-shoots and edits were not the only storms the ill-starred *Panic Room* had to weather. Midway through filming, cinematographer Darius Khondji was dismissed. 'It just wasn't working,' said the director. Khondji told *Dagsavisen Friday* that he was fired from the production after a conflict with one of the cast members: 'The problem was one of the actors, but I don't want to say who. The whole thing turned into a nightmare after a while. Sadly, I got to work too little with Jodie Foster. I did all the pre-production on *Panic Room* and it was a terrible thing when they took my baby away from me.' However, the cinematographer felt Conrad Hall Jr was a good choice to assume his position. '[Conrad] thought the whole thing was very sad, but I asked him sincerely to take over the job. That was the only way my look for the picture would stay intact.'

Fincher admitted that he and Khondji had disagreed on aspects of production. 'A number of the film's problems were created by my inability to allow the film to grow in the ways it wanted to. I had such a clear idea of what the film would be, but ultimately it's *nothing* like what I thought it would be. I consider Darius a great friend and one of the most talented cinematographers working today; we just had a really difficult time trying to develop a rhythm. Darius is completely focused and always gives a thousand per cent to his projects, and it's great if you're in synch with him. But if you're not in synch, it can be difficult and emotionally draining. We weren't able to find a rhythm with Darius, and we weren't really able to find one without him. It was just a big struggle every step of the way.'

According to Fincher, part of the conflict came from the lack of flexibility given to Khondji in his work. 'I think a lot of what cameramen want to do is not to be given a shot and be told to go to the light-meter. They want to be part of the decision-making process as to where the camera goes. Most of that had already been decided. Darius is a very experienced guy, he wants to watch the rehearsals, he wants to give input and be part of where the audience's eyes play, [but] half the job was done, and he felt he was just the light-meter guy.'

Fincher felt he was able to strike a balance with Hall. 'There are times when, as a director, you're seeing something no one else is seeing and you're saying, "I have to have this." There's always a lot of pressure on you, and sometimes you can articulate exactly what you want. But if you can't articulate it, then you might have to do it a bunch of times until you get it. Fortunately, Conrad sees things very similarly to the way I do in terms of staging and how things should be covered, and it was really helpful that he had worked with me as an A-camera operator for more than ten years. I never had any reservations about his ability to do the work; I was concerned about whether he would want to step into a somewhat nightmarish situation.'

Hall came on board, fully aware of the situation with Fincher and his design for the movie. 'Having operated for him, I think I offered a certain comfort level. I knew his language, so it was just a matter of figuring out what to do on this film. Once you figure out how David works, you're so far ahead of the game. He raises the bar so high that no matter what, you're going to walk out of there smelling like a rose. He knows enough about everyone's job to know what's possible and what isn't. What he wants to see is that you're fighting for him and giving him all you can. Toward that end, I told everybody that if they were delivering below par, it wasn't going to be good enough for David. Our goal on every single shot, every single take, was to give everything we had. That's what David expects from his crew. He's very precise, and if you have to do 25 takes, every single take has to be great. So by the end of the day, the end of the week, all the way to the end of the picture, you find yourself saying, "This is as good a job as any I've ever done in my life."'

The director's later comments underlined his intentions for the feature. 'Darius makes *films*, and *Panic Room* is a *movie*. There's a big difference – a *movie* is made for an audience and a *film* is made for both the audience and the film-makers. I think that *The Game* is a movie and I think *Fight Club*'s a film. I think that *Fight Club* is more than the sum of its parts, whereas *Panic Room* is the sum of its parts. I didn't look at *Panic Room* and think, "Wow, this is gonna set the world on fire." These are footnote movies, thrillers, woman-trapped-in-a-house movies. They're not particularly important. I like *Panic Room*, but I also think *Panic Room* is one of those little guilty pleasure popcorn movies. Scott Rudin, the producer, called me and said, "I saw your movie, I loved it. It's a cheesy popcorn movie produced to within an inch of its life." I thought, "I'd like to see that on the poster."'

The unsung 'star' of *Panic Room* was the 'townstone' house itself, a complex locale rendered in intricate detail on a soundstage at the Raleigh Studios lot by production designer Arthur Max. In order to introduce the audience to the shape and layout of the house, Fincher gently guides the camera through the interiors during the early establishing scenes – then kicks into high gear when the raiders break in and chase Meg and Sarah up and down the building before they make it to the relative safety of the panic room. The director felt it was important to give the camera total freedom to travel wherever it needed to inside the house, drawing from the similar shooting techniques developed and used in *Fight Club*.

'We wanted to really set up the omniscience of the camera, that the camera can go anywhere that it needs to go in order to tell you what it is that's going on, so, there are doorways that they run into that they can't get through or doors that shut in front of people and there's people separated by these different spaces, but the camera can easily move wherever it needs to. I like that, because it sort of sets up this feeling of dread, because you kind of know things can get bad given the personality types that are involved. Things can go south.'

Fincher effectively made the voyeuristic camera a source of dramatic tension. 'I liked the idea that you're sort of warning the audience – at some point you might see something you don't *want* to see. I think that it's always a balance between subjectivity and omniscience. That's always the thing you are trying to balance. In this movie's first two-thirds we try our best to establish a distance. The camera is completely unencumbered while the people are. The people run up, hit a door and fall back. They can't get through the wall, and then the camera just goes right through it.' He continues: 'The computer-generated camera movements made in the movie were not for the sake of being fantastic. On a set, every camera movement requires enough space for the crew that has to be behind the camera. What we were just trying to do with CG was to say, there's no camera operator, there's no crew, there's no track, and the camera can go everywhere. I think that there is something about that that tells the audience, "Scream all you want, no one can hear you. You can only watch."'

During the first half of the film, the camera behaves almost like a phantom spectator, a ghostly extra resident able to watch but not involve itself in any of the unfolding events. It's only when the action kicks off that the viewers – like Meg Altman – go from observing the story to being involved directly with it.

Three separate versions of the 6' by 14' panic room were used during the shoot, enabling Fincher to film it from lots of different angles. 'One of the reasons I wanted to do *Panic Room* was that I liked the idea of building this house on a soundstage by the airport, and having one place to go to every day. With *Fight Club*, we'd spent so much time waiting for trucks to be unloaded and then loaded up again, so this seemed like it would be easier. Of course, things went to shit and it wasn't easy at all.'

The director described Koepp's script as 'a brick road' through the story in terms of establishing tension and pitch, enabling him to spend his time on the setting of scenes. 'The biggest thing is finding, eight or ten weeks in, a new angle in a room that we've been inside a thousand times. "What can we do in this room that is reasonably realistic without being banal?" we would ask. It's a fairly stylised approach, there have to be a number of credible set-pieces and you have to engineer set-piece after set-piece. The whole movie is about twists. It's really an exercise in how much you can cram in, how many set-pieces in a row can an audience handle in this confined space?'

The hidden complexity inherent in the *Panic Room* production created logistical problems for the director. 'It's deceptive because you read a script and it reads like, these guys are doing things downstairs and it's being seen on video monitors then you cut to room where two people are trapped and they start talking. No script is really written in stone. There are things that you want to change or have the actors riff on. But you have to commit to what's on the video monitors behind the two actors in the panic room that you shot days before. A lot of times when you think it's really simple, you realise that you don't have enough footage to play on those monitors while the two actors talk, so you have to cover that stuff now. What was one set-up now becomes three set-ups.

'Another example is when Dwight starts smashing the ceiling to get into the panic room, so he's smashing the plaster. Now, you have to replace the plaster for every take, it's a 45-minute reset time, the plaster weighs 800 to 900 pounds, you have to build steel rails to get it up there. Also, you need to cut Take 3 with Take 11 so the smashed ceiling has to look the same in each and Dwight is actually breaking it so he needs to do it correctly. You're shooting something that's an eighth of a script page long, it should take half a day to shoot – instead it takes two days. It becomes an added element that has to be juggled ... it probably would have been easier to do it all with special effects, with greenscreens – in retrospect that would probably be less expensive than what we ended up doing.'

Angus Wall told *VFXPro*: 'There are I think 2073 set-ups in the movie, and I would say the majority of them have two cameras. That's quite a bit of material – there were basically two man-years going into it. Hopefully it paid off. For a 'simple' movie, it's very complex in the way that it's presented, there's a lot of interweaving.'

Fincher gives an example of the responsibility he feels from the *Panic Room* shoot. 'Today on the schedule it says we have to go down to the kitchen and shoot this scene, and a set of knives that were there in an early scene aren't there anymore, they've been stolen. Somebody walked by the set and stole them. I have to be the person who says, "Okay, we're not going to do this right now, go find some more knives. We're going upstairs to shoot something else, we'll come back to this later." You think that should be an easy decision to make, but it isn't, because then you have people who go, "You don't understand, the guy is here with the car and the car's rented by the day and we'll have to rent them some other time. Can't you shoot the scene another way without the knives?" And I have to be the person who either goes, "Okay, we'll do it another way without the knives," or who says, "No. Fuck you. Don't waste any more time talking about this. Get the knives. I want to shoot the fucking scene with the knives." I'm not in control of the knives getting stolen, but I'm responsible, I'm responsible for everything. Mainly, I'm responsible for the haemorrhaging of money it takes to keep 95 people employed for six months to make a movie.'

One of the film's unique qualities comes from a strong cast of actor-directors, an element of production that David Fincher embraced. 'It's great, I recommend it,' he said. 'For anyone who's directing a movie, direct directors. There are always moments in making movies where you ask somebody to do something and they're asking, "Why would my character do this?" With director-actors that never happened, because they went through this before, where a director should say, "Look, I don't fucking know why your character is doing that, but I need you to go to the window because for my next sequence I need to have seen you from there." Director-actors tend to go in that direction, "Okay, I'll do it, let me help you out." All the directors just go, "Fine," because they know you've only got so much time.'

He continues: 'I thought of Forest Whitaker and Dwight Yoakam initially ... at the time Nicole was cast in the movie. When she was injured and Jodie became available it was right after I met with her that I thought, "This is great, these people will know why I'm so neurotic." If you've directed before, the one thing you know is to just shut up and act. You do have to work to the audience's eye. That's what's funny about movie acting, that it is completely silly looking. The way people have to move around each other in a two-shot, if you saw people behaving like that in real life you would ask what the hell their problem is – but through the camera's lens, it works. When I asked these actors to do something they never said, "I don't think my character would do that." They just did it.'

'The film didn't faze me at all,' maintained Forest Whitaker. 'I understand stuff like, "We'll put it in later."' Jodie Foster agreed: 'David needs to work with experienced actors who have made a lot of movies. If you are just a young theatre actor who's never made a film before you could never make a film with him, he's much too exacting, so directors as actors really help him out, especially when they know why certain things will need to be cut out. Most of the time when you are getting direction from a director, nine times out of ten the direction is technical.'

Panic Room was the first film since *Alien 3* that allowed Fincher to focus his attention on a female lead and, like each of his movies, it was the core pairing of two people – in this case, mother and daughter – around which the entire plot revolved. Despite a short, steep learning curve for her characterisation of Megan Altman and the added personal constraints of her second pregnancy, Jodie Foster was able to bring her trademark strength and vitality to the part. 'It was really one of the most fun experiences I've ever had,' she noted. 'I loved the technical challenge. I loved the physical challenge. I loved not being bored.'

Her co-star Forest Whitaker described Foster as 'very centred, powerful, very strong and very focused; a very talented actress. I think this is an interesting film for her because she gets to play weak and insecure, which she doesn't [often] do.' According to Fincher, 'With Jodie it's all about her eyes, her thought process, the nature of the process and why she does the things she does. You're not going to give her a gun in each hand and have her running down an alley firing them in slow motion.' An able director in her own right, with films like *Little Man Tate* (1991) and *Home for the Holidays* (1995) to her credit, Foster described Fincher as 'the greatest technician I've ever worked with. He's some-body that I've wanted to work with for a very long time. He's just a magnificent director and somebody I've looked up to forever ... So I was ready to do anything he wanted.'

The part of Meg's daughter Sarah required a child actor with enough screen presence to hold her own with Foster; ironically, even before Foster had been cast, the girl who would fill the part had been chosen on the basis of her similarity to the actress. 'We saw Kristen Stewart,' said Fincher. 'We thought she was amazing, like a young Jodie Foster.'

Stewart recalls her initial reaction to winning the part: 'When I got *Panic Room* I'm like, "Oh my God, that's huge! It's bigger than huge!" I was kind of freaked out at first.' *Panic Room* represented Stewart's second feature film role after her debut in *The Safety of Objects* (2001); as Foster put it, 'She didn't need my advice. She's a great actress, she has great focus. She's wonderful. I spent a long time with her in that little room. She turned 11 on the movie. What's interesting is that she looks so much like me when I was a kid, and she sort of has the same quality, kind of stoic and very reserved emotionally and kind of a tough kid. I really enjoyed my time with her.'

Forest Whitaker was chosen to play the troubled Burnham, whose character was first pitched as a slick, technical type. 'Burnham was sort of glib and was originally the guy who designed the panic room, [but] I didn't buy talking that guy into breaking into a house,' Fincher decided. 'I think we had to make him the guy who installs them, the blue-collar guy. I loved the idea of Forest Whitaker; you can't get someone more physically imposing than him.' Like Jodie Foster, Whitaker is also a director and producer. His directing credits include *Waiting to Exhale* (1995) and *Hope Floats* (1998), and, prior to Fincher's involvement, he had briefly considered directing *Panic Room* himself, although he noted: 'For me I didn't find it very interesting as a filmmaker – but in David's hands, it's a perfect film.' He saw the script as similar to a theatre production. 'I felt that the first time when I read the script, [but] I knew it would be different than that, because David was involved.'

The director referred Whitaker to the movie *Key Largo* (1948) as a guide to Burnham's nature. 'He felt that my character was the Bogart character from that movie,' said the actor. 'The fact that he's conflicted was really attractive to me. It was really interesting to play. He's a guy who doesn't really want to cause any problems; he just wants to take care of himself and his family, and he just keeps getting sucked in. All of a sudden, it's too late.' This depth of character was what attracted the actor over the more villainous part of Raoul. 'What I liked about [Burnham] is that he keeps crossing these lines and he has to look at his own morality. He's just getting deeper and deeper until you think there's no escape, then there's that one extra line and he won't cross it. That's what's really fascinating to me. He does some reprehensible things. Maybe people don't notice it much, [but] he did come up with the idea of putting propane gas in the panic room. Just a little though!'

Country music singer Dwight Yoakam, who had recently written, directed and starred in his own project *South of Heaven, West of Hell* (2000), was cast as the violent wildcard Raoul. '[He] was originally written as a giant scary hulking guy,' said Fincher, 'but I thought, "What if he was this wiry, mean kind of ex-con white trash guy?" I remembered *Sling Blade* and I thought Dwight Yoakam would be cool.' Yoakam remembers his first impressions of the film set: 'It was literally a half a New York City block built on a sound stage and I became completely intrigued with how [Fincher] was going to approach filming this movie. It was very much a throwback to kind of the old studio-style filmmakers ... I said to [Fincher] when I first saw him, "This is very much like *Rear Window*," and he said, "Yeah, it's *Rear Window* meets *Straw Dogs*." I said, "Wow, Okay."'

Jared Leto came to Fincher's attention with his supporting role as the blond-haired Angel Face in *Fight Club*, the stereotypical pretty-boy punched into raw meat by an irate Edward Norton. As with that film, the handsome Leto – twice placed in *People Magazine*'s 50 Most Beautiful People list – suffers severe punishment in

Panic Room, getting burnt and then shot in the head. 'He's perfect for it, isn't he?' joked the director. 'If there is any guy you want to see get his face burned off, it's him.' Leto brings an ideal nervous energy to a character who is out of his depth during the house invasion. After casting the parts of Burnham and Raoul, Fincher jokes that he then turned into a casting agent, asking himself 'Who could I get to be in the middle?' 'It's got to be someone little and glib. Who has aspirations to be Latrell Sprewell [the New York Knicks basketball player]? Jared Leto – original gangsta. Jared came in, he had the gold teeth and he was doing this whole rap thing. I said, "I'm not too sure about that." So he went away, came back with cornrows in his hair. I thought it was awesome because it speaks so much to him being a wanna-be hard guy.'

With its small cast, the only other Finch Mob member in *Panic Room*'s ensemble is none other than scriptwriter Andrew Kevin Walker, making a cameo as the 'Sleepy Neighbour' who ignores Sarah's Morse code SOS message. Despite his work (credited and uncredited) on *The Game* and *Fight Club*, Walker had no part in the script for *Panic Room*. 'He and Koepp are best friends,' noted Fincher. 'If you're a professional screenwriter in Hollywood you get rewritten all the time ... I would tease David, "Andy's coming down. Just for a fitting!"'

The director's subdued, underlit vision of cinema is well suited to the gloom of *Panic Room*'s setting. At one point, Fincher considered shooting the first half of the burglary in near-total darkness. 'We talked about it, and we shot a lot of digital stills, but it was just asking too much of an audience to sit still for a scene where you can barely make out the people talking. I like the idea of doing that, and maybe you can do it in small doses, because that's what a house is like in the middle of the night.'

For the director, the shadowy ambience formed an important backdrop to the events unfolding around Meg and Sarah. 'I think almost everybody in life has been afraid of the dark,' he told *DFN*. 'I don't think this movie would be very scary if it took place during her lunch break. Everything has to funnel through what one thinks is aesthetically correct. Quite honestly, I don't like to justify sources of light in the shot so you end up doing top-lighting. You end up solving problems in similar ways because you have the same criteria for them. I also make movies that take place at night so you can't put people next to windows. That won't help you.' Fincher wanted *Panic Room*'s darkness to seem authentic, a conceit he had also aimed for in *The Game* and *Fight Club*. 'To my way of thinking, most movies are way too over-lit. It just doesn't look like real life to me, and this is a movie that had to take place at night, because it's about a break-in, so it's logical that it would be dark.'

The process of photogrammetry – mapping still images over the surface of computer-generated 'sets' – that Fincher used to such giddying effect in *Fight Club* turns the *Panic Room* house into a massive, multi-storey chess board in which the Altmans and the criminals are the pieces. The director talks through one of the shots: 'The first shot of Jodie when we pull back and we go through the banister, the banister is computer-generated – then when it tilts down, everything from that point on is CG. Then it goes down and passes by the columns and you see the car pull up and Forest comes forward. From that point on, it's a real camera. Then it goes over and as it wipes sideways and goes into the lock, it becomes CG. Then it comes back out and becomes a regular shot, just tracking along. Then as it pans over, it becomes CG and flies all the way across the kitchen, goes through the coffee machine, goes all the way to the back and then as Forest hops over the fence it becomes real again.'

Shooting these impossible elements, tracking back through virtual lock mechanisms and stair banisters, took up nine days on set but several months in post-production. The final, seamless shot lasts for almost three minutes without any apparent cuts. 'I think Koepp was trying to establish a really specific relationship between the windows and the burglars, the predators looking through. It's kind of like with fishbowls when cats press their noses up against them. Also, since we're in the shot where we float through the entire house, it established the geography. That's why the bad guys could have a conversation on the first floor and Jodie and her daughter can't hear them because she's so far away and we've shown that.'

Fincher's love of using a film's opening titles to set the tone for a storyline prompted the striking credits sequence for *Panic Room*. The director decided to 'book-end' the night-time narrative of the movie with daylight scenes; in Koepp's script, the opening titles were pitched as a staged series of shots of Manhattan Island, each closer than the next, finally zeroing in on the brownstone house. But Fincher chose instead to show a sequence of New York cityscapes with the credits hovering in front of major NYC landmarks. The final effect of these huge words floating just feet away from office blocks and churches is impressive and a little eerie, an impression deepened by Howard Shore's moody title theme.

Hollywood and New York visual effects studios The Picture Mill and Computer Café collaborated on the scene, which traverses Manhattan and ends near Central Park. Picture Mill creative director William Lebeda noted: 'By beginning the sequence just after dawn and moving through the morning to early afternoon, we were able to seamlessly link the titles directly to the first shot of the film, as the actors walk to the brownstone for the first time.' Lebeda and his team worked closely with Fincher and visual effects supervisor Kevin Haug to ensure the continuity of tone from titles to narrative. 'The fact that nothing happens in the sequence creates a tremendous amount of discomfort,' he adds. 'Another factor of the success of the sequence is its complete believability. When you see the final images, there is nothing out of the ordinary, except giant names floating above the city.'

Computer Café also provided visual effects for the outdoor scene of Burnham's arrest (actually shot on a soundstage). 'In that scene, Fincher wanted wet leaves and a pile of stolen savings bonds that drop from Forest Whitaker's hands to be caught up in a whirlwind, that spirals up and around him,' said digital effects supervisor David Ebner. 'Fincher knew there was no way to accomplish this shot with practical effects because of the rain and also because he was very specific about the motion he wanted.' Computer-generated effects provided the helical motion for the 'wind', as well as a few other elements, such as the burning propane, the flying gas bottle and the gunshot wounds.

The film also had its fair share of practical effects – most notably, the flaming gas burns suffered by Junior and the bloody makeup applied to actor Patrick Bauchau after Stephen Altman endures his savage beating, both creations of Alec Gillis and Tom Woodruff Jr. The director noted that a team of puppeteers was required to make one particular effect as nauseatingly real as possible: 'When the husband's collarbone was sticking out, we needed five guys to make it move.'

Both *Seven* and *Fight Club* had used special processes to deepen the coloration and texture of their 'answer prints', the print used as the root-stock for all transfers to other media and the reels sent out to cinemas, and *Panic Room* followed suit. The print was digitally colour-corrected through an intermediate process at Technicolor's Technique labs, after Fincher had seen the process during his supervision of an archival data master of *Seven* for New Line. 'That's when I said to the guys at Technique, "It would be great if we could use this technology to create all of the film's presentation formats." They then approached Technicolor and got the money to make it happen. We talked about doing *Panic Room* in High Definition, but the problem is, in these really enclosed spaces, the camera is huge. You can't stick it where you want.'

For the third time, Fincher brought in Howard Shore to score one of his films, following on from the soundtracks for *Seven* and *The Game*. After *Panic Room*, Shore would win an Oscar for his work on *The Lord of the Rings: The Fellowship of the Ring* (2001), a very different proposition to the measured dramatic tones of his music for Fincher's thriller. 'Scoring a movie is also about where *not* to put music in the movie,' said the composer. 'Using music in the film can express many different points of view. I think one of the points expressed specifically by the music ... is some lightness and a fanciful quality to the opening of the film, as if it was all happening in a dream.' The director sees Shore as someone with a daring creative drive: 'Howard is one of the best, most fearless collaborators you could ever work with. He is completely undaunted by what you are trying to achieve and totally pragmatic, and will tell you what does not work with the scene, and tell you how to fix it. He's a guy who will help you tell your story.'

Shore describes the process of development. 'I like to watch the film first as an audience does, because I want to feel something. The first screening is the most crucial screening for me ... I can usually start to write a lot of music just based on the first screening, then I might allow a week or two just to go through the initial dreaming, floating state where you are thinking about the movie. I write musical ideas based on what I'm feeling, watching the film over and over again, then what I do is go through a much more technical process of taking this material I created, which is essentially from my subconscious, and putting that into real composition ideas for the ideas of scoring scenes; applying this material to the actual film that Fincher has made.'

He continues: 'My compositional ideas are really based from an audience point of view. It's what I'm feeling when I see the film and there's certain imagery [in *Panic Room*] that made me see a homage to older films. That might have drawn me into certain areas of writing that might have been something from the 1950s and 1960s, so I think there were aspects of it that looked backwards towards films that were made mid-20th century.'

In the early stages of production, Fincher worked with David Koepp to keep the opening minutes of *Panic Room* as efficient as possible, wasting no time on superfluous action and cutting straight to the meat of the thriller. 'We kept saying, "There's no way you're not going to see fire on the ceiling in the trailer, so all this playing coy in the first three pages, it's stupid." It's like, let's get on with it, we know where we're going with it, we know where we're going to wind up.' It was also important to the director to keep the viewers one or two steps ahead of the characters. 'You get to see people working through processes, being forced to think physically. They find the fire-starter, they find the fire blanket. They – especially Jodie Foster's character – have to put things together, even though sometimes they can see but not hear what's going on. There are lots of misperceptions, and I love that irony, that we, the audience, know more about what's going on than the characters do. The tension of that is a very cinematic notion.'

Combined with Fincher's use of an omnipresent viewpoint, Koepp's story trades exposition for pace and makes an otherwise static environment dynamic. 'I always try to place the camera where the effect will be as dramatic as possible for any given moment,' the director said. 'I was looking for ways to move the story along – and it was written as a real page-turner – with a certain level of precision in the execution. I wanted it to feel like it was heading somewhere, like there was a sense of inevitability. I didn't want it to feel vague or happenstance. In a film like this, you don't want things to come together in a clumsy fashion; everything has to fit together. There are a lot of turns in the story that have everything to do with circumstances beyond the character's control, and I wanted the audience to be able to follow all of those twists and turns.

'Additionally, we always wanted the audience to be holding more of the cards than the characters in the film. We often had three or four characters, each with a separate agenda, on different floors of the brownstone. The audience needed to know what was happening in a somewhat chronological fashion, so stylistically we were trying to find interesting and efficient ways of moving the camera and getting the information across. Toward that end, we created some computer-generated motion-control shots that enabled us to make the camera sort of fly around the set, almost as if we were playing a game of three-dimensional chess. We could then show what was happening on three different levels at the same time. We also showed the action on various video monitors in the panic room, as well as by intercutting between the different characters.'

Notwithstanding the argument that *Panic Room* is a 'mere' thriller, the director sees the story as a modern-day metaphor. 'To me, it's about divorce. It's a movie about the destruction of the home and how far you're willing to go to hold on to what you have.' Having been through a separation himself, it's something Fincher can relate to. 'If there is a thematic underpinning to the movie, it's that. Bad things do happen to good people in that situation. But really, I just wanted the film to be an alternative. There are so many movies out there that tell the audience, "We don't want to make you uncomfortable, because this is your Friday night."'

The key terror of *Panic Room* comes from the spur of a parent defending the nest. 'You'd kill for your young,' says Fincher. 'There's the genius child and the polite child and the problem child. Your children are all different and they all require different things from you. That doesn't mean you love them any less.'

It's easy to draw the lines of victim and victimisers in the film between rich middle-class on one side and working class on the other, but in fact it's Junior, the instigator of the whole burglary, who is the uptown rich kid while homeowner Meg is the disenfranchised one. 'Obviously we needed a character wealthy enough to buy this kind of place,' said Fincher. 'I was not conscious of making any social comment with it. It was just for the pace of the story. Of course the character of Forest Whitaker represents blue-collar, but for Dwight's motivation, we never know clearly where he comes from. There was not an 'eat the rich' message. I don't see racial divisions in New York. Everybody's suffering the same and everybody's pawing their way. The most agonised and miserable guy in the movie is the one with the trust fund.'

Fincher commented that he sees the thriller as 'truly the guilty pleasure genre of moviemaking.' He goes on: 'I don't think there is any kind of importance to this kind of film ... a lurid kind of fear-based entertainment. Comedies are probably more important to the human psyche than movies that scare people, but it's nice every once in a while. One of the reasons I made this movie is because I like scaring people [but] I don't have a distinct particular need to make an audience terrified. I don't think this is a terrifying movie, it's a suspense movie with an implied threat throughout the film that is greater than what actually occurs. This is a movie I wanted to see. A lot of people have already done this kind of movie. Can I bring anything more to the party? I don't think, "Okay, I offended them at this point, so I have to make 'em nervous, to appease them." I don't think in those terms.

'It's got its humour and there is a bit of sadistic relish, especially with Dwight Yoakam's character. In the script we talk so much about this door that won't close, the door this and that, there was all this stuff about the safety mechanism, the fact that no one could ever get caught in it. So I have to see this door close on someone's hand. I said to David Koepp, "How can you have people talking about how dangerous the door is, and then we don't sever any limbs?" Koepp was like, "What is going to happen? This person is just going to scream and thrash through the whole scene. We can't have someone get a hand or a leg caught, they'd just sit in the background whimpering for the rest of the movie." I said, "Oh yeah. What's wrong with that?"'

Many observers saw the scene as pre-emptive payback for Raoul's later violence towards Meg and Sarah. 'You want a movie villain that people want to spit at,' says Fincher, referring to the moment where Raoul punches the young girl. 'I wanted to see her get really smashed, I wanted people to know this was not a movie that was going to play nice.' The original scene as scripted had Raoul slapping, not punching, Sarah. 'The fact is that the horrible reality of child abuse is that it isn't backhanded slaps. He is supposed to be an appalling character and you have to in some way get the kid out of the picture.'

'I'm just a hard-working interpreter,' stated the director, discussing his collaboration with Koepp. 'I like David and I liked his writing on this. He has a concept and a conceit. He has something that he wanted to do, not just in terms of cinema. The highest compliment that he's paid me since he saw the movie was that, "You weren't afraid to make it a genre movie." I said, "There was no reason for me not to, the script was good."' Fincher described the writer's methods in constructing *Panic Room* to *About.com*: 'Koepp's script, what he does so brilliantly, is place set-piece on top of set-piece on top of set-piece. I think that was the [intent] and I do think the movie is sort of an exercise in that respect. Koepp's whole thing was – How much can you cram in? How many set-pieces in a row can the audience handle and still be in this confined space?

Parallels between the films of Alfred Hitchcock and David Fincher had previously been drawn with *The Game*, and the director admits a definite influence in *Panic Room*. 'I saw a lot of Hitchcock when I was a kid; there were very few people that were that specifically true to their ideas and proclivities, so he was and is a very interesting filmmaker. His movies are so mainstream and so personal at the same time.'

Fincher echoes his comments to Yoakam in comparing the film to the work of Hitchcock and Sam Peckinpah: 'I sold the studio on this by telling them this was a cross between *Straw Dogs* and *Rear Window* – *Rear Window* was certainly a reference for *Panic Room*, because that film happens in one place, but I think there's a sort of middle-class approach to modern thrillers, that it will all turn out okay in the end. I wanted to make this film a bit dirtier than that, less safe.' One BBC radio journalist noted that the film's opening titles also recalled *The Trouble with Harry* (1955) and *North by Northwest* (1959). Fincher told *AICN*, 'Anytime you make a movie where there's suspense in a house with windows, you're kind of doomed to do a homage to *Rear Window*. I don't know if Hitchcock invented the rules, but he certainly implied that suspense was the product of the audience knowing more about the plot than the characters on screen. By doing this film, I couldn't do anything else *but* use some Hitchcock devices. The *problem* with this film is that, in the mindset of a modern audience, it sure does have more to do with *Home Alone* than with *Rear Window*.'

Certainly, viewers can wonder if Burnham's flippant line comparing Raoul to Joe Pesci is a veiled reference to that actor's appearance in *Home Alone* (1990). In fact, the 'home invasion' movie is an entire sub-genre that can be drawn back to films such as *The Desperate Hours* (1957, remade in 1990), *Lady in a Cage* (1964) and *Wait Until Dark* (1967). There are also antecedents in what *Sight & Sound*'s Linda Ruth Williams calls 'yuppie in peril movies' like *Pacific Heights* (1990), *Unlawful Entry* (1992) and *Sliver* (1993).

CUTS AND CHANGES

As stated above, the most important change to *Panic Room* was the departure and replacement of the lead actress, which necessitated a series of subtle alterations to Koepp's script. However, for the most part the film remains very close to the original outline, with only a few lines of dialogue and small moments differing from those in the final cut.

In the scene immediately after Meg and Sarah move in, where they split a pizza, the ensuing conversation that begins 'This place has too many stairs' originally took place beforehand, and was longer in the scripted version; it featured a spiky exchange between mother and daughter about some missing possessions and ended with Meg promising to cook something to eat, but discovering her cell-phone battery is flat – setting up the later scene with the charger. As Fincher notes earlier in this chapter, the changes were largely due to Jodie Foster's differing interpretation of the Meg Altman character.

Meg's heartfelt words to Sarah as she puts her to bed – 'It's disgusting how much I love you' – were improvised from the more ordinary line 'I really love you'.

Junior's rant to Raoul about being the 'loving grandson' originally included the line, 'Did you ever change a colostomy bag? Do you even know what it is?'

Despite Sarah's diabetic condition, the word 'diabetes' is never mentioned throughout the film, and the script's original description of the drug in her emergency syringe – the sugary solution Glucagon – was cut from all of the dialogue. Instead, the audience is tipped off to her illness by glimpses and subtle asides – Sarah's Coca-Cola intake, the medicine bottles in her bedside refrigerator, the medic-alert wristwatch and so on.

Burnham's line as he goes to give Sarah the injection – 'All I know about this is what I see on TV' – was changed from an explicit reference to the medical drama series *ER*.

AFTERMATH

The film's shooting concluded in November 2001 and Fincher set to work on post-production and editing. But even after dissuading Columbia from using an alternate ending, the director come into conflict over the Motion Picture Association of America's rating for *Panic Room*. Fincher refused Columbia's requests to cut down the violence in the film in order to get it under the wire for a PG-13 certification. 'I told them, "I can't make a PG-13 version of this movie, because I don't know how you'd do it." It would be too light.' Fincher's final cut ensured that *Panic Room* reached movie screens in the USA with an R – Restricted – rating.

Furthermore, the key themes of *Panic Room* – security against invaders, defence of your loved ones against impossible odds – had taken on a different, more pertinent resonance by the time the film finished production. The terrorist attack on the World Trade Center in New York City, the setting for the film, linked the story with a larger, real-life threat for many viewers. But like *Fight Club*, which came under fire because it followed the Columbine shootings, *Panic Room*'s storyline was less about 9/11 than it was about the more basic, animal concerns of defending the nest. 'If there is a message in the movie, it's *do not get a panic room,*' noted Jodie Foster. 'The film says, if anything, instead of thinking of a scenario where something bad can happen to you, you should be vigilant and listen to your instincts beforehand. The minute [Meg] walked into the house, she didn't like it, she didn't like the panic room but she was suckered into it by someone who told her that she should get it to get back at her husband. She didn't listen to her instincts.'

The film opened in March 2002 on over 3000 screens across America; the first weekend netted $30 million, leading to a gross of more than $95 million that made it Fincher's second most lucrative feature after *Seven*. The movie also allowed Fincher a box-office rematch with actress Ashley Judd, whose film *Double Jeopardy* had trumped *Fight Club*'s opening weekend in 1999; this time the director came out the winner, as *Panic Room* beat out Judd's *High Crimes* to the top slot. However, despite an impressive showing earlier in the year, *Panic Room* remained outside the highest grossing films for 2002, losing out to the *Star Wars*, *Harry Potter* and *Lord of The Rings* sequels – and, ironically, another movie scripted by David Koepp, *Spider-Man*.

Despite the film's comparative success, Fincher was not happy with the way the movie was sold to cinemagoers. '*Panic Room* was a disaster in terms of the marketing of it,' he said. 'It was just so painful. The things that movie studios are willing to do to get people into the theatre are just not things that I'm willing to have my name used in conjunction with. When Sony went to put together a recruited screening for *Panic Room*, I said, "Be aware that if you go onto the internet and if you go into the shopping malls and you say, 'Would you like to see the new movie from the director of *Seven* and *Fight Club*, starring the star of *The Silence of the Lambs*?', you're going to get the kind of cross-section of audience that this movie was *not* made for. This movie is made for people who went to see *Kiss the Girls*, this movie is made for people who went to see *The Bone Collector*, this is a fast ball down the centre of the plate, this is a popcorn movie. I want that audience."

'They said, "No, no, no, we know what we're doing," so they went and recruited people on the basis of the director of *Seven* and *Fight Club* starring the star of *Silence of the Lambs* and they got a bunch of people there who were expecting *Fight Club* who were totally disappointed with the movie. Then the studio goes, "Okay, you were right," but then they want to go out with television commercials that say "from the director of *Fight Club*, from the director of *Seven*" and I said, "This is *not* that kind of movie – why do you even want to use *Fight Club* if nobody went to see it? What value are you trying to cash in on here?"'

As perhaps the only aspect of filmmaking that is beyond his control as a director, Fincher's bugbear with the marketing of his works concerns him greatly. 'They say everything ... "This is the most terrifying movie ever made." But it's not. "Oh, but you have to say that because the audience expects that, it has to be the most terrifying movie ever made." But it's not terrifying, it's suspenseful, it's a thriller ...can't you say thrilling? It's the Hollywood hucksterism, it's the way that this not very sensitive, not very thoughtful, not very interested multinational media hierarchy looks at their product like widgets, just the way that Michelin looks at fucking radials – it's like this one, this one's got white-walls on it, and the guy who designed the tyre is going, "No, but this has the grooves to take the water out..." And everyone else in the country is rolling their eyes and going, "It's a tyre, it's made out of black rubber, it goes on a car, who gives a shit?" That's how movie companies look at the movies, so you've got to go in and fight for what you think is right in the end.'

He mentions the *Panic Room* poster as an example. 'I wanted the slot with the eyes [the design that they used] because it kind of talked about the thing that the movie was. We fought and fought and fought for the poster, and then for the DVD I said, "Don't use the poster, people have already seen it, just use a black cover." [They said] "No, no, no, the audience have to be reminded of the experience they had that they liked." Hopefully, you're going to get people who never went to see the movie reconsider it, but it's like this Pavlovian thing. "We love the poster!" But they *didn't* love the poster when I brought it to them for the movie.'

Commentators on Fincher's other thriller *The Game* had been critical of that movie's chilly emotional tone, but in *Panic Room* they felt he had created a high-tension narrative. 'Tense, terrific, sweaty-palmed fun,' in the words of *Miami Herald* reviewer Rene Rodriguez, and to Stephen Hunter of the *Washington Post* it was 'powerfully manipulative, quite clever and full of evil ambition'. Jeff Vice of the *Deseret News* praised 'Fincher's characteristically startling visual style and an almost palpable sense of intensity', while for *Detroit News*' Susan Stark it 'confirmed Fincher's status as a filmmaker who artfully bends technical know-how to the service of psychological insight.' Roger Ebert's review in the *Chicago Sun-Times* touched on the structure of the movie: 'Once we sense *Panic Room* isn't going to cheat, it gathers in tension, because the characters are operating out of their own resources, and that makes them the players, not the pawns.'

Others, such as the BBC's Neil Smith, made the inevitable comparisons, calling it a 'hugely accomplished slice of Hitchcockian suspense.' Robert Wilonsky of the *New Times Los Angeles* was less polite: 'A collage of clichés and a dim echo of allusions to other films,' while Kenneth Turan at the *Los Angeles Times* damned it with faint praise: 'What's surprising about this traditional thriller, moderately successful but not completely satisfying, is exactly how genteel and unsurprising the execution turns out to be.' Some critics argued that *Panic Room* was 'too mainstream' after the challenging *Fight Club*. 'I think most movies are,' said Fincher. 'How many *Fight Clubs* are going to come along, the projects that make you want to kill to get involved with?' But criticism of Fincher's direction and Koepp's script aside, the film's box-office success against a dozen family movies proved that cinema audiences were hungry for taut suspense drama, for a film that CNN's Paul Clinton called 'a classy, intelligent thriller for grownups'.

After the film had completed its theatrical run, the *Panic Room* DVD was released at the end of 2002 and, despite rumours to the contrary, was a 'plain vanilla' product with none of the added value of the extras-laden *Seven* and *Fight Club* special editions. Pre-vis supervisor Ron Frankel had hoped some of the story-board animation would be available on the disc to show audiences how the early designs translated into the finished film, but no commentary or supplementary footage was forthcoming, much to the disappointment of the director's fans. Fincher stated that any such release would not include Nicole Kidman's scenes: 'I've had people ask me about putting [them] on the DVD, but you just don't do that to actors.'

With regard to a 'special edition' of *Panic Room*, the director replied, 'Who knows? It may end up being too much trouble. I refused to do a commentary for them on the DVD they put out. I refused to do it because they were just like, "Let's crank it out, don't get precious about it, the movie was a hit, just get it out on DVD, more money for everyone". We may do [a special edition] if there is enough interest, there's a lot of stuff, a lot of interesting pre-vis and pre-production shot on video, but I hate it when there's like nine different versions of a DVD out. It pisses me off, because I buy DVDs, I don't call my friends at Warner Bros and go, "Hey man, you got a *Matrix* DVD?" I go out and buy the things and I get pissed off that I've got so many *Godfather* DVDs…' However, in April 2003, screenwriter Roger Avary – at work on the script for *The Lords of Dogtown* – let slip that a *Panic Room* Special Edition featuring all the movie's extensive pre-visualisation would be released later that year.

On several occasions, David Fincher's comments about *Panic Room* throw up the remark that this is 'a *movie* movie'; he speaks about thrillers as 'guilty pleasures' and 'footnote movies', almost as if he's on the brink of apologising for creating a film that might *just* be classified as conventional. But one only has to watch his movies to know that Fincher simply isn't capable of making something that fits in that category.

Panic Room doesn't blow apart thriller conventions in the same way that *Seven* blasted the cop drama and serial killer genres, it doesn't challenge the viewer in the same way that *Fight Club* smacks you in the face and dares you to keep up. Rather, it's the twin sister to *The Game*, outwardly a standard suspense drama but inwardly an intricate mechanism to extract tension from an audience. It may not transcend its genre, but it does represent a finely tooled archetype of it. Until the release of his next picture, viewers are free to debate if *Panic Room*'s 'normality' represents a sea change in Fincher's creative style, or if it was a calculated move on the part of the director, perhaps to soften his nonconformist reputation and allow him greater freedom with future projects. But it's more likely that neither is true, and that Fincher simply applied the same criteria to this script as he has to all his projects: 'Can I do something new with it?'

While *The Game* played with movie logic in a realistic setting, *Panic Room* doesn't stray outside the suspended reality of its 'reel' world – none of which makes it any less valid as a film. Meg Altman begins the story in the same place as the audience, as a passive observer of the unfolding events through the panic room's monitor screens; but soon she's acting instead of reacting. First, she takes over the territory of the film – the house – from the 'cast' of housebreakers, becoming a player on the 'stage'. And then she moves up to eventually become the 'director' of the story. Like Fincher, by the last reel of *Panic Room*, Meg is making the criminals go where she wants them to, rewriting their script and even *lighting* them to her orders; the conclusion of the movie comes together by her design. Intentional or not, her arc through *Panic Room* can be read as a representation of the audience-author relationship.

On my first viewing of *Panic Room*, I fell into the trap that a lot of viewers did; I unfairly expected Fincher to top *Fight Club*, tritely remarking that the movie had more *room* than it did *panic*. But, returning to the film for the purposes of this book, my opinion shifted as I studied the artistry of it in greater detail. Fincher is a master of what *Sight & Sound* called 'the potent single shot' and *Panic Room* represents the cleanest, most economic example of that in the director's canon to date. The perfectionist nature of the direction is matched by solid performances from an excellent cast. In this movie, nothing is wasted, no actor's turn of the head, no pan or zoom, no sound or flicker of light goes where it isn't needed; this is a work of pinpoint accuracy where the director has ensured that every element is *exactly* where he wanted it.

Some might argue that a film so rigorously planned and pre-designed is without imagination or spontaneity – until you consider that in cinema nothing is ever truly unrehearsed; every time a director places a camera and blocks a shot, it becomes a fraction of a planned blueprint from which the whole movie is assembled. *Panic Room* is a very well-engineered work, with Koepp's frugal and apt writing providing the solid framework on which Fincher can display his command of technique. It's not a triumph of style over substance; this is a triumph of style *and* proficiency.

SEVEN

Fincher's Future

'If you have a clue and a passion, people will get out of your way because people want someone to follow.'

DAVID FINCHER'S WORK continues to make him a much sought-after filmmaker, a director and producer whose unique style draws in actors, writers and other creative talents who are eager to work with him. With the successes of his studio pictures, Fincher finds himself in a position to pick and chose projects that interest him; the director can afford to take the time to mould feature scripts and concepts to suit his purposes without, one hopes, the need to submit to producing more conventional fare. The trademark Fincher 'look' remains emblazoned on every frame of film he shoots.

For several months after the release of *Panic Room*, it was widely accepted that the director's next feature would be the action sequel *Mission: Impossible 3*; but, in fact, Fincher would pass on the blockbuster project early in 2003 in favour of a far smaller, but no less dynamic film, *The Lords of Dogtown*. Written by Stacey Peralta, one of the founders of the contemporary skateboarding scene, *Lords* is an asphalt-eye view of the birth of the skate punk culture from its early days at California's Venice Beach.

At first, the film was pinned to rapper-turned-director Fred Durst, of the band Limp Bizkit; Fincher told *Variety* in 2002, 'This is a movie about iconoclasts, it is about youth and energy and anger and fulfilment. How could one not think of Fred Durst?' He added: 'I'm just trying to produce a movie with Art and John. I met Fred Durst years ago, and [*Lords*] is something he'd really like to do and it's something we'd really like to make happen.'

Durst had experience in directing rock videos for groups like Staind and Puddle of Mudd, and his involvement with Fincher had begun with the script *Runt*. Written by William J Cloakley and Christian Van Gregg, *Runt*'s script is a harsh cycle of high school violence sparked by a mousy young artist whose unrequited love earns him a beating from the local sports hero; when the artist's dog (the titular 'runt of the litter') becomes a victim of this little war, he goes out on a collision course with revenge. In reference to the spate of school disorders in the wake of the Columbine shootings, Durst noted that 'There are so many movie studios that are scared to touch subject matter like this, but I think it's real. I think it will help people understand the underdog.'

Fincher's willingness to go to the mat for a darker theme was no doubt part of his attraction to the project. 'David ... worked out killer,' the performer said during an MTV interview. 'The greatest part of it is, for two and a half months he took me in his office and taught me how to direct. Broke the script down, page by page, shot by shot. It always turned into a killer conversation just about whatever. Then we got into the script an hour later and he'd say, "Okay, today you got to go home and rent *Lawrence of Arabia*." Relive the experience, and look at this scene and tell me what it did for you.' He made me go through all these different movies, from *Badlands* to *Chinatown*, just for shots, just for themes ... He opened my mind so much, and taught me so much.'

However, *Runt* fell by the wayside early in 2002. Durst and Fincher instead shifted to making *Lords of Dogtown*, but by the end of 2002 it was Fincher who looked set to sit in the director's chair. Casting began on the film in early 2003 and, as this book went to press, plans were proceeding to shoot the movie on location in Los Angeles during the summer. The two men may yet work together on *Wanna-Be*, a drama about growing up in an organised crime family.

The script behind *The Lords of Dogtown* grew from G Beato's 1999 article of the same name in *Spin* magazine. Beato wrote about skateboarding mavericks Tony Alva, Jay Adams, Shogo Kubo and Stacy Peralta, about their radical development of skating skills and the emergence of the sport from the shadow of surfing in the 1970s, about the formation of the rule-busting Zephyr Competition Skate Team and the rock-star rise to fame that followed. While Peralta was working on a script that dramatised the real-life events Beato recounts, the *Spin* article led to the production of a documentary, *Dogtown and the Z-Boys* (2002), which Peralta directed.

While still working at 20th Century Fox, Art Linson was involved with the *Dogtown* project prior to it being developed into a script, and the producer recruited Peralta after Fox put the concept into turnaround while the documentary was in production. 'This is a cool story about young kids growing up in a tough section of Venice,' Linson said, 'trying to carve out a surf spot for themselves and discovering through skateboarding who they really are. These guys were hijacking swimming pools in Brentwood, draining them and skating in them, and they were outlaws in Venice at the time. Some got famous and some got run over by the experience. It's a fantastic tale.'

Sony Pictures purchased Peralta's original manuscript in January 2003 and screenwriter Roger Avary, of *The Rules of Attraction* (2002) and *Killing Zoe* (1994), joined the production to develop the script with Fincher. While some commentators have already wondered if Fincher's dark outlook is suited to a rites of passage drama, one only has to look back at the *Spin* article to see that this won't be *The Fast and the Furious* on skateboards; *The Lords of Dogtown* promises to be an edgy ride fuelled by aggression, substance abuse and attitude. The movie is set to be released in 2004 as an Indelible Pictures film.

After *The Lords of Dogtown*, the director's dance card remains packed, with a handful of projects shifting in and out of favour from the back-burner limbo that Hollywood knows as 'development hell'. Adaptations, crime thrillers, science fiction, horror and war stories are all stacked in David Fincher's in-tray as vehicles for his direction or as projects to manage in an executive producer role; each is waiting for the right moment, the right script, the right wallet to open and a green light to blink on. Given the mercurial nature of Tinseltown, any one of these potential projects has the capacity to become an instant certainty overnight and fast-tracked into production in months; conversely, each of them could also sink into the depths of the studio vaults and, like so many movie scripts, never see the light of day again. Whatever their eventual fate, it remains enticing to consider the ghostly possibility of these David Fincher movies-in-waiting and imagine how he would bring them to the screen...

Chemical Pink

AFTER FINCHER'S SUCCESS in adapting Chuck Palahniuk's novel *Fight Club* to the screen, it was perhaps inevitable that these two creatives would work together on another feature. After *Fight Club*, rumours circulated that Fincher was considering scripts based on other books by Palahniuk, including *Invisible Monsters*, *Survivor*, *Choke* and *Lullaby*, or that the author was penning an original script for the director. At present, *Invisible Monsters* has been optioned for the screen by fledgling British director Jesse Peyronel's Bounder Productions, while *Choke* has been taken on by Beau Flynn's Bandeira Entertainment, and Fincher's interest in developing *Lullaby*, a scary tale about a nursery rhyme that kills those who hear it, is a fairy story itself.

Palahniuk's script for Fincher is actually an adaptation of another writer's work – author Katie Arnoldi's debut novel *Chemical Pink*. An award-winning bodybuilder and surfing champion, first-time writer Arnoldi's book is set in the ultra-competitive world of professional female bodybuilding, following the character of Aurora Johnson into a strong mixture of sex, drugs and Hollywood gloss; the writer gives a sound-bite description of the story as a 'twisted *Pygmalion*'. Arriving in California, single mother Aurora is ensnared by Charles Worthington III, a rich and sociopathic Svengali-like 'sponsor' sexually obsessed with muscle-girls, who dreams of moulding the ultimate woman bodybuilder through a regimen of intensive training, physical sculpting and colossal doses of drugs. As *Chemical Pink* unfolds, Aurora and Charles enter into a perverted relationship where he plies her with horrific amounts of hormones, anabolic and androgenic steroids in return for her partnering him in sadistic torments and warped sex games.

The story questions what lines can be crossed in order to become the physical ideal. Arnoldi's sharp, eye-witness insight into the body-god culture of Hollywood gyms unveils monstrous details, like the side-effects that give women body-builders metabolic overload and secondary masculine characteristics like hairy backs, boils, beards and clitorihypertrophy, where the clitoris becomes enlarged to a penis-like state.

Palahniuk put a mini-series project in development with cable channel HBO on indefinite hold because of an offer from Fincher to craft a *Chemical Pink* screenplay for him. In Palahniuk's words, he described the premise as 'a dark film', tagging *Seven* star Kevin Spacey for a key role (most likely that of Worthington) and admitting that the chance to work with Fincher and Spacey was one he was unwilling to pass up. The director was impressed enough with Arnoldi's novel to purchase the film rights before the book even hit the book-shops, at one point considering shooting the movie in a High Definition film process.

The abundant drug-fuelled body fascism of *Chemical Pink* instantly strikes a chord with the themes of *Fight Club*, recalling the ill-fated character Robert Paulson ('Bob. Bob had bitch tits.'), a steroid-pumping juicer cursed with testicular cancer and riddled with chemical imbalances. *Chemical Pink* also parallels *Fight Club*'s motif of physical prowess as a means to liberate the self from a society that weakens it – no matter how twisted the motivation. The theme of obsession as a force to distort both body and mind shows up strongly in the director's work and Palahniuk's too, making Arnoldi's novel a prime choice to adapt as their second feature collaboration.

However, while Fincher's dark approach to filmmaking seems a perfect fit for *Chemical Pink*'s translation to the screen, his involvement in the project is currently only as a producer. '*Chemical Pink* is a movie that I'm hoping Jonas Akerlund is going to direct,' he notes. Like Fincher, Akerlund's career kick-started in music video, with his 'Ray of Light' and 'Music' promos for Madonna, as well as work for acts like U2, Moby, The Prodigy and Ozzy Osbourne. Ackerlund's kinetic and hyper-lit style combined with Arnoldi's twisted characters promises an eye-popping feature film.

Fertig

BASED ON THE 1963 book *They Fought Alone* by John Keats, this is the true story of Lieutenant Colonel Wendell Fertig, an American officer in the Second World War who led his rag-tag unit of soldiers against enemy forces in the

Pacific, gathering up local support to create a guerrilla force capable of opposing the Imperial Japanese army.

In 1942, as the Japanese invaders pressed their assault on the islands of the Philippines, US forces were pushed to the very brink of destruction until their commanding officer ordered them to lay down their weapons and surrender rather than face annihilation. However, the Japanese occupation army were soon being harried by guerrilla forces made up of Filipino and American soldiers, and on the island of Mindanao, an officer named Wendell Fertig rallied an army of nearly 38,000 men, effectively denying Mindanao to the enemy for the duration of the conflict. Allegedly, the guerrilla leader announced himself as 'Brigadier General' Fertig in a radio message to General Douglas MacArthur, although in fact he was a reserve lieutenant colonel serving in the US Army's Corps of Engineers, who had been reported missing in action on the island of Luzon.

With the secret assistance of the recently created OSS covert operations force, Fertig and his men were kept supplied even as the American government were compelled to deny any official support for their activities. Forced to dig in and await the return of MacArthur, Fertig's troops kept the pressure up against the invaders for two years until relief eventually arrived. Colonel Fertig's story is classic war movie stuff, a grim tale of heroism against impossible odds; as well as Keats' book, W E B Griffin also wrote about Fertig's odyssey in his novels *Behind the Lines* and *The Fighting Agents*.

In the midst of Hollywood's resurgence in war stories, exemplified by *Pearl Harbor* (2001), the *Band of Brothers* television mini-series, the remake of *The Thin Red Line* and the Vietnam-era *We Were Soldiers* (2002), *Fertig* came forward as an excellent feature property. William Nicholson, writer of *First Knight* (1995) and *Gladiator* (2000), penned a script for Columbia Pictures and in 2000 actor Tom Cruise was reputedly in consideration to take on the titular role. Cruise eventually passed on *Fertig*, electing instead to play the lead in another war movie, *The Last Samurai*, but both he and David Fincher expressed an interest in working together on a future feature.

In the interim, Fincher maintains an interest in *Fertig* and the lead role has since been connected with Brad Pitt. For the director, the war film is a genre he has yet to try his hand at, and helming a movie like *Fertig*, with all the harsh drama this true-life tale has to offer, would be a unique challenge to him. In late 2002, Fincher noted: '*Fertig* is a movie that I hope to direct, and we're in the process of location scouting.' Possible locales tipped to double for the Philippines include Panama and Hawaii.

Nicholson spoke about working on the feature at the Orange Screenwriters Season Lecture in February 2003: 'I'm doing a thing with David Fincher at present, and I have to sort of become David Fincher, and think, "How is he seeing this?", so that he will be able to direct it ... and then the actor comes on board, and it's Brad Pitt. I'm sitting there thinking, "I should be so lucky to have these people actually wanting to do – I was going to say *my* movie, but of course, it's not *my* movie and when it eventually comes out, it'll be *David Fincher's* movie.'

Hard Boiled

DAVID FINCHER WAS first made aware of *Hard Boiled* when actor Nicolas Cage approached him with the concept, intent on adapting this comic book series for the big screen. Cage had been impressed enough by the comic to personally purchase the rights for his production company Saturn Films, with Warner Bros in line to distribute the final product.

Writer and artist Frank Miller, creator of comics such as the defining *Batman* saga *The Dark Knight Returns*, the noir-style *Sin City* crime tales and the science fiction samurai drama *Ronin*, wrote this violent and destructive tale with artist Geoff Darrow, earning them the 1990 Eisner award, the comics industry's most coveted prize. Cage's intention is to play the lead role of Carl Seltz, an insurance investigator in a near-future world with an idyllic home life and loving family; but Seltz's calm existence is shattered by the shocking discovery of his own dual identity. The Carl personality is just a cover for a vicious tax collector called Nixon, a robot-hating homicidal killer with the blood of hundreds of innocents on his hands. Worse still, Nixon soon learns that even *this* is a lie, that he is really a machine himself, a cyborg warrior called Unit 4 with a destiny to free the intelligent robot slaves of the future. Fincher puts it simply: 'It's about a robot who thinks robots are despicable and can't believe he's a robot himself.'

Darrow's hyper-detailed artwork represents a ready-made storyboard for the potential *Hard Boiled* feature film, and this is not the first time that Nicolas Cage has been connected with comicbook characters, with both *Superman* and *Ghost Rider* movies linked to the actor. In addition, writer Frank Miller's practice in features as a co-writer on *Robocop 2* (1990) and *Robocop 3* (1992) lends him the experience to shift the pitch of the comic to a film script. Both Miller and Darrow have a relationship in place with Warner Bros., with the writer developing the *Batman: Year One* project for the studio and Darrow involved in design work on *The Matrix* movies.

Prior to David Fincher's connection to *Hard Boiled*, *Matrix* writer/director duo Larry and Andy Wachowski had been considered to handle the project, but Miller had been uninterested in their concepts for the feature as a traditionally animated movie. *Variety* later reported Fincher in the frame to helm the picture, with the director intent on creating a fully computer-generated feature, like *Final Fantasy: The Spirits Within* (2001). 'I wanted to do it as a series of animated shorts at first to introduce the character,' he notes. 'We have these R-rated animated shorts, and then we kind of unleash [the character] and then do it as a complete CG animation.' At present the director seems content to let the writer drive the project and develop *Hard Boiled* as he sees best. 'It's a thing that we're talking about; I don't know what we're going to do with this. Frank has an idea, and I think he's a genius so I'll follow him anywhere … but I don't know what he's got in mind yet.'

Hard Boiled's visually complex nature, a narrative packed with kinetic action and layers of detail, is an interesting fit with Fincher's approach to cinema, and in addition the double-think identity crisis plotline ramps up the split personality themes of *Fight Club* to fever pitch. The project may also mark Fincher's first foray into a fully computer-created feature film.

Mank

AS FAR BACK as 1997, this biographical story of Herman J Mankiewicz, the writer of Orson Welles' epic motion picture *Citizen Kane*, was rumoured as a pet project for David Fincher. From a script written by his father, Howard Fincher, the director's black and white biopic targeted *Seven* star Kevin Spacey as the lead, with *Panic Room*'s Jodie Foster in a co-starring role as movie actress Marion Davies. In production at the same time was HBO's telemovie *RKO 281*, which also covered the backstory of *Citizen Kane* (casting John Malkovich in the Mankiewicz role and Melanie Griffith as Davies). Still, the true story behind the creation of this mould-shattering movie and the writer behind it has enough scope for the production of a further feature by Fincher and his father.

Mankiewicz was a cynical but extremely talented scriptwriter, a former theatre critic for the *New Yorker* and the *New York Times* who left his job for the glitter of early Hollywood. Dropping out of the elite circle of New York's high society, specifically the so-called 'Algonquin Round Table', Mankiewicz began with scripts for silent films, starting with *The Road to Mandalay* in 1926, working on more than 70 features during his lifetime. He once famously described Hollywood to a fellow writer in NYC by saying: 'Millions are to be grabbed out here and your only competition is idiots. Don't let this get around.' As film technology evolved in the late twenties, Mankiewicz changed gears and moved seamlessly into talkies, continuing to write stories or dialogue for films like *Man of the World* (1942), *The Lost Squadron* (1932), *Dinner at Eight* (1933) and *It's a Wonderful World* (1939), as well as an uncredited rewrite on *The Wizard of Oz*; he also worked with the Marx Brothers as an executive producer on movies like *Horse Feathers* (1932) and *Duck Soup* (1933).

With his career flagging as the thirties ended and with his comedic hits behind him, Mankiewicz's Oscar-winning success with Welles' *Citizen Kane* in 1942 gave him a brief respite. However, his alcoholism and large gambling debts eventually got the better of him and he died, penniless, of uremic poisoning in 1953. Remembered for Welles' powerfully directed feature about a ruthless newspaper mogul, Mankiewicz no doubt drew on his personal experiences as a former associate of real-life magnate William Randolph Hearst and as a partygoer at Hearst's huge Hollywood mansion. Although Mankiewicz was forced to share *Citizen Kane*'s Academy Award for Best Writing with Welles, the great majority of the script was the writer's own work, and it was not only a source of friction between the two men but of debate among film critics to this day.

Last mooted as a Propaganda Films movie, Howard and David Fincher's *Mank* may yet be produced as a project at Indelible Pictures. Fincher has previously spoken of his intent to use a special film stock to shoot *Mank*, a black and white negative type no longer used in the contemporary industry that would have to be recreated from the original 'recipe'. For the director, this feature represents an opportunity to produce a fundamentally different film from his earlier works in a genre he has yet to explore; at the same time, the life of Herman J Mankiewicz retains the streak of darkness that has always appealed to Fincher's sensibilities. '*Mank* is a script that I've been working to get exactly right for ten years,' said Fincher, 'and I hope, some day, to make it as one of the definitive 'writer in Hollywood' stories.'

The Reincarnation of Peter Proud

A FAVOURITE FILM of the director's youth, Fincher liked the 'sense of irony' present in this 1975 horror feature starring Michael Sarrazin, Jennifer O'Neill and Margot Kidder. J Lee Thompson, who worked on *Ice Cold in Alex* (1958), *The Guns of Navarone* (1962) and *Cape Fear* (1961), directed the film from a script by Max Ehrlich, who wrote 'The Apple' for the original *Star Trek* television series plus *Zero Population Growth* (1972), a doom-laden science fiction movie about birth control. Fincher's love for the key concepts of the film led him to consider a modern version, in partnership with *Changing Lanes* (2002) producer Scott Rudin at Paramount Pictures. Rudin purchased the remake rights to *The Reincarnation of Peter Proud* in late 2001 for $700,000 against a fee of $2.2 million.

In the story, the titular character is a college professor who inexplicably starts to experience haunting visions from a past life, slowly being drawn into the behaviour patterns of his earlier self. Visiting the places glimpsed in his dreams, including a sinister lake, Proud encounters Marcia Curtis and feels some strange connection to her. Soon he begins to fall in love with her daughter Ann, but when Peter starts to exhibit the mannerisms of her dead husband,

Marcia realises that Peter is the reincarnation of Ann's father Jeff. With Jeff's mysterious death still unresolved after decades, Proud struggles to discover the truth while Marcia tries to keep the 'incestuous' relationship between Peter and Ann from progressing; and it becomes clear that only Marcia knows exactly what happened to her husband. As the film draws to a climax, Proud returns to the lake once more, unwittingly duplicating the actions that led Jeff Curtis to his death.

A dark and gloomy piece of seventies psychological horror, *The Reincarnation of Peter Proud* is viewed by some as a forgotten classic, overlooked and deleted on video, occasionally appearing in backwater slots on late-night television. Fincher's razor-edged twist endings, last-minute reversals and cinematic sucker-punches trace a direct line back to the rug-pull conclusion of *Peter Proud*, which influenced the young David in the same way as the finales of *Planet of the Apes* (1967) and *The Last of Sheila* (1973). In reference to the similarly grim ending of *Seven*, Fincher defended the use of darker conclusions so: 'You can make a movie where people don't walk off into the sunset and which is still fiscally productive.'

A script for the remake is currently being developed with Hillary Seitz, who previously wrote the screenplay for *Insomnia* (2002) and the adaptation of Isaac Azimov's science fiction classic *I, Robot*, due to shoot in 2004. Although still something of a wish-fulfilment project for the director, perhaps to repay a debt of influence to this unsung movie, a remake of *The Reincarnation of Peter Proud* remains on David Fincher's back-burner for the foreseeable future.

Rendezvous With Rama

A HIGHLY REGARDED science fiction novel by Arthur C Clarke, the author of *2001: A Space Odyssey* and its sequels, this book from the mid-seventies won both the Nebula and Hugo awards in the same year. Later expanded in sequels like *Rama II, The Gardens of Rama* and *Rama Revealed*, *Rendezvous with Rama* has frequently appeared on the wish-lists of producers in the 30 years since it was written. The story's connection with David Fincher arose early in 1997, when *Seven* actor Morgan Freeman approached the director with the concept after purchasing the rights for his production company Revelations Entertainment. Originally planned for a New Year's Eve release in 1999, *Rendezvous with Rama* has since slipped back along Fincher's schedule on a number of occasions.

The novel's plotline centres around the first human contact with an alien space vessel, a massive cylindrical craft codenamed Rama after the Hindu deity. A few hundred years hence, the crew of the *Endeavour*, a 'space-guard' ship employed to hunt down and destroy Earth-threatening asteroids, are sent to investigate what at first appears to be another stray rock, discovering the gargantuan mechanism as it passes through the solar system on a mysterious mission. With their commanders back home unable to launch a full-scale investigation team, the *Endeavour*'s Captain Norton and his rag-tag crew are sent to board Rama and probe its secrets. ('It's a survival movie,' said Fincher. 'It's what it would be like if five satellite repairmen rather than scientists had first contact with extraterrestrial intelligence.') Once inside the hollow interior of the ship, Norton's team discovers an alien ghost town inhabited by organic machines called biots, which appears to be abandoned – but is it?

Freeman's involvement in *Rendezvous with Rama* places him in the role of Captain Norton, as well as serving as executive producer with Revelations' Lori McCreary. French fantasy artist Jean Giraud (also known as 'Moebius'), who worked on films like *The Abyss*, *Blade Runner* and *Heavy Metal*, is working with the producers as a conceptual design artist and, most notably, computing technology giant Intel have joined the project as a major partner. Freeman commented, 'The current trend toward more digital effects in film will continue until digital cinematography is the norm, not the event that it is now. Lori McCreary and I created Revelations with this kind of technological leap in mind.'

Intel's involvement in the film points to plans for *Rendezvous with Rama* to use an unprecedented amount of computer-generated imagery to create the alien world of the massive spaceship. 'Around 99 per cent of it would be CGI,' Fincher notes. 'Technology's close to being able to do that.' On features such as *Star Wars Episode I: The Phantom Menace*, actors were shot against greenscreen backdrops before being digitally inserted into completed artificial sets; *Rendezvous with Rama*'s production plans to reverse this process, creating the CGI sets first so that the cast can relate to an image in their minds rather than acting off 'thin air'. Fincher describes the intent: 'It's basically a motion-capture movie. The environment is completely synthetic, the actors are performing in real-time, but you're editing the real-time component so you can introduce the weightlessness and get the performance that you want.'

The director plans to shoot the film with digital cameras instead of regular Panavision equipment and, unlike a fully CGI feature such as *Final Fantasy* or *Toy Story* (1995), *Rendezvous with Rama*'s cast will be human beings and not virtual 'avatars'. In mid-2001, Freeman and McCreary wowed audiences at the Comdex computer industry show with digital test footage from the film, of the Rama ship itself and a spider-like biot, exhibiting the first proof that Intel's partnership in the project is set to pay dividends in the form of incredible visual effects.

'*Rama* is a really good script, but the technology may not exist [now] to pull it off,' says Fincher. 'It's mostly CG, even for the human faces. I think we'll motion-capture human faces and put them into spacesuits and make it completely photo-realistic. The first half of [the film] takes place in total darkness.' The director clearly sees the film as a way to push forward the frontiers of visual effects. '*Rama* is being budgeted and we're trying to get a budget that's under $140 million. The research and development that Digital Domain are trying to do with facial motion capture [is amazing], and we're working with the Institute of Creative Technology and trying to figure out ways to do High-Def photogrammetry, like interlocking High-Def cameras on bases and using that to drive a 3D model, then putting the actors into spacesuits that would be 3D animation. It's pretty interesting – if it works.'

Meanwhile, the film's script remains a sticking point for the production, a hard science fiction narrative that must be translated to the screen and still retain its impact; but, as one SF's best-known books, Clarke's novel has also been plundered for its tropes for decades. 'It's a very tricky adaptation,' Fincher notes. 'It's probably one of the most pilfered books of the last 30 years. There are so many science fiction films that owe at least a narrative twist or a notion to *Rendezvous with Rama* – *Star Trek: The Motion Picture*, *Alien*, *Armageddon*, *Independence Day* ... all of these movies have plot devices and elements that are taken from it, so I don't feel you can just *do* the book. I think you have to re-invent it.' Another difficulty inherent in adapting the source material is the length; at one point Fincher spoke of 'trying to get a script together of fewer than 300 pages'.

The process of adapting *Rendezvous with Rama* began with screenwriter and Finch Mob regular Andrew Kevin Walker, who was approached to take the novel through development in 1997, to evolve a script that kept Clarke's open-ended conclusion. Walker specifically noted the challenge of writing an alien contact feature where the aliens never actually appear. However, the writer was unable to commit to the movie, offering to pen a production draft at a later date, so in 2000 it was industry newcomer Scott Brick who took on the writing duties. A former comics journalist, Brick's work met with glowing praise, and Walker later took a pass over the story before the script moved on to *Band of Brothers* writer Bruce McKenna, who most recently was involved in polishing the material in tandem with Fincher; it is the McKenna and Fincher draft that is currently circulating among investors for the feature.

'I'm interested in how these NASA guys sleep when they're inside a 50-kilometre-long, pitch-black, weightless tin can,' says the director. 'Who could sleep in that? You're on the verge of doing something great for mankind, but think of the human frailty aspect.' He continues: 'This is a movie that you want, when 12-year-olds come out of seeing it, you want them to run out and buy a telescope and not an action doll. With that in mind, we've got to keep the costs down to do the Arthur Clarke version.'

Fincher admits he's made 'a lot of radical changes' to the narrative, including the removal of a subplot about the *Dragonfly*, a zero-gravity glider. 'We cut a lot of stuff that I know people will freak out about, but I want to do *Rama* as *Into Thin Air*,' he says, referring to Jon Krakhauer's 1996 book covering a true account of an ill-fated expedition up Mount Everest. 'I want to do it as like an assault on Everest, I want it to be about the physical concerns. How many oxygen bottles do you have? How do you get in? How much wire do you leave behind, what kind of markers, what trails do you take, where's your base camp, what happened to that shit that you left here, where's your garbage? So, it's really all brought back down to opposable thumb interests, as opposed to the bigger, psycho-spiritual 'next evolution of man' stuff.'

Despite earning a place in cinema history as a benchmark science fiction movie, the Stanley Kubrick version of Arthur C Clarke's *2001: A Space Odyssey* was not a mainstream hit, and the lacklustre performance of the sequel *2010: Odyssey Two* (1984) did little to elevate the writer's other works to the big screen. At present, only one other Clarke novel, *Childhood's End*, is currently under feature development, with Beacon Pictures. However, the adaptation of *Rendezvous with Rama* has the potential to go blockbuster, merging cutting-edge visual effects with a strong script and David Fincher's hand at the helm. The director's first and last foray into science fiction to date was the cramped and confined horror of *Alien 3*, and while this film may touch on similar themes, the scope of *Rendezvous with Rama* could make this the 'biggest' Fincher feature to date; in addition, Fincher's skill at crafting stories set close to the protagonists may save the movie from becoming swamped by its own eye candy and preserve the novel's non-Hollywood ending.

Rendezvous with Rama appears to be one of the more viable concepts on the director's slate, with a script nearing completion and computer generated pre-visualisation already under way. As well as the film, Freeman's Revelations Entertainment production company also hopes to create tie-ins such as on-line material, television shows and an IMAX movie using a subset of the feature film's footage matched with new material.

One of the occupational hazards of being a film director is deflecting the constant storm of rumour and counter-rumour surrounding just what feature project will be the next to go in front of your camera. For example, in the past Fincher has been connected with movies such as *8mm* and *The Avengers*; and while these were both films he did at one time consider directing, for every script he evaluates, eager pundits link him to a dozen others. Most recently, during his work on *Panic Room*, Fincher was tipped to be the director of such diverse features as *Spider-Man* or the adaptation of the stage musical *Chicago*. His name has also been linked – wrongly – with screen versions of other novels by *Fight Club*'s Chuck Palahniuk (see above), comic book superhero flicks *Shi*, *Spawn II* and *Superman Lives*, as well as unproduced action-thrillers like *Solace* and *Pathfinder*.

For over a year, Fincher had been firmly placed in the director's chair for the third movie in the *Mission: Impossible* series, only to leave the project mere days before the deadline for this book. For followers of the director's work, it's hard not to speculate on the possibilities of some of Fincher's more interesting 'near-misses', including *M: I-3*, the military drama *Squids*, the science fiction horror of *Passengers*, the sex comedy *Seared*, the gloomy *Stay* and the remake of Hitchcock's *Strangers on a Train*.

In early 2002, Fincher announced that his next project would be to take on another big-name movie franchise and helm the third film in the *Mission: Impossible* series, following in the footsteps of Brian DePalma's 1996 original adaptation of the 1960s TV show and John Woo's bullet-ballet sequel *M: I-2* (2000). Some observers considered that Fincher's agreement to do another 'threequel' might put to rest the critical ghosts stirred up by his debut movie *Alien 3* – or perhaps reawaken them. 'We're working on it,' he joked at the time, 'and there's a beautiful symmetry.' With the possibility of being placed once more at the helm of a license that had earned a billion dollars in global ticket sales, both his fans and the Hollywood movie community were watching Fincher closely and critically to see how he would handle the film; but in February 2003, he parted company with the franchise, to be replaced by *Narc* director Joe Carnahan, who also worked on *The Hire Phase 2* with the short *Ticker*.

Fincher's involvement with the *Mission: Impossible* series grew from his brief association with actor Tom Cruise on the unfilmed *Fertig* project (see above); while Cruise passed on *Fertig* in favour of *The Last Samurai* (2003), the actor and director affirmed their interest in working together. In his role as an executive producer on the *Mission: Impossible* movies with Paula Wagner, Cruise selected Fincher as a potential helmer on *M: I-3*, opening up pre-production discussions with franchise owners Paramount Productions for shooting to commence in 2003. In June 2002, Cruise told interviewers: 'I'm talking to David and hopefully it will all come together. To see Fincher unload on *M: I-3* ... Well, I'd like to see that.'

In early 2000, a script centred on a plot to destroy the Seven Wonders of the World had been in consideration with Ang Lee as director, but the terrorist acts of 11 September 2001 likely derailed any plot where the destruction of major landmarks was a key element. For his take on *Mission: Impossible 3*, Fincher planned to up the ante, noting: 'I have some specific ideas that Cruise and I discussed that I think would make it interesting, kind of shocking. It's a particularly extreme take on espionage without having anything to do with terrorism or spying.' In an interview with the *Irish Times*, the director hinted that the storyline would cover the illegal trade in human organs and body parts from Africa to the West, and later comments from Paramount confirmed that location scouting in the United Arab Emirates had taken place, with the city of Dubai set to feature as a key location in the movie. 'It's a really cool idea, really violent,' Fincher told the *Guardian*, 'if [Paramount] let us do even half of what we want, it should make for a pretty interesting film.'

Given the high-profile nature of the *Mission: Impossible* films, many observers considered that Fincher's darker directing style might have taken a back seat to the high-octane action/adventure storytelling that the previous movies showcased. 'I'm unaware of my reputation,' the director joked during an interview. 'I know Oliver Stone was supposed to do the first one, but he didn't ... Making *M: I-3* would be a challenge for me. I didn't have enough clout to do [*Alien 3*] as I wanted to. I've never had a deal with a movie that had to open on a certain date or get box-office results to justify its existence.'

After being burned on the third *Alien* feature, Fincher is well aware that in Hollywood 'You can never make exactly the movie you want to make. I met Tom Cruise, and he has a very healthy attitude towards making movies which is, "Let's only do it if we can do something that's really great," which is the antithesis of the *Alien 3* situation, which was, "We've gotta have the movie, it's got to be out in theatres, that's the only thing that matters." He is saying to me, "See if you can come up with a story that surprises me, tell it to me over the phone and if I get excited lets go and make it. Let's only do something if you are excited about it, and I'm excited about it, and Robert Towne is excited." That's what we've been doing and after five months, we've got a first act...'

Even with Cruise as both lead actor and executive producer on the movies, Fincher had nonetheless expressed his desire to preserve final cut, hoping to retain the promise that *Mission: Impossible 3* would remain 'A David Fincher Film'. But the director's commitment to *The Lords of Dogtown* and Paramount's desire to bring *Mission: Impossible 3* out as a tent-pole blockbuster release in 2004 made the point moot, and potentially what might have been Fincher's most conventional movie to date will go ahead without him. 'I pulled out to do a skateboard movie instead,' he noted dryly.

Squids was jokingly considered by some to be a monster movie about mutant sea creatures when it was first announced in connection with Fincher; from the pen of David Ayers, *Squids* is in fact a tense tale set on a US Navy submarine. The story is a rite-of-passage narrative about a young sailor during the late 1980s, in the latter days of the Cold War.

Fincher equates the plotline with the boat journey into the Cambodian jungle from *Apocalypse Now*, 'except on a $200 million submarine with nuclear warheads'. The US Navy submariners are nicknamed 'squids', and Ayers' script draws heavily on his time as a serving member of the US Marines. Ayers' first feature script, the historically challenged World War II drama *U-571*, proved his familiarity with submariners and *Squids* could be conceived in terms of the tension and claustrophobia seen in *Alien 3* and *Panic Room*, if Fincher were to direct it.

'It's a really interesting coming of age movie, [but] it's really about American foreign policy, it's about American *military* foreign policy at the end of the Reagan era. It's about life in a nuclear submarine for an 18-year-old white kid from South Central LA, whose had the shit kicked out of him his whole life, who sees some very atrocious behaviour by American military personnel, and some really dangerous politically compromised and morally compromised situations, [so] that he eventually decides he doesn't want to be a sailor any more.' Fincher's discussion of the script indicates a film-in-waiting that eschews the trappings of conventional technothrillers: 'I think that everybody felt, given the world as is it right now, this script was *persona non grata*. So David Ayers, to his credit, bought the script back from New Line rather than make the changes, and so he owns it now, and if he ever decides he wants to do it...'

Speaking in early 2002, in a global climate still reeling from the terrorist attacks on the World Trade Center and the Pentagon, Fincher notes that 'it's exactly the wrong time to be making this movie. I think it's a looking glass held a little *too* close.' In the pro-government, gung-ho America of post-September 11th, *Squids* may be a hard sell for some time to come; in the director's words, 'The white power structure very rarely wants to look at its shortcomings.' However, in the 9/11 aftermath, the United States government *was* willing to look at Fincher's comments and those of several other movie creatives, including Spike Jonze, as part of a working group convened to theorise possible terrorist attack scenarios for federal intelligence officials.

Seared was pitched as a loose adaptation of *Kitchen Confidential: Adventures in the Culinary Underbelly*, the autobiography of chef Anthony Bourdain. The book is a testosterone-fuelled caper, a *Fight Club* with pepper-mills and Sabatier knives, snapshots from the author's earliest days as a low-life kitchen stooge to his current posting as executive chef at New York's Les Halles. *Kitchen Confidential* paints a picture of haute cuisine behind the scenes as a world filled with thugs and thieves, hard-assed wheeler-dealers stripping staff from each other's restaurants, swearing, fighting, screwing, drinking and doing drugs in among the creation of delicious food.

But the anecdotal book lends itself poorly to a feature script. Instead, Jesse Wigutow fictionalised the work as *Seared*, cherry-picking the best moments and the key themes. Wigutow worked on *Sweet Friggin' Daisies* (2002) and *It Runs in the Family* (2003), as well as *Urban Townie*, a script Brad Pitt was briefly connected with. Pitt was in the running for the lead in *Seared* too, playing erstwhile chef Jake Casdin, but the role has also been pinned to actor Benicio del Toro. 'It's a kind of sex comedy about celebrity chefs in New York,' said Fincher in 2001. 'But it's too obscure to really explain how it became a script... It'd be like *Shampoo*, only with food.' The script casts the fictional Casdin as the star chef of a swanky Manhattan eatery, balancing his decadent, high-pressure lifestyle between his art student girlfriend and restaurant critic mistress. Jake is under pressure from a coke-fiend sous-chef, with a massive wedding banquet to cater and an offer of his own kitchen to mull over; and, amidst it all, the arrogant, irresponsible but ultimately gifted cook has to pull his life together before it self-destructs.

It's easy to make a connection between this story and *Fight Club*, spinning off from the scenes of culinary terrorism perpetrated by Tyler Durden. 'It [would be] sort of a romp,' Fincher noted, 'or as much of a romp as I could do.' Fincher spoke of *Seared* as something different from his previous studio films: 'It's what [Steven] Soderbergh calls 'a purification project', like Dogme.' (The director refers to the Dogme '95 filmmakers' manifesto for creating movies without the technical gewgaws of modern production: 'You've got to do it all hand-held, with no storyboards, no pre-visualisation.') In September 2002, Fincher was still involved with *Seared*, intending to produce with *What's Eating Gilbert Grape* (1993) and *The Cider House Rules* (1999) director Lasse Hallström behind the camera, but early in 2003 he left the project entirely; Fincher had stated previously that the film was possibly too expensive to produce. 'Sex comedies are only as expensive as the people you want to see fuck, and I wanted to see expensive people fuck.'

Stay is an original script penned by novelist David Benioff, and it was the subject of a frenzied bidding war in late 2001, the like of which had not been seen since the multi-million dollar paycheques of the mid-1990s, when writers like Shane Black and Joe Ezterhas pulled in fees of $4 million for *The Long Kiss Goodnight* (1996) and $2 million for *Showgirls* (1995). Purchased for the princely sum of $1.8 million by Regency Enterprises, a production company based at the 20th Century Fox studio, Benioff's script is a supernatural thriller; the protagonist is a professor of psychology at a prestigious Ivy League university who must prevent an ill-fated student from committing suicide.

Despite Benioff's neophyte status as a screenwriter, Regency were forced to outbid five other studios for the right to make *Stay*, and in the interim the writer sold a second, untitled pitch (described as an 'epic') to Warner Bros. Benioff's previous novel of drug-dealers and lowlifes, *The 25th Hour*, was adapted as a feature starring Edward Norton, directed by Spike Lee in 2002. Like the previously mentioned remake of *The Reincarnation of Peter Proud*, *Stay* offered Fincher the opportunity to craft a dark narrative in a supernatural horror vein. In late 2002 the director noted, 'I'm meeting and discussing *Stay* with David Benioff, we're in final rewrites to see if I can get out of it what I *think* I can do best with it. It may or may not pan out ... There's a big twist at the end, which I think is problematic for an audience to buy, given my experience on *Fight Club*.' It may have been this aspect of the project which eventually saw Fincher bow out in early 2003, with Marc Forster, director of *Monster's Ball* (2002), taking his place.

Strangers was first mentioned in early 2000 with David Fincher to direct. Producer Arnold Kopelson described the updated *Strangers on a Train* script by Rand Ravich, writer on *The Astronaut's Wife* (1999) and *Candyman II: Farewell to the Flesh* (1995), as 'not a remake per se, but a reconceptualisation of the novel'.

Patricia Highsmith's crime novel *Strangers on a Train* is best known to movie-goers in its incarnation as a 1951 feature directed by Alfred Hitchcock. First adapted for the screen by Whitfield Cook, Raymond Chandler and Czenzi Ormonde, the original film centres on tennis star Guy Haines, whose idle conversation in a railway carriage with Bruno Antony leads to a horrific homicide plot in which Bruno offers to kill Guy's wife in return for Guy killing Bruno's father. A fresh take on Highsmith's 1950 book would actually be the fourth interpretation of *Strangers on a Train*, counting the Hitchcock film, Robert Starr's little-known 1969 version *Once You Kiss a Stranger* and the 1987 Danny De Vito/Billy Crystal black comedy *Throw Momma from the Train*.

Ravich's script apparently altered the focus from Cook's adaptation, recasting the Guy role as a reporter who has to clear his name after a criminal kills his wife and frames him; in a very nineties addition to the narrative, the reporter must also struggle to regain custody of his son. Kopelson, who worked with Fincher on *Seven*, previously produced *A Perfect Murder*, a remake of Hitchcock's *Dial M for Murder* (1953) starring Michael Douglas and Viggo Mortensen, which suffered a critical beating similar to Gus Van Sant's revisionist version of *Psycho* (1998).

Fincher's affection for Hitchcock's work is well documented, but his approach to the project was not a good fit for the producers. '*Strangers* was something that I was involved with for about six seconds,' says the director. 'I went in and had a meeting with Arnold Kopelson and Lorenzo di Bonaventura. I said, "Here's the cast that I would make it with," and they said, "That's it?" and I said, "Yeah, those are the two guys I would make the movie with," and they said, "Well, what if they won't do it?" I said, "You've got to rewrite the script, because I don't think you would interest them with the script that you have," and they said, "We don't want to tie ourselves down." And they went off on their merry way to do it...' Fincher would not be drawn on who his choice for the two male leads were, but some have speculated that it would have been *Fight Club* duo Edward Norton and Brad Pitt.

Without Fincher, the adaptation still remains in flux, with David Seltzer, writer on *Dragonfly* (2002), *My Giant* (1998) and *Bird on a Wire* (1990) penning a new draft of *Strangers* for Warner Bros in 2002. Late that year, Fincher's fellow Propaganda Films alumni Antoine Fuqua, who directed *The Replacement Killers* (1998), was tipped to shoot the feature.

'There are many more movies I'd like to see made than I could possibly make,' states Fincher. Whatever course he takes from here will be defined by what fresh challenges this innovative director chooses to set himself. But for his audiences one thing remains certain. Wherever his films take us, they will provoke us, divide us and push us to study all the dark places where the light seldom falls.

Filmography

'I just do my work and try to live it down.'

DOCUMENTARY (as director)
The Beat of the Live Drum (1985)

FEATURE FILMS (as director)
Alien 3 (1992)
Seven (1995)
The Game (1997)
Fight Club (1999)
Panic Room (2002)

SHORT FILMS (as producer or executive producer)
Ambush (2001)
Chosen (2001)
The Follow (2001)
Star (2001)
Powder Keg (2001)
The Car Thief and the Hit Man (2001)
The Hit Man and the Investigator (2001)
The Investigator and the Man in the Tan Jacket (2001)
The Man in the Tan Jacket and the Motel Maid (2001)
The Motel Maid and the Package (2001)

SHORT FILMS (as director)
The Hire: Driving Techniques (2001)
The Making of The Hire (2001)

FEATURE FILMS (other credits)
Twice Upon a Time (1983) (Special Photographic Effects)
Return of the Jedi (1983) (Assistant Cameraman, Miniature & Optical Effects Unit)

The NeverEnding Story (1984) (Matte Photography Assistant)
Indiana Jones and the Temple of Doom (1984) (Matte Photography)
Being John Malkovich (1999) (Christopher Bing, uncredited role)
Full Frontal (2002) (himself)

COMMERCIALS
'Smoking Foetus', The American Cancer Society (1984)
'Barclay on Broadway', Nike (1992)
'The Director', Chanel (1992)
'BladeRoller', Coca-Cola Japan (1993)
'Children', Nike (1993)
'Ginger or Marianne?' aka 'Pool Hall', Budweiser (1993)
'Instant Karma', Nike (1993)
'The Ref', Nike (1993)
'Find Something', Nike (1993)
'Temple of Flight', Nike (1993)
'Young Miss' aka 'Demolition', YM Magazine (1993)
'Magazine Wars', Nike Tennis (1994)
'Restaurant', Levis Japan (1994)
'Escape', Honda (1995)
'You Will', AT&T (1995)
'Chase', Levis (1996)
'Reason #259' aka 'Rivet', Levis (1998)
'Invincible', Nike (2000)
'Mechanical Legs', Adidas (2002)
'Real', Coca-Cola (2002)

MUSIC VIDEOS
'Shame', The Motels (1985)
'Shock', The Motels (1985)
'All the Love in the World', The Outfield (1986)
'Everytime You Cry', The Outfield (1986)
'Don't Tell Me the Time', Martha Davis (1987)
'Downtown Train', Patti Smith (1987)
'Endless Nights', Eddie Money (1987)
'Englishman in New York', Sting (1987)
'Get Rhythm', Ry Cooder (1987)
'Johnny B', The Hooters (1987)
'No Surrender', The Outfield (1987)

'Notorious', Loverboy (1987)
'She Comes On', Wire Train (1987)
'Storybook', Mark Knopfler (1987)
'Heart of Gold', Johnny Hates Jazz (1988)
'(It's Just) The Way That You Love Me (version 2)', Paula Abdul (1988)
'Roll With It', Steve Winwood (1988)
'Shattered Dreams' (US version), Johnny Hates Jazz (1988)
'Cold Hearted', Paula Abdul (1989)
'The End of Innocence', Don Henley (1989)
'Express Yourself', Madonna (1989)
'Forever Your Girl', Paula Abdul (1989, unfinished)
'Janie's Got a Gun', Aerosmith (1989)
'Real Love', Jody Watley (1989)
'Straight Up', Paula Abdul (1989)
'Cradle of Love', Billy Idol (1990)
'Freedom '90', George Michael (1990)
'Home', Iggy Pop (1990)
'LA Woman', Billy Idol (1990, unfinished)
'Oh Father', Madonna (1990)
'Vogue', Madonna (1990)
'Who Is It (version 2 Break-up Dangerous Story)', Michael Jackson (1992)
'Bad Girl', Madonna (1993)
'Love is Strong', The Rolling Stones (1994)
'6th Avenue Heartache', The Wallflowers (1996)
'Judith', A Perfect Circle (2000)

References

DVD and Video

Alien 3 (1999), '*Alien* Legacy' edition DVD.
The Making of Alien 3 (1992), video boxed set promotional tape.
Seven (2000), Special Edition DVD commentary tracks & supplementary material.
The Game (1998), Criterion Collection Laserdisc commentary tracks & supplementary material.
Fight Club (2000), Special Edition DVD commentary tracks & supplementary material.
Panic Room (2002), DVD.

Scripts

Brancato, John & Ferris, Michael – *The Game*, October 1995.
Brancato, John & Ferris, Michael and Gross, Larry and Walker, Andrew Kevin – *The Game*, February 1996.
Gibson, William – *Alien III*, 1987.
Hill, Walter & Giler, David – *Alien III*, April 1991.
Koepp, David – *The Panic Room*, February 2001.
Pickett, Rex – *Alien III*, January 1991.
Red, Eric – *Alien 3*, 1989.
Twohy, David – *Alien III*, October 1989.
Uhls, Jim – *Fight Club*, February 1998.
Walker, Andrew Kevin – *Seven*, January 1992.
Walker, Andrew Kevin – *Seven*, August 1994.
Ward, Vincent & Fasano, John – *Alien III*, March 1990.

Websites

A.Fincher.News.Site – www.davidfincher.cjb.net
DFN: David Fincher.Net – www.davidfincher.net/index.html
Alien 3 (The Official Site) – www.alien-movies.com/html/alien3/alien3_frames.html
Seven (The Official Site) – www.se7enmovie.com
The Seven Cult – www.se7en-cult.com
Fight Club (The Official Site) – www.foxmovies.com/fightclub
Panic Room (The Official Site) – www.spe.sony.com/movies/panicroom

Panic Room: Home Safe? – talie.underground.net/panicroom/index.html
The Hire (The Official Site) – www.bmwfilms.com
Chuck Palahniuk: A Writer's Cult – www.chuckpalahniuk.net
Chemical Pink – www.katiearnoldi.com/books.html
Rendezvous With Rama (The Official Site) – www.rendezvouswithrama.com

Bibliography

BOOKS

Arnoldi, Katie – *Chemical Pink*, Forge Books, 2002.

Bourdain, Anthony – *Kitchen Confidential: Adventures in the Culinary Underbelly*, Bloomsbury Publishing, 2000.

Bruno, Anthony – *Seven: A Novel* (novelisation), St. Martins Press, 1995.

Clarke, Arthur C – *Rendezvous with Rama*, Victor Gollancz, 1973.

Dyer, Richard – *BFI Modern Classics: Seven*, BFI Publishing, 1999.

Ellison, James – *Panic Room* (novelisation), Pocket Books, 2002.

Foster, Alan Dean – *Alien 3* (novelisation), Warner Books, 1992.

Highsmith, Patricia – *Strangers on a Train*, W W Norton, 2001.

Keats, John – *They Fought Alone (Classics of War 2: Secret War Series)*, Time Life, 1990.

Lacey, Nick – *The Ultimate Film Guides: Se7en*, York Press, 2001.

Linson, Art – *What Just Happened? Bitter Hollywood Tales from the Front Line*, Bloomsbury, 2002.

Maltin, Leonard – *Leonard Maltin's Movie Encyclopedia*, Penguin Putnam, 1994.

Miller, Frank & Darrow, Geof – *Hard Boiled*, Dark Horse Comics, 1993.

Palahniuk, Chuck – *Fight Club*, W W Norton, 1996.

Prendergast, Tom & Prendergast, Sara – *The International Dictionary of Films & Filmmakers*, fourth edition, St James Press, 2000.

Pym, John (ed) – *Time Out Film Guide*, tenth edition, Penguin, 2002.

Schnelle, Frank (ed) – *David Fincher*, Bertz Verlag, 2002.

Silverberg, Robert – *Moonferns & Starsongs*, Ballantine Books, 1971.

Uhls, Jim – *Fight Club: The Original Screenplay*, ScreenPress Publishing, 2002.

Walker, Andrew Kevin – *Seven & 8mm*, Faber & Faber, 1999.

ARTICLES

Barry, Chris – 'Give Me Dogme or Give Me Death!', *FilmFodder.com*, June 2002.

Beato, G – 'The Lords of Dogtown', *Spin*, March 1999.

Biskind, Peter – 'Extreme Norton', *Vanity Fair*, August 1999.

Blair, Iain – 'David Fincher interview', *Film & Video*, October 1997.

Bond, Jeff – 'Lust in Space', *DreamWatch*, April 2000.

Braund, Simon – 'Retro: David Fincher', *Empire*, May 2002.

Brooks, Xan – 'Directing is Masochism', the *Guardian*, April 2002.

Buckland, Carol – 'Seven – Deadly Cinema?', CNN.com, September 1995.
Burman, Mark – 'David Fincher's Alienation', Starburst Special, April 1993.
Burman, Mark – 'A Real Horror Show', the Independent, August 1992
Busch, Anita – 'Fight Club review', the Hollywood Reporter, October 1999.
Clark, Mike – 'In Seven, Deadly Sins Receive a Stylish Sheen', USA Today, December 1998.
Clinton, Paul – 'Panic Room review', CNN.com, March 2002.
Cooney, Jenny – 'The Head Master', Empire, November 1997.
D'Angelo, Mike – 'The Game review', Entertainment Weekly, 1997.
Darke, Chris – 'Inside the Light', Sight & Sound, April 1996.
Day, Sydney – 'Space Gothic', Marquee, May 1992
Doherty, Thomas – 'Alien 3 review', Cinefantastique, October 1992.
Donadoni, Serena – 'Heavyweight anti-heroes', the Orlando Weekly, October 1999.
Doogan, Todd – 'David Fincher interview', The Digital Bits, May 2000.
Dyer, Richard – 'Kill and Kill Again', Sight & Sound, September 1997.
Ebert, Roger – 'Seven review', the Chicago Sun-Times, September 1995.
Ebert, Roger – 'The Game review', the Chicago Sun-Times, November 1997.
Ebert, Roger – 'Fight Club review', the Chicago Sun-Times, October 1999.
Ebert, Roger – 'Panic Room review', the Chicago Sun-Times, March 2002.
Elmer, David – 'Game Boy', Time Out, October 1997.
Elzer, Steve – 'Squids press release', April 2000.
Emerson, Jim, 'The Critics Duke it Out Over a Knockout Movie', Reel.com, 1999.
Epstein, Dan – 'David Fincher interview', DFN.com, 2002.
Epstein, Dan – 'Forrest Whitaker interview', DFN.com, 2002.
Epstein, Dan – 'Howard Shore interview', DFN.com, 2002.
Epstein, Dan – 'Jodie Foster interview', DFN.com, 2002.
Farber, Stephen – 'A Whole New Game' the New York Times, September 1997.
Fordham, Joe – 'Kevin Haug interview', VFXPro, November 1999.
Fordham, Joe – 'The VFX of Fight Club', VFXPro, November 1999.
Fuller, Graham – 'Fighting Talk', Interview, November 1999.
Gilbey, Ryan – 'Precocious Prankster...', Independent Eye, October 1997.
Gilbey, Ryan – 'Four walls and a Funeral', the Independent, 2002.
Goldberg, Adam – 'Alien 3 review', All Movie Guide, 1992.
Gonzalez, Ed – 'Fight Club review' Slant Magazine, 1999.
'Grozilla' – 'Interview with David Fincher', AICN.com, 2002.
Guthmann, Edward – 'Seven's Lurid Monster Mash', San Francisco Chronicle, September 1995.
Guyot, Paul – 'A Talk with David Fincher', DVDTalk.com, 2002.
Haflidason, Almar – 'Seven review', BBCi, April 2001.
Haflidason, Almar – 'Fight Club review', BBCi, 2001.

Harris, Mark – 'Five Things We Hate About You, *Fight Club*', *Entertainment Weekly*, October 1999.

Henkel, Guido – 'David Fincher interview', *DVD Review*, May 2000.

Howe, Desson – '*Alien 3* review', the *Washington Post*, May 1992.

Howe, Desson – '*Seven* review', the *Washington Post*, September 1995.

Hunt, Bill – '*Alien 3* DVD review', *The Digital Bits*, 1999.

Hunt, Bill – 'David Prior interview', *The Digital Bits*, May 2000.

Hunter, Stephen – '*Panic Room* review', the *Washington Post*, March 2002.

Johnsen, Frank – 'Darius Khondji interview', *Dagsavisen Friday*, July 2002.

Jolin, Dan – 'The *Total Film* Interview: David Fincher', *Total Film*, May 2002.

Jensen, Jeff – 'Cause For Alarm', *Entertainment Weekly*, March 2001.

Kennedy, Dana – '*Stay* script sale', the *New York Times*, December 2001.

Kermode, Mark – '*Alien 3* video review', *Sight & Sound*, March 1993.

Lauten, Erin K – 'Editing *Panic Room*', *VFXPro*, April 2002.

Longsdorf, Amy – 'Foster Battles Bad Guys in *Panic Room*', the *North Jersey Record*, March 2002.

Mackle, Rob – 'What's all the fuss about...David Fincher?', the *Guardian*, September 1997.

Magid, Ron – 'Speeding up the Screams in *Alien 3*', *American Cinematographer*, December 1992.

Makal, Kaite – 'Designing the *Fight Club* brain sequence', *EditorsNet*, November 1999.

Makal, Kaite – '*Panic Room* Title Design', *VFXPro*, 2002.

Martin, Kevin A – 'A World of Hurt', *Cinefex*, January 2000.

Maslin, Janet – '*The Game* review', the *New York Times*, November 1997.

Maslin, Janet – '*Fight Club* review', the *New York Times*, October 1999.

Mitchell, Ben – '*Seven* video review', *Neon*, October 1997.

'Moriarty' – 'Art Linson interview', *AICN.com*, May 2002.

Mottram, James – 'Dwight Yoakam interview', *BBCi*, March 2002.

Mottram, James – 'Forest Whitaker interview', *BBCi*, March 2002.

Newman, Kim – '*The Game* review', *Empire Online*, 2000.

Norton, Bill – 'Zealots & Xenomorphs', *Cinefex*, May 1992.

Nguyen, Tommy & Goldsmith, Meehna – 'Fincher Returns to Music Videos', *EditorsNet*, March 2000.

O'Hehir, Andrew – '*Panic Room* review', *Sight & Sound*, May 2002.

O'Leary, Devin D – 'Steve Golin interview', *Film Vault*, September 1997.

Palahniuk, Chuck – 'Behind the Scenes: *Fight Club*', *Us Magazine*, August 1999.

Palahniuk, Chuck – 'I Made Most of it Up, Honest!', the *Los Angeles Times*, September 1999.

Palmer, Martin – 'Biff-fest with a conscience', the *Times*, November 1999.

Pearce, Gareth – 'Return to the Forbidden Planet', *Empire*, September 1992.

Pickle, Betsy – 'Is *Fight Club* a Rebel With a Cause?' the *Deseret News*, October 1999.

Potter, Maximillian – 'Do These Men Represent the Future of Hollywood Filmmaking?', *Premiere*, February 1998.

Probst, Christopher – 'Playing for Keeps on *The Game*', *American Cinematographer*, September 1997.

Probst, Christopher – 'Anarchy in the USA', *American Cinematographer*, November 1999.

Probst, Christopher – 'Home Invasion', *American Cinematographer*, March 2002.

Pulver, Andrew – 'Prince of Darkness', the *Guardian Guide*, October 1997.

Pulver, Andrew – 'Fight the good fight', the *Guardian*, October 1999.

Pulver, Andrew – 'High Art, Low Road?', the *Guardian Unlimited*, May 2001.

'RS' – 'Vile Bodies', *Time*, September 1995.

Richardson, John H – 'Mother From Another Planet', *Premiere*, May 1992.

Rodriguez, Rene – '*Panic Room* review', The *Miami Herald*, March 2002.

Salisbury, Mark – 'Seventh Hell', *Empire*, February 1996.

Sauriol, Patrick – '*Rendezvous with Rama* script review', *Coming Attractions*, February 2002.

Savlov, Marc – '*Alien 3* review', the *Austin Chronicle*, May 1992.

Savlov, Marc – '*The Game* review', the *Austin Chronicle*, November 1997.

Schaefer, Steven – 'Brad Pitt & Edward Norton interview', *MrShowbiz.com*, October 1999.

Schneller, Johanna – 'Two Heavy Hitters Put Their Muscle Behind the Controversial *Fight Club*' *Premiere*, August 1999.

Schweiger, Daniel – 'The Many Mutations of *Alien 3*', *Horrorzone*, August 1992.

Shulgasser, Barbara – '*Seven*: Thrill-less thriller', *San Francisco Examiner*, September 1995.

Sloane, Judy – 'Killer Movie', *Film Review*, February 1996.

Slotek, Jim – 'Cruisin' for a Bruisin'', the *Toronto Sun*, October 1999.

Smith, Adam – '*The Game* review', *Empire*, November 1997.

Smith, Christopher Allan & Tunison, Michael – 'David Fincher interview', *Cinescape*, May 2002.

Smith, Gavin – 'Inside Out', *Film Comment*, September/October 1999.

Smith, Neil – '*Panic Room* review', *BBCi*, May 2002.

Smith, Sean M – 'Jodie's Choice', *Premiere*, March 2002.

Smithouser, Bob – '*Fight Club* review', *Focus on the Family*, 1999.

Stark, Susan – '*Panic Room* review', The *Detroit News*, March 2002.

'Stax' – 'The Stax Report: *Passengers* script review', *IGN.com*, December 2000.

'Stax' – 'The Stax Report: *Seared* script review', *IGN.com*, November 2001.

'Stax' – 'Remakes on a Train', *IGN.com*, February 2002.

Strick, Phillip – '*The Game* review', *Sight & Sound*, November 1997.

Sturm, Rüdiger – 'David Fincher interview', *Spiegel Online*, 2002.

Svetkey, Benjamin – 'Blood, Sweat & Fears', *Entertainment Weekly*, October 1999.

Taubin, Amy – 'Invading Bodies: *Alien 3* and the Trilogy', *Sight & Sound*, August 1992.

Taubin, Amy – 'The Allure of Decay', *Sight & Sound*, January 1996.

Taubin, Amy – '*Se7en* and violence', *Sight & Sound*, March 1996.

Taubin, Amy – 'So Good it Hurts', *Sight & Sound*, November 1999.

Taylor, Charles – '*The Game* review', *Salon.com*, November 1997.

Teasdall, Barbara – 'Edward Norton Fights His Way to the Top', *Reel.com*, 1999.

Thompson, Bob – 'Playing *The Game*', the *Toronto Sun*, August 1997.

Thoresen, Bjorn – 'Digital Domain Brings Nike Olympic Campaign Into Focus', *VFXPro*, 2000.

Travers, Peter – '*Alien 3* review', *Rolling Stone*, 1992.

Travers, Peter – '*Seven* review', *Rolling Stone*, 1995.

Travers, Peter – '*Fight Club* review', *Rolling Stone*, 1999.

Turan, Kenneth – '*Seven* Offers a Punishing Look at Some Deadly Sins', *Los Angeles Times*, September 1995.

Turan, Kenneth – '*Fight Club* review', *Los Angeles Times*, 1999.

Turan, Kenneth – '*Panic Room* review', *Los Angeles Times*, March 2002.

Vercammen, Paul – 'Brad Pitt Spars with *Fight Club* Critics', *CNN.com*, October 1999.

Vice, Jeff – '*Panic Room* review', The *Deseret News*, March 2002.

Walker, Alexander – '*Fight Club* review', *London Evening Standard*, November 1999.

Walker, Andrew Kevin – 'David Fincher Director Profile', *Interview*, March 2002.

Webber, Paul – 'Jodie Foster interview', *BBCi*, March 2002.

Westerbrook, Caroline – 'Killer Instinct', *Empire*, February 1996.

Whitehouse, Charles – '*Fight Club* review', *Sight & Sound*, December 1999.

Wijnsma, Jo – 'Scott Brick interview', *A.Fincher.News.Site*, 2002.

Williams, David E – 'The Sins of a Serial Killer', *American Cinematographer*, October 1995.

Williams, Linda Ruth – 'Mother Courage', *Sight & Sound*, May 2002.

Wilonsky, Robert – '*Panic Room* review', *New Times Los Angeles*, March 2002.

Wise, Damon – 'David Fincher interview', *Neon*, November 1997.

Wise, Damon – 'Menace II Society', *Empire*, December 1999.

Wrathall, John – '*Seven* review', *Sight & Sound*, January 1996.

Uncredited – 'Brad Pitt interview', *Entertainment Weekly*, January 1998.

Uncredited – 'The Business', *Sight & Sound*, August 1996.

Uncredited – '*Seven* production notes', 1997.

Uncredited – '*Fight Club* Censored in U.K.', *VFXPro*, December 1999.

Uncredited – '*Fight Club* production notes', 1999.

Uncredited – 'How to Start a Fight: *Fight Club* DVD booklet', 2000.

Uncredited – 'Web Closes in on Fincher', *Starburst*, February 2000.

Uncredited – 'Behind the *Fight Club* DVD', *Barnes & Noble.com*, July 2000.

Uncredited – 'Fred Durst interview', *MTV.com*, March 2001.

Uncredited – 'The Making of *Panic Room*', *About.com*, 2002.

Uncredited – 'Panic Attack: An interview with David Fincher', *Amazon.co.uk*, 2002.

Uncredited – '*Panic Room* production notes', 2002.

Uncredited – 'David Fincher interview', *BBCi*, March 2002.

Uncredited – 'Fincher in the frame for *Mission: Impossible 3*' the *Guardian Unlimited*, April 2002.

Index